Happy Birthday
Leon.

Love from Mam.

Oct 2020.

WHAT A
FLANKER

WHAT A FLANKER

JAMES HASKELL

HarperCollins*Publishers*

HarperCollins*Publishers*
1 London Bridge Street
London SE1 9GF

www.harpercollins.co.uk

First published by HarperCollins*Publishers* 2020

1 3 5 7 9 10 8 6 4 2

A catalogue record of this book is
available from the British Library

HB ISBN 978-0-00-840368-3
PB ISBN 978-0-00-840369-0

Printed and bound in Great Britain by
CPI Group (UK) Ltd, Croydon

MIX
Paper from
responsible sources
FSC™ C007454

FSC
www.fsc.org

This book is produced from independently certified FSC™ paper
to ensure responsible forest management.

For more information visit: www.harpercollins.co.uk/green

'The best revenge is living well.'

CONTENTS

FORWARD

When news broke that I was writing a book about my career, I felt a great disturbance in the rugby community, as if millions of voices suddenly cried out in terror. But do not fear, I won't be throwing anyone under the bus in the coming pages. Well, maybe a couple of people. But if this book fails and hundreds of unsold copies are pulped, I will atone by having the resulting porridge reconstituted as a trestle table in a home for battered rugby players.

What follows is not a blow-by-blow account of my life. You won't find out where I was born (Windsor), the name of my first pet (Jet, as in Jet from TV's *Gladiators*) or the name of my first school (Papplewick). But you will find out which bastard always skimmed the top off the fruit crumble before Wasps games, why props are still so fat (I've no idea to be honest, unacceptable) and what the hell went wrong at the 2015 World Cup. That's right, there is some serious stuff as well.

I am well aware that I've always been marmite ('Oh, for God's sake, why him?' Not my words but those of Ireland legend Rory Best on hearing that I'd been picked for the Lions). But I hope this book shows that I always gave my all for club and country, and just wanted to have a bit of fun on the side. I do hope you enjoy. And to the man who stuck a bottle of beer up his arse and did a handstand on a boat: thank your lucky stars I didn't name you.

P.S. Yes, I know I spelt 'foreword' wrong at the top of the previous page. Needless to say, I will have the last laugh.

1

WHEN TEAM SOCIALS GO WRONG

THE BOAT TRIP, PT I

There's no getting away from it: she's lost control. Like that old Joy Division song: '*Confusion in her eyes that says it all. She's lost control. And she's clinging to the nearest passer-by.*' When I say 'she', I mean me. Because I'm standing on a boat in a wig and a dress, a woman for the day. A skipper in drag witnessing a full-blown mutiny. And when I say 'skipper', I don't mean skipper of the boat. He's the 60-year-old bloke cowering behind the DJ decks, whose jam-jar glasses can't hide the terror in his eyes. I mean skipper of Wasps, one of the proudest rugby union teams in England. So, in truth, I've got no passers-by to cling to. I'm meant to be the boss. The guv'nor. The rock. People are supposed to be clinging to me. Fat chance. We've only been drinking for a couple of hours and already I'm thinking, 'You're Captain Bligh and that bloke over there with his pants around his ankles doing a handstand on a chair with a bottle of lager up his arse is Fletcher Christian.' This is going to get ugly.

That's the problem with academy kids. They always get giddy and feel the need to impress their team-mates. There might have been a time (doubtful) when a young kid wanting

3

to impress his team-mates quoted an inspiring passage from Shakespeare – 'Once more unto the breach, dear friends!' – but not nowadays. Instead, they do handstands with bottles of lager up their arses. A week in Hell, with the Devil's little All Black imps stamping all over my testicles, could not have prepared me for what happens next ...

The academy kid flips off the chair and back onto his feet. The bottle of lager exits his arse like a bat out of hell. Closely followed by its former contents. Closely followed by a jet of excrement. The bar ladies below deck have a particularly good view of this literal shit show. They're screaming and saucer-eyed and clinging to each other as if we're 10 miles out at sea and under attack from the dreadful spindly killer fish. The vessel's skipper is open-mouthed. I think I can detect a solitary tear running down his cheek. If this were a scene in a movie, he'd rip the needle off the record and silence would ensue. Instead, people are running in all directions and retching over the side of the boat.

Time to muster as much gravitas as a 6 ft 3 in, 19-stone man can while wearing a wig and a dress. I chuck several fucks into the arse-lager-shit magician and tell him to clean up his mess, before rushing below deck, apologising profusely to the bar ladies and grabbing a bucket, sponge and some Jif. As the academy kid is on his knees, scrubbing the deck clean of poo that should, by rights, still be up his backside, I think to myself, 'What a tragic episode. But we must carry on.'

AN ESSENTIAL RELEASE

I know what you're thinking: how can professional sportsmen be so unprofessional? How can an England international allow such shenanigans to go on in his midst? I sometimes think the same. Then again, you try keeping control of a squad of professional rugby players let off the leash after a long, hard season. And, let's face it, young men are known to be quite daft. Groups of young men even dafter. And groups of young sportsmen dafter still.

But perhaps a more compelling explanation for professional sportsmen's occasional lapses in professionalism is because they spend so much time being professional. Being a professional rugby player is bloody hard work. It involves a lot of sacrifices. Getting battered and bruised in training and on match days. Repeated blows to the head, snapped and twisted muscles and broken bones. Eating the right things, drinking the right things, keeping strictly to the rota. Going to bed early and hardly ever going out. It's not like working down a mine – we love it and we get paid well – but it takes its toll, physically and mentally. So the odd team social serves a purpose. It's an essential release and bonding experience, not much different to a miner having a few pints in the pub with his mates on a Friday night.

There are two main ways a team bonds: by suffering on the field together, in training and on match days, and by sharing nights out together. I look at team socials as like a play or a film. Not that anyone else would want to watch it, but they are little pieces of human drama for those that take part. Team socials have their heroes (the team-mate – normally Danny Cipriani – who walks off with the most beautiful woman anyone has ever laid eyes on), their anti-heroes (the team-mate who sticks a bottle of lager up his arse, does a handstand and shits himself) and their villains (the team-mate who punches someone for no good reason). There are the jokers (the team-mate who can destroy a man with a single quip, while reducing the rest of his pals to eye-watering, stitch-inducing laughter), the fools (the team-mate who gets drunk, falls over and suffers a comedy injury), the foils (the team-mate who kneels behind a man who then gets pushed over, preferably into someone's garden), the eternal victims (the team-mate who spends all night chatting up a woman only to get custard-pied – again), the stock characters and bit-part players (the team-mate who passes out in the toilets after a couple of tequilas or is found curled up under a table, mumbling about mummy). A great team social has comedy, farce, absurdity, cruelty and tragedy. And preferably some singing.

I hesitate to compare rugby players to soldiers. God knows those boys and girls do a more important job than we do, but there are similarities in the way we behave when we're not on the front line or field of play. Team socials, for soldiers and sportspeople, are about building camaraderie. They are about creating communal history. Team socials top up the well of comedy, so that the lads can keep going back for laughs, time and time again.

Professional rugby players, like players in any team sport, are adults who never stop laughing like children. Because nothing in the world bonds a team better than laughter. I must have laughed 100 times every single day for 18 and a half seasons. Everything I did – and I did a lot of stupid things – I did for the story. It's like that line delivered by Jeremy in *Peep Show*, after Mark has made a tit of himself again: 'At least you've got a funny story to tell.' All I ever wanted was to sit at the back of the coach, swap stupid tales and make people giggle.

ABOMINABLE VISIONS

I've never really recovered from my first proper team social. I was a teenager playing for Maidenhead when we went on tour to France (the clubhouse coffers must have been a bit bare that year), taking in the exotic rugby outposts of Boulogne and

Calais. I was just about old enough to have the odd shandy if I asked nicely, but the dads in our group, excited beyond belief at being away from their wives for a couple of days, were under no such restrictions. And when groups of middle-aged men are away from their wives and under no restrictions, things often go horribly and disturbingly wrong.

One traumatic evening, I was wandering around the hotel, no doubt bored and wanting a piece of some action, and heard an almighty racket coming from the bar. Curious but also slightly scared, I gingerly pushed the door open and was greeted by the sight of my father dancing on a table, as naked as the day he was born. The abominable vision shocked me to the very core. You can't un-see something like that: your father, legs splayed, backside exposed for all to see, cock and balls swinging in time to some banging Europop. I caught his eye, then quietly closed the door, hoping no-one else had seen me, and sloped off to bed. We never spoke of this episode. But it's why I haven't been able to look him square in the eye for the best part of 20 years. Sometimes I wake up in a cold sweat, having revisited the scene in my dreams. I'll start muttering to myself, 'The horror … the horror …', like Marlon Brando in *Apocalypse Now*.

Such a disturbing experience might have left a more delicate soul scarred for life, but when I finally came of age and it was my time to get involved, I dived right in. No holds barred. Full tilt. Right in the thick of it. A psychologist might deduce that my unbridled enthusiasm for team socials was a coping mechanism, me trying to assert control and take ownership of chaotic situations. Or maybe they'd just say I was a bit of a dickhead. Not that I had much choice. Just like no-one had a choice back then. It was drummed into me from the very beginning that team socials are as integral to rugby as scrums, line-outs and filling a team-mate's shoes with shaving cream.

I was still at school when I went on Wasps' pre-season trip to Poland, a fresh-faced 17-year-old about to enter the upper sixth. And while I was a bit nervous about the training side of things, I was terrified of what might happen if we were allowed a night on the beers. I'd been told about some horrific initiations, including the time Lawrence Dallaglio was dangled by his ankles from a balcony by Dean Ryan and his captain Mark Rigby. It was only when one of the other back-rows, Francis Emeruwa, a softly spoken giant who put the fear of God into everyone, told them to stop, that they did so. I dread to think how hard Emeruwa was, because Ryan and Rigby were no shrinking violets. Lawrence would have been a teenager, like me, so I had sleepless nights thinking about all the things that might happen to me in the Polish boondocks.

We were in Poland for 10 days, training four times a day, with one evening off. But that's all it takes. Some brainbox had organised a trip to Auschwitz the following day, so the plan was to go out for pizza and a few beers. I didn't believe in drinking – when I was at school, I ran the school bar but never took advantage because I thought it would affect my fitness – so I told myself I was going to turn up at this restaurant and stay well out of the way. I hated hangovers with a passion. They killed me. And who wants to be hungover at Auschwitz? The last place in the world you want to be hungover is at Auschwitz. Are you even allowed to be hungover at Auschwitz? But I soon learned that trying to stay out of the way at a rugby team social is like trying to avoid punches from Mike Tyson while stuck with him in a phone box.

So there we were, a few of us younger players, tucked away in the corner of this open-air restaurant-cum-nightclub. And over swans first-team fly-half Alex King, holding two pints of lager. And the first thing 'Kinger' ever says to me is, 'Haskell, Lawrence doesn't think you can drink. Show him you can.'

Not only is Lawrence the current Wasps captain, he's also the Godfather, not doing much apart from lurking menacingly and sending his foot soldiers on various errands with the message: 'Make him an offer he can't refuse.'

I think, 'Let's just get this over with,' grab a pint and chin it in one. Five minutes later, Fraser Waters swans over and says, 'Haskell, Lawrence doesn't think you can drink ...' Another pint chinned. Five minutes later, Paul Volley swans over. Same chat, same outcome. Five minutes later, Josh Lewsey swans over. Five minutes later, Simon Shaw swans over. After about six pints, Lawrence finally deigns to swan over himself. 'Good to see you drinking,' he says, with an evil glint in his eye. 'Have another one.' Now I'm absolutely steaming and starting to panic. Do I make a tactical retreat? No, that's not a good look. Just grin and bear it. But what about Auschwitz? 'Never mind Auschwitz,' says Mark Denney, all two of him, 'have another drink ...'

There followed a kangaroo court session, beloved of rugby teams all over the world, during which Peter Scrivener, forever injured, won the stealing a career award and Josh Lewsey the most likely to get shot by your own side award. But after about 10 pints, I was feeling very dusty indeed and had to be rescued by Shaun Edwards, chief deputy to Wasps head coach Warren Gatland. Shaun grabbed me by the scruff of the neck and said to me, 'Right, kid, I'm taking you home.' But to get home, we had to walk through the woods in the dark, so now I was shitting myself because I found Shaun scary even when I was stone cold sober. Mercifully, I made it back to the barracks – which is what our accommodation was – located my room and found Rob Howley, the great Wales scrum-half, shirt off, shredded to the bone and eating jelly babies on his bed. I remember thinking, 'I thought these people were elite professionals, and all this guy appears to eat are jelly babies and toasted cheese sandwiches.' Rob, clearly not a fan of Polish food, had even brought his own Breville toastie-maker and a bag full of condiments. The room, which had no windows or air conditioning, was like a sauna, my mattress felt like a Jacob's cream cracker and we'd run out of water. Well, I'd run out of water, was too scared to ask for any of Rob's and too drunk to venture out of the room. As a result, and despite my colossal alcohol intake, I had the worst night's sleep ever, a fitful few hours of tossing and turning punctuated by terrifying thoughts of how I might disgrace myself at Auschwitz and the odd beer-fuelled nightmare.

When I woke up the following morning, I could still taste cheap Polish lager and Rob Howley was on his second bag of jelly babies. All I could think was, 'I can't go to Auschwitz. I'd like to go to Auschwitz. Actually, that's a lie. Auschwitz is not a place you ever want to go, but it's somewhere I feel I should probably go.' Whatever I was thinking, my immediate desire was to stay in bed for as long as possible. But realising that that probably wasn't going to be an option, I dragged myself out and went in search of the only person more drunk than me the night before, Garth Chamberlain. Garth was the same age as me but even less experienced at drinking. In fact, before that trip, Garth had never touched a drop, so when the boys made him drink, it was like taking a wrecking ball to a temple. When I tracked him down, he was cowering in the shower, sobbing. Through bubbles of phlegm and snot, he explained that not only had he been made to drink 10 pints, he'd also drunk tap water, so was wrestling (not very well) with the twin demons of alcohol poisoning and dysentery. Apparently, when Garth's room-mate found him crying and being sick, Garth had claimed he was dying and demanded an air ambulance be called. A few wise heads, by which I mean some senior players who were still quite drunk, comforted him by telling that he wasn't dying but now he had drunk the tap water he'd probably end up in a body bag. As you can imagine, this was music to Garth's anxious ears. The details are hazy, although I do recall being very jealous, because Garth managed to dodge the trip. Bastard.

About 20 minutes later, I was wedged into a seat at the back of this rickety old shitbox of a coach with no aircon. And who sat next to me? Prop Craig Dowd, All Blacks legend and the only man more hungover than me. Craig was very much an old-school Kiwi – 'do not speak until you're spoken to' – who already hated me because I'd chipped his tooth in my first-ever Wasps training session, when we went head-to-head in some wrestling. Picture it: hardened, humble Kiwi and gobshite English public schoolboy, all aboard the coach trip to Hell. How could we not end up as best friends? The reality was, while this coach was rattling along, bunny-hopping through potholes, bouncing my head off the window, all I could think was, 'Do *not* spew on Craig Dowd … do *not* spew on Craig Dowd.'

I was on that coach for four hours. And it's not like we were on our way to a water park, where we could pass out on a sunbed for the afternoon, we were on our way to a place where over a million Jews were exterminated by the Nazis. Craig fell asleep after about 10 minutes, having drunk all the water, and I wasn't able to move him for the rest of the journey. And his legs were spread so wide that by the time we arrived, I'd lost all feeling in my thighs.

I got off the coach and retched a couple of times, before being taken on a guided tour with the rest of the lads. Each room was more horrible than the last, and my head was spinning the whole time. 'I can't be sick here. Not at Auschwitz. Never at Auschwitz.' That might have been the most taxing and depressing two hours of my life. I managed not to puke and finally located some bottled water that at least eased my Hitler-shaped horror of a hangover. But just as the world was starting to feel a little bit normal again, I had to endure another four hours of Craig Dowd's extravagant manspreading. The chat was non-existent, the heat unbearable and the smell most foul. Take it from me, Craig Dowd is not a man you'd ever want to sit next to on the Tube, or any mode of transport for that matter. But even though the next few days' training were an appalling slog, I'd done what I had to do to be accepted: worked hard, played hard and fulfilled my off-field commitments.

BOYS OUT OF THE BARRACKS

My first proper team social at Wasps – as in when I was a fully paid-up member of the first-team squad, aged 19 – was after we did the Premiership–Heineken Cup double in 2004. That was never going to be a quiet one, and rightly so. The theme was Hawaiian, so I turned up at the Mitre pub in Fulham in a Hawaiian shirt, a pair of flip-flops and some expensive Burberry jeans I'd got for Christmas (but not Burberry check – my fashion sense has been questioned down the years, but even I'd balk at wearing Burberry check jeans). If I remember rightly, and there's a lot I don't remember rightly about that evening, it was the first time I'd worn them. It was a beautiful early summer's day in London, I could smell the barbecue from across the street, and when I walked in with my mate James Wellwood the kitty cash was already flying. Any man who has been in a similar situation with his mates will recognise that these are classic ingredients for chaos.

The second Fraser Waters clocked my outfit, he said to me, 'Mate, that outfit is not Hawaiian.' Fraser is so posh it hurts. In fact, he's a big posh sod with plums in his mouth. But he was also an unbelievable rugby player, a top team-mate, tough as nails and an animal on the piss. And now he sounded properly affronted. I felt like a recruit being shouted at by a sergeant major during uniform inspection, but I decided to fight my corner.

'Everyone looks like this in Honolulu,' I finally replied, indignantly.

Big mistake. I'd provoked the mob.

'Haskell, you wanker!' said someone.

'That's not fucking Hawaiian!' hissed another.

'Cut his jeans off!' shouted someone else.

With that, Martin Purdy and Simon Shaw, who I always suspected were gorillas in human suits, grabbed my arms. There is young man strength and there is 'dad strength'. Dad strength doesn't come from lifting weights in the gym, it naturally develops with age and from doing battle in thousands of rucks and mauls. And Simon Shaw had ultimate dad strength, which made resistance futile. Fraser pulled out a pair of scissors – from where, I do not know – and started hacking away at my very expensive and beloved jeans. Trevor Leota and Phil Greening were scrabbling about on the floor, putting their big sausage fingers into the holes Fraser was cutting and pulling furiously, and about 30 seconds later I was wearing a pair of denim hot pants, so short that they had even cut the pockets off and my boxer shorts were hanging out of the bottom.

Fraser then turned on Wellwood. It was like a scene from a 1970s slasher flick – the assailant, fresh from a kill, a crazed expression on his face, brandishing a pair of scissors. Five minutes later, Fraser had fashioned Wellwood's brogues – handmade, Church's, probably cost him (or more likely his mum and dad) about 500 quid a shoe – into a pair of flip-flops. But because Fraser wasn't a shoemaker, especially after 10 pints of Stella, the flip-flops soon disintegrated. So to save him from walking about barefoot for the rest of the day, the lads gaffer-taped the strips of leather to his feet and calves, so that Wellwood now looked vaguely like a posh Hawaiian in calipers.

Unprovoked mob attacks aside, I soon realised that drinking could be a good laugh. Chatting shit in the sun, swapping funny stories, taking the piss. Back then, there was no pretence of organised fun. It was a simple case of herding everyone into the same space, drinking as much as possible, seeing what panned out and hoping no-one died. Before that day in the Mitre, Tom Rees hadn't been much of a drinker either. But Phil Greening spotted him hiding in a corner nursing a Coke, marched over, shoved a pint into his chest and roared, 'Drink this, Robot Nause!' (Reesy was nicknamed Robot Nause or Robot Wars or Rees Bot, all because I told everyone that his dad and him built robots in their garage and once appeared on *Robot Wars* with a machine called Thunder Claw. All lies, of course, and I probably wouldn't have made it up if I'd known how big my team-mates' appetites were for morsels of nonsense that painted anyone in an unflattering light.)

'Sorry, Phil, I can't,' replied Reesy. 'England Under-21 training tomorrow.'

It was like that scene from the screwball comedy *Old School*. Remember Will Ferrell as Frank the Tank? Phil was looking at Reesy in utter disbelief, as if Reesy had just told him he was going shopping at Home Depot in the morning for wallpaper and flooring. Maybe Bed Bath & Beyond, but only if he had time.

'Haskell, why is your mate Rees bot not drinking?' said Phil eventually.

A brave man, and a good friend, might have told Phil to piss off and leave Reesy alone. Instead, I smirked and shrugged, and suddenly Reesy was surrounded by baying team-mates.

'Robot Wars! We're gonna hit you 'til you drink!'

All these lads started piling into him, hitting his legs, around the back of the head, in the gut. Have you ever seen the film *Scum*? Well, it was a bit like that. Except with a load of big posh blokes. I half expected Fraser to come flying in, swinging a sock full of billiard balls. But still Reesy resisted. He was curled into a ball, shouting and screaming about England training, until he realised that the only way to stop them hitting him was to agree to drink. And the second Reesy took his first sip he was Frank the Tank, a straight-shooter transformed into a beer monster: 'Fill it up again! Fill it up again! Once it hits your lips, it's so good!' The last I saw of Reesy that day, he wasn't running down the middle of the road naked, he was spewing in a urinal. And in case you were wondering, Reesy did make it to England camp the following day – and trained the bloody house down. They'd never seen him play so well. Maybe it was the guilt. Maybe lager just agreed with him. But he never stopped drinking.

The rest of that day is pretty hazy. I do recall Purdy playing the guitar, making up a song about team-mates to the tune of Damien Rice's 'Cannonball' (a song that is still sung at Wasps today, with lyrics tailored for current players), and someone creeping up behind him and setting his linen shirt on fire. Typical Purdy, he just carried on playing while people were putting him out. I also recall Purdy (who got a double first from Cambridge and now makes furniture in France), who had one of those early fitness watches that told him his heart-rate, running on the spot in the middle of the dancefloor – a massive second row, with a bottle of lager in one hand, properly sprinting, knees up to his chest. He actually did that quite often, way more than anyone else would think was normal. If someone asked him what he was doing, he'd say, 'What the fuck does it look like? I'm doing a fat burner,' and he'd carry on running for another 20 minutes.

It's difficult to say whether Lawrence Dallaglio was there that day or not. It's quite likely that he swanned in at some point, although Lawrence always had something else on and didn't like to mix with the rabble – or what I like to call 'bin juice'. Bin juice are those players who, when they turn up to pre-season training, get issued with a bib and a tackle bag, act as cannon fodder for the first team, have a lot of awkward conversations with coaches about selection that never happens, get roped into all the community commitments but come into their own at team socials, get steaming and cause lots of drama. Don't get me wrong, bin juice players are integral to any successful team, essential for the group's energy and morale. Because if the bin juice goes off the boil, they'll bring the house down from the inside. Not that I blamed Lawrence for his reluctance to wade into the bin juice nonsense. He was the skipper, after all, a Wasps legend, an England World Cup winner, a British and Irish Lion. He couldn't be seen slumming it with bin juice, not when they were cutting off clothes, making people drink and setting people on fire.

After hours of drinking in the sun, we all decided to move the party to Purple, this horrific nightclub attached to Chelsea's Stamford Bridge ground. As we were strolling down the Fulham Palace Road in the lazy early evening, surrounded by roaring football fans and families heading to dinner, Kenny Logan grabbed me from behind and Paul Volley gripped the bottom of my exposed boxer shorts and gave me a horrific wedgie, which led to my boxers being torn in half. Paul chucked the two tattered pieces of cloth into a bin and with that, him and Kenny took off down the Fulham Palace Road, crying tears of maniacal laughter. I was left standing there, like Alan Partridge and his tiny shorts with the perished inner lining, my boys firmly out of the barracks. What to do? Going home wasn't an option. I'd never hear the last of it, and I lived in the butt fuck of nowhere. So I made the best of a bad situation, balanced one testicle precariously on the gusset of my denim hot pants and left the other one hanging. One out of two ain't bad. Although I do sometimes think, 'If camera phones had been around back then, I might never have played for England, or been allowed near playgrounds.'

I walked into Purple, took one look at the bar and shuddered. Purple was a terrible mess of humanity, as always – and that was just my team-mates. I wasn't sure I'd make it through the night without a girl accusing me of exposing myself and getting filled in by the bouncers, so I got a few pints of water down my neck, and me and a couple of other lads got a cab back to some girl's house in Fulham. So there I was, wedged into this old-fashioned armchair, the kind of thing Scrooge would have sat in, trying to flirt with these girls. The boys were still out of the barracks (I'd given up trying to stop them making an appearance many hours earlier, and luckily I was still a young man – a senior player might have had to tuck them into his socks), and I was chatting away as nonchalantly as a man can with his testicles on display, when James Dunne, a fellow academy player, stormed into the living room and started doing a flamethrower with a can of hair mousse and a cigarette lighter. Clearly James had been spurned by a woman, so he did what any spurned and very drunk rugby player did back then – regressed to a childlike state and became hellbent on ruining everyone else's chances of pulling. He became the true personification of a cock blocker: if he wasn't getting any, then none of us were.

Dunney's catchphrase was, 'I'm not scared of it.' And whatever it was, he wasn't. That's all the man used to say. Someone would say to him, 'Dunney, there is no way you can fit your head in those railings.' And he'd reply, 'Yeah, why not, I'm not scared of it.' Or they'd say, 'Dunney, are you going to have a fight with that bloke over there?' And he'd reply, 'Yeah, why not, I'm not scared of it.' Some nights, Dunney would go to bed, set his alarm for 1 am and drive down to the Oceana nightclub in Kingston, which was only 10 minutes from his academy digs. He'd enjoy the last two hours of partying, chat up a girl and take her home. He was like an early Uber service. We used to say, 'Dunney, isn't that a bit weird?' And he'd say, 'I'm not scared of it.' Had I lived next door to a nightclub in London, I might not have been scared of it either.

Anyway, I was wedged into Scrooge's armchair in some strange girl's living room, my testicles were hanging out and there were flames whizzing past my face. Hair mousse, when flamed, turns into something resembling napalm, and this stuff was landing on the furniture and all over my exposed legs, so that the room smelled of burning hair. Next thing I knew, I was waking up in this strange living room with the worst hangover known to man. My tongue was stuck to the roof of my mouth and some imaginary being was smacking me over the head with an invisible lump hammer. I was half-standing, half-sitting in this armchair and my joints had seized up. I had terrible tendinitis in my knees at the time, so my bottom half had gone rigor mortis. As I tried to unfold myself, whimpering as I did so, 'Help me! Someone please help me!' this girl strolled in and asked, almost airily – as if it was the most normal thing in the world to see some 6 ft 3 in boy-man, wearing a Hawaiian shirt, hot pants and with his bollocks hanging out, trying to extricate himself from her armchair on a Sunday morning – if I was okay.

'Not really,' I replied meekly. 'Where am I?'

'You're in Fulham. Would you like some breakfast?'

The smell of bacon started wafting in from the kitchen – such a beautiful aroma when you're in the right mood, but a hellish aroma after a ferocious all-day booze-up and the realisation that your mother might see your pixelated testicles in tomorrow's *Sun* – and I almost spewed. I had to get out of that place. So without bidding farewell, I fled the scene, leaving Dunney to mop up the mess that, to be fair, he'd made. Alas, I didn't know London from Adam. I was a homebody from a small town in Berkshire. And I'd lost my phone, probably because that bastard Waters had cut my pockets off. So I begged for some change and called my mum from a payphone. The conversation that followed was a bit like that scene in *Pulp Fiction*, when Vince blows the kid's head off in the car and gang boss Marsellus Wallace summons Winston Wolfe to clean things up. My mum didn't tell me that she was on the motherfucker and to wait for The Wolf, but she did tell me that she was sending Mladen. Shit. That's all you had to say! Mladen was this guy who worked for my parents, a kind of gardener/handyman/chauffeur/all-round hero and a person, like The Wolf, who could get you out of sticky situations.

I managed to find my way back to the Mitre, having asked directions from various perturbed early risers, and Mladen was there waiting for me, like the legend he was. Mladen had always been one of my biggest fans (still is) and thought I was destined for great things in rugby. But he was also a strict Seventh-day Adventist and had never touched a drop of drink. So when I fell sideways into the passenger seat, bleary eyed, stinking of sambuca, my Hawaiian shirt open to the waist, balls hanging out, he looked at me like I was the second coming of Beelzebub. But Mladen did what Mladen does best – drove fast and asked no questions – and I stuck my head out of the window all the way back to Berkshire. I didn't say a word, even when Mladen wound the window up and slowly crushed my arm and head in the door.

Back in Berkshire, I tumbled out of Mladen's car, staggered into the garden, fell flat on my face on the lawn and passed out. We were having some building work done at the time and a concerned builder rushed inside and said to my mum, 'Mrs Haskell, we don't mean to alarm you, but there appears to be a vagrant asleep on your lawn. Wearing hot pants.' My mum, a very proud woman who liked to tell everyone everything about me (at least the good stuff) popped her head out of the kitchen window and said, 'Oh, don't worry, that's just my son.' How proud she must have been that morning.

DANGEROUS PEOPLE

There is a misunderstanding among the public that professional rugby players are the same as university rugby players, which is why a lot of people immediately take against us, because they assume that all we do is drink and play games involving biscuits. But university rugby players are mad bastards who do stuff we'd never do – drinking piss and sick, bullying the fringe members of the team into shaving various parts of their bodies, being louts and smashing things up. I'd go as far as to say that if I'd been made to do some of the initiations my schoolmates were made to do at university, I wouldn't have been a professional rugby player. Luckily, I never went to university. When I hear those stories, I just think it's odd. There's nothing fun about it.

I've been made to drink seven raw eggs, vodka-soaked tampons and plenty of 'dirty' pints, consisting of a bar's top shelf and various other bits and bobs. But nothing seriously weird. That's not to say some serious drinking didn't go on, and the thing you feared most was being caught trying to avoid it. Wasps and England prop Tim Payne was a hero of a man but a grimly determined drinker when he needed to be. While I was never a heavy drinker, even in my early days, Payner was a stickler for commitment, on and off the pitch, and never failed to notice a player's absence from post-match festivities. He'd phone me after games and growl down the phone.

'Haskell, it's Payner. You coming on the piss tonight?'

'Erm, no. I mean, yes. Maybe. Probably not. I've got something else to ...'

'Fuck off, you cunt!'

And the phone would go dead. I'd be sat there thinking, 'Shit, maybe I should have gone out. Maybe this will be held against me.' But on Monday, I'd rock up to training and all would be forgotten, as long as I worked my bollocks off. James Brooks, another lovely guy and a top player, was another strange one when it came to drink. One minute you'd be talking to him and he'd be his perfectly normal, calm and collected self. But after three pints he'd transform into his alter ego, who was this this unbearable nightmare of a human being called Hank. And once Hank was out of the box, he would just refuse to go away. When people saw Hank marching in their general direction in a bar or nightclub, they'd start running. And if you didn't run fast enough, he'd pin you in a corner and start nausing your ear off.

'You don't understand, Haskell, you're not tough enough [*that's hard to take from a 5 ft 4 in fly-half*]. You need to be doing this, you need to be doing that ...'

'Sure Hank ... what's that over there?'

'No! You're not listening to me!'

Hank had this heavy lead (as in the metal) finger and he'd prod you in the chest with it for an hour, telling you how good you could be if only you stuck with him and wanted it enough. (I should note that Hank's lead finger wasn't as heavy as Craig Dowd's lead finger after he'd put away a couple of bottles of red wine – after a few minutes of Dowd's lead fingering, you were struggling to breathe.) Hank just loved having these horrific, steaming deep and meaningfuls. His intentions were pure and noble, but it was difficult to take. And if his victim was also steaming, these chats could go on for two or three hours. Hank also had two fights (*two?!*) with Shaun Edwards, which only a fully fledged madman would do. Seriously, who goes back for seconds with Shaun Edwards? Certainly not me, and I'm twice his size.

The players who presented most danger to life and limb on team socials tended to be boys from the South Pacific. Pacific Islanders are the loveliest people and unbelievable players, but they often have a huge amount of pressure on their shoulders because of the shoddy contracts they are cajoled into signing and the number of dependants they have. They're often supporting big families and sometimes whole villages back home. One player told me he had 100 people relying on him, which must be tremendously stressful. People might go hungry based on the bad decisions they make, and imagine having to phone home and tell your folks your contract isn't being renewed and no other clubs are interested. I also found the South Pacific boys, like most men, weren't very good at communicating their problems. Whether any of that's got anything to do with their wildness on the booze, I don't know. But it was definitely a trend and something former Samoa international and my old Wasps team-mate Dan Leo spoke about eloquently and at length on my *House of Rugby* podcast, which is now known as *The Good, The Bad and The Rugby*.

Some know themselves well enough not to drink at all, but I'd often hear those that did drink say, 'We'll just have one beer,' and I'd watch them chin it in one and know it was all going to go wrong. I'll have to leave out some of the names because they got up to some seriously mad shit after a few beers, as we all have done, but there was the time two Fijians, a Samoan and an England international walked into a pub

– yes, this is a joke, kind of – and the older Fijian ended up punching the younger Fijian in the face. And because of their strictly observed rules of social hierarchy, the younger Fijian couldn't hit him back. This was a nice pub in Coventry, full of families trying to eat their Sunday lunches in peace, so the England international tried to calm things down. But the Samoan, who was normally quite an unassuming guy and was as confused by the Fijians' disagreement as anyone else, started shouting, 'Why are you fucking fighting? If you want to fight, fight me!' before punching himself repeatedly in the face. I can only assume he felt left out. Unsurprisingly, the Fijians weren't interested in fighting the Samoan, and the barman had to ask the Samoan to stop punching himself in the face, because he was scaring the customers. In the end, with the barman having failed to calm the Samoan down, the bouncer pepper-sprayed him. Bizarrely, it was the Samoan who ended up in the back of a police car, for fighting himself. How did he know if he'd won or not? As you can imagine, when we heard about it in the Monday morning changing-room debrief, we all found it hilarious, albeit a little bit shocking.

There is a lot of social hierarchy in the Pacific Island nations, stuff that is difficult for British people to get their heads around. But the basics are understanding your heritage, knowing your place and respecting your elders. For example, when it comes to England's Mako and Billy Vunipola, whose heritage is Tongan, Mako rules the roost. And it's the same with the Tuilagi brothers. Manu, the youngest, used to carry Alesana's kit bag for him at Leicester, and up the chain it went. If I asked my younger brother to carry anything, he'd tell me to get fucked and walk off. After England won the Grand Slam in 2016, all the friends and family who had travelled over to Paris joined us in a nightclub to celebrate, including Henry Tuilagi, who is just about the biggest man I have ever met. A long table of drinks had been laid on and when I wandered over to wet my beak, big Henry was blocking my path. I'm not ashamed to say that I was too scared to serve myself, even though Henry wasn't even in the team, because I knew that Samoans were quite strict about stuff like that. So I asked Henry's permission to take a beverage and he said, 'Of course, bro, they're not my drinks.' And I started stuttering like an idiot: 'Thank you Henry, thank you sir, you are so, so generous ...'

While I pride myself on being culturally aware, there was another reason for my reluctance to cut in front of Henry at the bar. I had been told about one Leicester team social where Henry made it clear, or thought he did, that he was the king of a particular table and therefore it was his job to serve the drinks. If you wanted one, you just had to ask and he'd pour it. So when a slightly addled physio forgot his place and served himself, he was given a stern warning by Henry not to do it again. Fast forward 20 minutes and the physio, even more drunk and forgetful, did it again, before Henry, without any hesitation, chinned him. There was some concern that the physio might be dead, but it having been decided that he was in fact still alive, the party continued around his lifeless body. And when the physio eventually came round and made the mistake of getting to his feet, Henry chinned him again, or so the story goes.

When I told that story on the *House of Rugby* podcast, I got a direct message on Instagram from Henry the following day. When I saw his name, I shat myself. Henry is lovely, but he is also one of the scariest men I have ever met. And he is very clearly a stickler for the rules. But when I opened up the message it read, 'Bro! Love that story, it's not all true!' If you listen intently on a quiet day, you may still be able to hear my sigh of relief.

TOTAL COMMITMENT

While on the 2017 Lions tour, me and Rory Best got into a very deep discussion about team socials and he told me a strange story about his Ulster and Ireland team-mate Jared Payne. When Payne told his captain Rory he didn't enjoy the socials that were being laid on, Rory asked him what he'd like to do instead. Payne, who was born and raised in New Zealand, replied, 'We could do a hermit half-dozen.'

'What the fuck is a hermit half-dozen?'

'Well, each player gets six beers, they all find a tree, climb the tree and drink the beers on their own as quickly as possible. Before meeting up again.'

'That doesn't sound like much fun. It just sounds a bit weird.'

'Well, we could do a house hermit half-dozen instead?'

'What does it involve?'

'Well, each player gets six beers, you all find a separate room in the house, sit in the room and drink the beers. As quickly as possible.'

'I don't think you understand, Jared. It's a team social ...'

Who in their right mind wants to sit in a room, or up a tree, drinking six beers on their own in silence when they could be out drinking with their team-mates? The answer to that question is Kiwis. Apparently, this hermit half-dozen is an actual thing, loved not only by Kiwis, but also by Trappist monks and serial killers. I recently spoke to one of the Northampton lads and they told me that, under pressure from their Kiwi cohort, they tried the hermit half-dozen. Having necked six beers in about half an hour, they reconvened for the main part of the evening and everyone was spewing in the bin by 11.

Clearly, different people have different interpretations of what a team social should be. I think a team social should be fun. I never liked the idea of being locked in a room with a load of lunatics and made to neck pints. I loved the socials which were planned to the letter, with almost military precision. Nowadays, they almost have to be like that, because if you think modern kids have short attention spans due to prolonged exposure to mobile devices, try keeping a rugby team amused, organised and focused for longer than 10 minutes. During my second stint at Wasps, Sam Jones was a meticulous social secretary and ran some of the best socials I was ever involved in (although, let's be honest, the boat trip was a bit of a black mark against his name – I'd give him two stars on Tripadvisor for that one). One time, Sam organised for the whole team to go on a pub crawl round Leamington Spa before jumping on the train and heading down to London. We had to do daft things to win points, like presenting a random woman with flowers while she was walking along with her bloke. That didn't always go down too well. There were quizzes, mandatory selfies in front of landmarks, and more points awarded for various challenges, ranging from 10 points for getting a fit girl's number to 100 points for getting a tattoo. The assumption being that no-one was stupid enough to get a tattoo on a team social. They assumed wrong, as four lads came home with them. There were more points to be won if your team managed to make it home without breaking a precious golden egg that everyone was given at the start of the day. We'd do pretty much anything to break up the drinking. One of the challenges was to snog a celebrity for 200 points, so I snogged Danny Cipriani. Alas, the jury wouldn't accept it, on the grounds that he wasn't famous enough. However, I can reveal that Cips is a wonderful kisser, with lovely soft lips like velvet.

There were players who didn't enjoy team socials. That was fine, to a point. But it could be a problem when certain players isolated themselves completely, because refusing to be a team man is not good for morale and not something most team-mates take kindly to. A player should never be pressured into doing something he doesn't want to do. He should have his own mind. But sometimes you have to do things you might not want to do for the greater good. That doesn't mean you have to be drinking dirty pints from a wellington boot. You don't even have to drink. Just turn up for a couple of hours, have a chat and leave if it's getting a bit tasty for your liking. Job done. Sadly, I can recall many players who wanted no part of it and became outcasts.

Whether it's making a few tackles in a contact session or turning up to a team social, it's about telling your team-mates that on match day, they can rely on you, you'll be 100 per cent committed to the cause, be by their side when the flak is flying and never flinch. That's why if a social was fancy dress, I expected everyone to go to every length to make their outfit as good as possible. And most of the time, the lads would go above and beyond the call of duty. One fancy dress social that springs to mind was after we won the Heineken Cup for the second time in 2007. Everyone except two lads pulled their fingers out, and the assembled squad would have given the costume department at Pinewood Studios a run for its money. We met at 11 am in Fulham, and the sight was a magnificent one. Pete Richards and Joe Mbu turned up as Björn Borg and Venus Williams respectively, and promptly started playing tennis in the middle of the road. Naturally, I was Lawrence Dallaglio (his mum supplied me with one of his old England kits and I even had a custom face-mask made). Alex King was a peeping Tom affectionally known as 'The Pest', wearing a trench coat and just an elephant's trunk posing pouch under-neath. Matt Dawson was the lead singer of The Darkness and Martin Purdy was our friend Frank the Tank from *Old School*.

One of our props, whose blushes I will spare, came as a tumble dryer, with his head poking out of the top of the cardboard box. That related to another night he'd taken a woman back to his flat and the following morning she looked like she'd been through a tumble dryer. When they came down the stairs, she was clinging to him like a koala, her legs were shaking, her hair was all over the place and she kept telling him how much she loved him. That's what I call doing a professional job in the bedroom. Everyone was someone or something else that day and it was magnificent to be a part of. When us old team-mates meet up today, it's those stories we share, rather than stories of glorious victories.

LADY-PLEASERS

In rugby days of old, backs would be the main lady-pleasers on an evening out, with the forwards bumbling about in the shadows, hoping for a few scraps. The modern forward is paid to be in good shape and a lot of modern ladies like a bigger gentleman. Back in the day, I enjoyed my singledom like the rest. I wouldn't describe myself as a lady's man as I always had a body like *Baywatch* and face like *Crimewatch*. I was never one for getting incoherently drunk and being sick on myself, like some team-mates. My sole purpose on a night out was to get to know various members of the fairer sex better. I liked to have a nice chat with a girl and see how things progressed. Sometimes it did, sometimes it didn't. As with most forwards, it was about putting in the graft and playing the numbers game.

I think it's fair to say that certain backs operated on a different level altogether. Danny Care in his heyday was something to behold. Thom Evans, who once appeared full-frontal naked on a French 'arthouse' calendar called the Dieux du Stade (more of which later), dated Kelly Brook and was last seen on the red carpet with Nicole Scherzinger at the Golden Globes, would have women dripping off him. Presumably, Nicole bought him a shitty stick for Valentine's Day. Then there was the man I don't wish to embarrass but who I'll call The Special One. The Special One was devastatingly handsome and in the habit of telling women he loved them after half an hour. You'd overhear the poor girl telling her mate, 'I can't believe he loves me!' But The Special One's chat, horrific as it was, wasn't as bad as another one of my England team-mates', who I'll call Harry (in case you were wondering, his name isn't actually Harry. I wouldn't be that horrible). One time, Harry was chatting to this very attractive girl, and she broke off the conversation to tell me that while my mate was incredibly good looking, he was also extremely boring, and that if I told him to 'shut the fuck up', she'd sleep with him anyway.

But however good looking a rugby player might be, he will never be able to compete with a footballer or elite boxer. Those boys are in a different stratosphere when it comes to wooing ladies, owing to their fame and worldly riches. Without mentioning his name, let me tell you about an evening I once spent with a famous boxer. He phoned me and said, 'James, do you want to come to dinner at Stringfellows?'

'Do they do food at Stringfellows?'

'Yeah, including dessert …'

I was thinking, 'Is he talking in code? Is *dessert* a euphemism?'

I didn't even like strip clubs. I hated the fakery and pretence of it. All that foreplay and none of the fun was not my vibe. Plus, I didn't need any more women in my life pretending they loved me. But, of course, I accepted his invitation anyway. On the night, we pulled up to the gate in his Mercedes, he lobbed the keys to the valet, and our entrance was like that scene out of *Goodfellas*, where Henry Hill leads his new girlfriend through the restaurant before being seated right at the front. Everyone knew him, people were winking, bowing and slapping him on the back. And the strippers were almost drooling, so that I thought my mate might be ravaged at any moment.

When we sat down – he had a golden throne at the head of the table, no word of a lie – he started going on about this amazing chocolate fudge cake they had on the menu, and again I was convinced he was speaking in metaphors. I was in a permanent state of confusion, not knowing if what came out of his mouth was real or a double entendre. Out of nowhere, some of the most beautiful women I'd ever seen, none of them wearing much, started processing past. And my mate was passing comment on them, like a judge in a dog show. After a couple of minutes, he gave one of them the nod, like a holy seal of approval, and she sat on his lap, before one of her rivals, who had drawn the short straw, sat next to me. I said to her, 'Listen, I'm going to be up front with you, you don't have to talk to me because I don't want a dance and I've got no money anyway. I'll just eat my chocolate fudge cake and you can dance for someone else.' She didn't get the message and I spent a very uncomfortable few minutes spooning chocolate fudge cake into my gob while she hovered over my shoulder.

Eventually, one of the boxer's mates said to me, 'Can I buy you a dance?'

'Nah, I'm all right. The fudge cake is very nice, though …'

'Come on, let me buy you a dance.'

Meanwhile, the boxer had disappeared with the stripper who had been perched on his knee, so I agreed to a dance just to break the awkwardness.

By the time this stripper had led me to a booth, the boxer had returned to the table, where he was speaking to two random female punters. So the whole time this stripper was dancing, grinding against me and jiggling her breasts in my face, she was looking over my shoulder and saying, in this thick eastern European accent, 'Who are those women he is talking to?'

'I don't know.'

'What do you mean, *you don't know*?'

'I mean, I don't know. Please, can you just dance? Let's get this over with.'

'But who are they?'

'They must be his friends.'

'Friends? What friends? Friends how?'

As soon as my time was up, she jumped off me, put her bra and knickers back on – so hastily that she was stumbling all over the place on her eight-inch heels – and literally ran back to our table. Being interrogated while having a fanny thrust in your face might float some blokes' boats, but I pitied the poor man who had paid so much on my behalf for such a distant, workmanlike performance.

When I got back to the table, the boxer asked me how it had gone. 'Not great,' I replied. 'She was asking questions about you the whole time.' Soon after, I left the club and headed home. The following morning, I had a text message from the boxer, sent at 4 am. 'That stripper from last night who mugged you off. I put her on trial, found her guilty and punished her.' Don't worry, before you start digging up patios, that just meant he had sex with her. As I said, he liked speaking in code. There were also pictures. But don't go flicking, you won't find them in the middle of this book. That boxer was a horrible yet magnificent machine. He did more drilling than Shell and never went home alone.

On the 2017 Lions tour, I did have the misfortune of rooming from time to time with someone who ran this boxer close, shagging-wise. He'd say to me, 'Hask, I need to borrow the room.'

'What do you mean?'

'I mean I need a bit of privacy for a couple of hours.'

'For fuck's sake. I've got a game tomorrow!'

Part of my preparation for the midweek game against the Hurricanes was sitting in the corridor for three hours while he was having his wicked way.

But most rugby players are strictly second division when it comes to attracting ladies. Usually, when I told a woman I played rugby, she'd ask me a couple of questions about the All Blacks – 'Oh, did you ever play against that team that does the dance? Were you scared of the Haka?' – and that would be the end of the conversation. For most of my career, I would just pretend I did something else when talking to women. Not only is rugby not interesting to anyone who isn't properly into it, rugby players don't earn anywhere near what most Premier League footballers earn, which certain women are quite attuned to. Also, when you do actually meet a woman who loves her rugby, that is a huge red flag in itself for a whole host of reasons.

Fan: 'So what did you think of Bath's performance this weekend?'

Me: 'Oh, is that the time? I have to go and return some video tapes …'

I could fill another entire book with stories about demented fans, and why you need to run away as fast as your legs will carry you.

I've been in nightclubs with footballers – when I say 'with', they were usually behind a velvet rope, drinking Cristal champagne – and seen women literally fighting to get near them. I was in a club in Vegas once and women were treading all over me to reach some Chelsea bench-warmer I'd never heard of.

Meanwhile, I was probably telling some poor girl I was a property developer or a plumber who specialised in laying heavy pipe. Funnily enough, they'd usually walk off after that gem.

A footballer's level of spending and debauchery makes rugby players look like monks. However, we will have a good go at it when the time is right. I've seen rugby lads stick their credit cards behind a bar and get lumbered with an eight-grand bill, because all the lads pissed off and left them in the lurch. They'd spend the rest of the season desperately trying to claw the money back, from people who would do anything to avoid paying them. Not because they couldn't afford it, but because it was funny or they were tighter than cramp and you'd need a crowbar to get anything out of them.

One of my favourite stitch-up stories involved a former team-mate and England captain, who stole a bottle of champagne from behind a bar, which the owner then claimed was worth 12 grand. Because this player didn't have the necessary funds, he had to phone his mum and get her to pay for it. When I heard what had happened, I said to him, 'No club leaves a 12-grand bottle of champagne sitting on the bar. You've been done over.' It was probably a bottle of Lambrini worth three quid.

Interestingly, no record of this story seems to exist, so I think the England coach who made this guy captain must have got his forensic media team to erase it from the internet. I wish someone would do that for me.

STOP BEING MUPPETS

Camera phones have put the kibosh on a lot of the rowdier stuff. I suppose you could argue that's good in one way, because it means that no unsuspecting member of the public will ever have to see a rugby player's testicles again. The downside is that no-one is safe on a night out anymore because people film everything. Nowadays, a player can get into trouble just for being snapped in a nightclub, let alone strolling down the Fulham Palace Road with his balls hanging out. Look at what happened to Danny Cipriani, who was dropped before he was meant to make his England debut, simply for being photographed dropping off tickets to some mates at a nightclub. Brian Ashton, the England head coach, overreacted in dropping Cips before getting the full facts. However, I have to be a little wary about leaping to Cips's defence because he did once get run over by a bus on a team social.

It's not just camera phones that make things difficult; it's the fact that certain members of the public think they can gain something from seeing players a bit worse for wear. One time, one of the lads jumped off the team coach and had a wee behind a tree at around 2 o'clock in the afternoon. A couple of days later, Wasps received a letter from some irate woman claiming that her children were traumatised at seeing a rugby player 'expose' himself. This letter went on for ages and ended with the killer line, 'If you could see fit to provide us with season tickets, we might be appeased.' People see a bit of rowdy behaviour, discover it's a rugby team, and their eyes suddenly widen and their ears prick up. They see it as an opportunity, an easy way of cashing in. Consequently, a lot of team socials nowadays take place behind closed doors, away from the general public. That's sad, because rugby players don't want to be kept separate from the rest of society, as if we're exotic zoo animals and too dangerous to mix with.

But I can't just blame camera phones for the tempering of behaviour. Players being hit by team-mates until they take a drink, for example, is a thing of the past because a player not wanting to drink is to be respected nowadays. It is not uncommon for younger players to be teetotal nowadays, because they want to keep themselves in as good nick as possible, while there are other players who know that drinking too much will turn them into out-of-control mutants. I certainly never put any pressure on anyone to drink when I was Wasps captain. As soon as they said they weren't drinking, that was the end of it, unless they gave an unacceptable reason, like having to go shopping with their girlfriend the following morning. Then I'd maybe have a word. But the most important thing in any sports team is the players all being in it together.

The game has changed in terms of how professional it needs to be. The older I got, and the more responsibilities I had as a senior Wasps and England player, the more I realised that I had to look after my image as well. I'd rarely get steaming drunk, I just couldn't afford to. It was tricky sometimes, because I wanted kids to have the same amount of fun as I did coming through and reap the benefits of off-field bonding, but it became abundantly clear that's the way it had to be. Towards the end of my career, I spent a lot of time at team socials sharpening kids up, telling them to stop being muppets, calm down, just relax and enjoy themselves. It might have been the only time we'd all drunk together for six months, but with members of the public wanting to be offended, it only took one person to do something stupid.

ALMOST KILLING RORY BEST

There aren't many kids to sharpen up on Lions tours, which is maybe why players relax, have so much fun, and at times enjoy themselves a bit too much. While I don't consider myself to be a proper Lion, because I didn't play in any of the Tests, the 2017 tour of New Zealand was the best I ever went on. The midweek team had a job to do, which was to win those dirt-tracker games to keep the tour on track. And off the field on a Lions tour, a key part of team bin juice's job description is to keep morale up. I think I played my part, because what I remember most about that tour was laughing hysterically every day and bonding with all my team-mates.

Rory Best and his fellow Ulsterman Iain Henderson were like Shrek and Donkey on that trip. They were inseparable and always cracking jokes, although I could only understand about half of what they were saying. I honestly thought Hendy was speaking Irish for the first few days. And while Rory is incredibly clever, I've never met a man who could drink so much without falling over. To be honest, both of them had hollow legs when it came to putting the drink away: if you tried to go head-to-head with either one of them, it would have been goodnight Vienna. So when I came down for breakfast the morning after the final Test, and Rory and Hendy wandered in steaming drunk, I knew there might be trouble ahead. The first thing Rory said was, 'Want a drink, Hask?' I didn't really want a drink because it was only eight in the morning. But they persuaded me to have a cider with my eggs on toast, and once the bubbles hit my lips, that was it. We barely moved from that table for the next 15 hours. That's not even hyperbole. We just sat there from 8.30 to 10 o'clock at night, shooting the shit, crying with laughter and ploughing through more drinks than George Best on a good day.

We were soon joined by Jack Nowell, who had been asleep on a portable hospital bed in the team room, as well as C. J. Stander from Ireland and England props Dan Cole and Joe Marler. It quickly became clear that despite Rory's cleverness, his drinking games were rather rudimentary. One was called 'toothpicks', which involved sticking toothpicks in our faces. Nothing more complicated than that. I have photos somewhere of me looking like that bloke from *Hellraiser*, with blood dripping down my cheeks. Another was called 'drink', which involved necking whatever drink you had in front of you whenever Rory said 'drink'. After a few hours, we all had beer boxes on our heads, with holes cut out for eyes and faces drawn on them. Because Dan Cole was so negative (more in appearance than demeanour), he had a big, sad mouth carved into his.

After about seven hours, I noticed that Rory was starting to drift off. To be fair to him, he had been drinking for about 20 hours. So I said to him, 'Come on old fella, let's have a little lie down.' I wheeled in the hospital bed that had been Jack Nowell's place of rest the night before, and we put Rory on it and tucked him in, so that he looked like a corpse. Arms folded across his chest, like he had been read the last rites, blanket up to chin, his little bald head poking out the top. He tried to fight it but because he was so dreadfully old and wonderfully comfortable, within about 30 seconds he was asleep and happily snoring away. Then I said, 'Why don't we wheel him outside and leave him on the street?' We pushed him through the hotel, all still with boxes on our heads, sniggering like children and shushing each other, so that we were making even more noise than normal, while telling each other to quieten down. When we got him outside I said, 'Why don't we push him down that hill?' Our Lions hotel was right on top of a huge hill in Auckland that sloped down for miles to the sea. Without waiting for a response, I kicked the back of his bed and off he went.

For the first 10 seconds or so, we all thought this was one of the funniest things we'd ever seen – Rory Best, a pale corpse, gently rolling down a hill in a hospital bed. People were literally on the floor, unable to breathe. But, quick as a flash, it turned into a scene from a Norman Wisdom film. As the hill became steeper, the bed picked up speed and panic set in. Now there were four or five of us chasing Rory in this bed, with beer boxes on our heads, shouting and screaming, as people in suits wandered past, on their way home from work.

For a few moments, I thought we'd killed Rory Best, one of Ireland's great rugby heroes, the pride of Ulster. But we – and, more importantly, Rory – were saved by a fortuitous bend in the road, which sent him swerving into a bus stop, scattering commuters and depositing Rory onto the pavement. People were screaming because they thought he was a runaway corpse that had rolled out the back of some undertaker's ambulance. Rory was just very confused. One minute he'd been playing toothpicks, the next he was sprawled in a bus stop, surrounded by people with boxes on their heads.

But almost killing Rory Best wasn't a spectacular enough way to crown a series draw with the All Blacks. The day before we flew home, we got on it again. And this time I suggested a game of 'fire pussy'. I learned fire pussy while at the 2011 World Cup in New Zealand. I was doing some filming in Dunedin, and one day me and a few of the lads visited the city's student quarter, which is famous for being like a slum. There were burnt-out sofas in front yards, boarded-up windows and front doors hanging off hinges, and it soon became apparent that Dunedin students lived like crackheads in the 1980s Bronx.

We spent the afternoon sitting on the roof of a house water-bombing people, before being given a guided tour of the inside. It was like a Victorian hovel. There was a hole in a wall next to where a door should have been, a leaking roof and an outside toilet with no lightbulb, so that you had a choice of shitting with the door open or in the pitch dark. In the kitchen, some bloke was cooking what looked like a bit of dead person in a pan. These students appeared to have spent no money on anything. There were children in Africa living in better conditions. Yet, bizarrely, they were all wearing really expensive shoes. That confounds me to this day. Why would you shit in the dark and eat roadkill while being able to afford the naughtiest pair of trainers going?

But the most notable thing about this hovel was that the living room was covered in scorch marks, which started on the table and snaked across the floor, up the walls and halfway across the ceiling. Naturally, I asked, 'What the hell has happened here?'

'Oh, that's just fire pussy.'

'What the fuck is fire pussy?' I thought it was some kind of very painful women's STD.

'It's a game. You set something on fire and the first person to put it out is the fire pussy. As punishment, the fire pussy has to do all the chores. And he doesn't stop being fire pussy until he plays another game and someone else puts the fire out.'

What. A. Game. Although maybe not one to play with the family on Christmas Day. And clearly no-one had been enforcing the rules in that house, because no-one had done any chores in there for at least a decade.

Anyway, back to Auckland in 2017. My suggestion of a game of fire pussy with my Lions team-mates was surprisingly well received (I say 'surprisingly', but most of the lads had been drinking for a day and a half), and someone immediately tore one of Johnny Sexton's sleeves off and set it alight. Someone dropped a cardboard box on top and soon we had a small fire on our hands. Everyone stared at it for 30 seconds or so, with a mixture of excitement, awe and dread, and I could see people getting nervous, as in almost shitting themselves nervous, before Jack Nowell came out of nowhere and started stamping the flames out. It's quite possible that Jack rescued a magnificent tour from a sour end, or he bottled it, but I'll let you the reader decide. Common sense suggests he probably did the right thing. But because neither he nor any of us are ever likely to play another game, he will forever be known as 'Fire Pussy'.

THE BOAT TRIP, PT II

Which, in a roundabout way, brings us back to the boat trip that went horribly wrong. How, you might have been thinking, did the entire Wasps squad end up on a stag-do boat on the Thames? Well, I thought we'd be able to contain things on a boat. And yes, I have seen *Jaws*. Blame the social secretaries, it was their idea. 'Skipper, we're going to hire a stag-do boat, sail up the Thames, have a few drinks, get dropped off at a bar. No problems.' But within an hour of meeting in Richmond, we had problems. And quite a lot of them.

Because the skipper of the boat had got the tides wrong, he was an hour late, which should have rung alarm bells. How the hell does a skipper get the one thing wrong that a skipper is supposed to know? Had I not been drunk and trying to control a baying mob, I might have flagged this up with Captain Rum. Perhaps I would have grabbed his hands and said, 'I'd wager those pinkies have never weighed anchor in a storm?' But what with all the delays, which meant far too much pre-trip Prosecco, some of the lads ended up going feral (rugby players lose concentration very quickly if they're not kept entertained). It was a steaming hot early summer's day, the towpath was rammed and people were starting to recognise us. Especially me, despite – or, more likely, because of – the fact I looked like that bearded Austrian woman who won the Eurovision Song Contest (the dress I was wearing actually belonged to my now wife's mum). One of the academy lads was caught trying to steal a bottle of vodka from a restaurant (I made him return it and apologise, like a good little schoolboy), and another almost got into a fight because he kept picking up passing dogs and pretending they were his, and people tend to get a bit funny about you touching their dogs. I was trying to calm everyone down and apologising to irate members of the public, everyone was digging out the social team for the lack of organisation and by the time the boat turned up, things were already descending into all-out carnage.

As we were piling on the boat, this middle-aged woman who looked suspiciously like a stripper turned up. At first, I thought she was one of the people whose dogs had been molested. When I asked one of the social secretaries who she was, they told me she was indeed a stripper. My immediate thought was, 'Hmmm, I didn't know they made strippers that old.' My second thought, riding in on the coattails of the first, was, 'That's interesting, inviting a stripper onto a boat full of rugby players in the age of camera phones.' One of the social secretaries assured me that all phones would be confiscated and locked away, and that there were actually supposed to be three strippers, so it was all I could do to thank God for small mercies that the other two hadn't shown up. Perhaps they had missed their dial-a-bus from the old people's home. Anyway, the boat pulled away, the lads started a singalong and I made sure the skipper, who was very apologetic about being late, had turned the CCTV off. It was not like I was planning anything untoward, but experience had told me that in a world of fact-twisting media and the easily offended, it was best not to have evidence of anything. About 30 seconds after leaving shore, with complimentary cocktails being passed around as an apology from Captain Rum, a graduate of the same maritime school as the skipper of the *Costa Concordia*, the antique stripper decides to drop her coat and start wandering around in her lingerie. Some of the lads start cheering like American frat boys, and I am thinking, 'This has got all the hallmarks of a car crash.'

About half an hour later, we pull into this lock and the stripper is standing on the front of the boat with her tits out. It's like that scene from *One Flew Over the Cuckoo's Nest* when the asylum inmates return from their fishing trip, all looking proud as punch. The families in the pub and on the towpath don't look so happy. There are disgusted mums clasping hands over children's eyes, ice cream cones falling from children's hands, startled couples almost toppling sideways off tandems. I run to the other end of the boat, to put as much distance between me and the stripper as possible, while shouting, 'Lads! You haven't thought this through! Get her below deck! I repeat, get the woman below deck!'

We set sail again, and I discovered that the 800 quid we put behind the bar had already run out, which was impossible in my estimation, unless the lads were drinking Cristal. Which they weren't, as we were on a stag-do boat on the Thames and the height of glamour was a warm can of Red Stripe. Due to the lateness, malleable accounting by the barmaids, and the fact that because the skipper got the tides wrong we could not get to the bar upriver where we were supposed to be going, we ended up just doing big circles of the Thames. So our relationship with the skipper went downhill pretty quickly. Back up on deck, I got a court session underway. We'd had a number of captains that season, so the boys laid down a challenge to all those who had worn the armband: who was the real skipper of Wasps? A 'boat race' was called and I chinned my pint quickest to settle the argument. My leadership rubber-stamped, my next port of call dictated by the fines committee was to punish two of the academy lads with three lashes on the arse with a riding crop. They knew what they'd done wrong. One had called me the worst word of all and the other had ignored team rules – both heinous offences, and without order we have chaos. As the lashes rained down on their bare buttocks, the rest of the lads cheered, knowing justice was being done.

Every club has a fines committee that marks down all the misdemeanours throughout the season. No-one is safe from their roving eye, and team socials/court sessions are where these crimes are brought to the team's attention, tried and punished. This could range from crimes against fashion, lateness, breaking team rules, or in one player's case consistently being put in the friend zone by women. His punishment for this was to spend the entire team social in his own paddling pool or friend zone, filled with beers to be drunk, and shamed. Being captain, I was often the executioner or had the final word on sentencing. However, when Captain Rum saw what was going on, his eyes were on stalks, because where there is rum and the lash, sodomy is sure to follow. And then it happened, that thing that no-one who witnessed it will ever be able to unsee. The handstand. The bottle of strong European lager. The Devil's evacuation. The horror … the horror …

Having docked many hours later, and being more of a sprinter than a marathon man on team socials, I decided to skip the evening's entertainment and get an early night. But the following morning, I phoned Sam Jones and said, 'Any fallout from the boat trip?'

'Yes. I've had a call from the owner. They've had to get the boat chemically cleaned. But he said as long as we leave a good review, he's happy. Oh, and the stripper has been on to one of the lads. The idiot paid for the team show with his PayPal account, so she had his email. And she wants her blouse and petticoats back.'

'Right. Tell the skipper we'll pay for the chemical cleaning. But do not leave a review until it's all sorted. Fuck knows who's got the stripper's blouse – probably one of the backs – but tell him to give her some money and we'll take it out of the kitty.'

I thought it was all sorted until my dad got an email from some bloke claiming to be John Terry's agent, saying that the boat staff had never seen such debauchery (do bear in mind that the boat was used solely for stag-dos, so the whiff of bullshit was strong from the off), and that the staff were suffering from post-traumatic stress disorder and were considering taking legal action. I told my dad and he suggested setting up a meeting, but the bloke was very cagey and kept threatening to tell our bosses at Wasps unless we paid him/them a satisfactory amount of compensation. They were on the make, because they thought we were all minted sportsmen with money to burn. I knew things were going to get far weirder when I phoned John Terry, told him what was going on and he told me he'd never heard of this 'agent'.

Things quickly got worse. This so-called agent didn't wait for a meeting, and with a big pay day on his mind he went ahead and told Wasps we'd had a gay sex orgy on the boat. Supposedly, we were all sucking each other off and shagging each other; we were all off our heads on drugs; one lad in a pig mask was being particularly sinister and intimidating all the staff; someone shat themselves; and 'the big one in the wig and dress, James Haskett' (*who?*) was the ringleader and had personally inserted bottles of lager up team-mates' arses. This Walter Mitty of an agent produced affidavits from the crew that were a joke. The bit about someone shitting themselves was true, as was the bit about me hitting people on the arse with a riding crop. Nothing else was. But when I told the club that this bloke was a charlatan, and pleaded with them not to pay compensation, they were already in damage-limitation mode and arranging an investigation.

Wasps' legal team arranged meetings with the lads and read them reports from the staff. It was frankly ridiculous. Players were asked if it was true that they'd dumped their girlfriends for the weekend to have a gay boat orgy. They were asked if it was true that I'd made them do all sorts of weird things.

'Did James insert a bottle of lager up your bottom? Did James make you perform a sex act? And remember, it's okay if you did … this is a safe place.' The legal team's mistrust of our version of events could only have been made clearer if they'd produced a doll and asked the lads to point to where I'd touched them.

I'd been on an England tour to Australia when the interviews took place and was now conducting conference calls with the club from Ibiza. None of the affidavits matched, and I told the club it was all bullshit and that they shouldn't let this cat fish of an 'agent' bully them. But the club were panicking. As is almost always the case with sports teams, it was a case of manage reputational damage first and worry about personnel second. And then this lunatic played his trump card and asked for £8 million compensation. *Yes, £8 million!* He'd gone full-on Dr Evil. I imagined him sitting in a boardroom (his mum's kitchen?) with the boat people, saying, 'We will hold Wasps ransom for … eight million pounds!' before raising his little finger to his lips and sniggering. One kid shat himself and cleaned it up himself, and they wanted £8 million. The survivors of the terrible Alton Towers rollercoaster accident didn't get that much between them, and they tragically lost limbs. PTSD? That's what soldiers get when they see their mates get blown up in battle, not when you see someone get hit on the arse with a riding crop.

A few months later, the agent who had promised the world and not even delivered a globe to his bosses decided to cut his losses and sell the story himself. I don't know how much he got for it, but it was very, very far short of £8 million. They couldn't report all the allegations because they had no concrete evidence. And the legal team had redacted so much that the article didn't even make sense. But there was a lot of coded chat about 'debauchery' and 'sex acts' and people feeling overwhelmed and terrified. Of course, I was the only player mentioned, accompanied by a big photo of me with my top off. Meanwhile, the agent had written to the RFU, suggesting it would be a travesty if I ever played for England again. His letter read, 'I am shocked and appalled that you have allowed James Haskell to go off to Australia and play for his country and gain cult status with his performances when he is a deviant. To make matters worse you allowed him to swan off to Ibiza with his pop star girlfriend.' (I was livid, Chloe incandescent – a pop star, how dare they?)

The club spent something like 70 grand on legal fees and tried to take it out of the lads' salaries, which we weren't having. They then sacked me as captain, although they claim they didn't. They made up some story about me needing time to recover from injury, and that I would be away a lot with England, so they gave the job to Joe Launchbury (who is a great captain). I told them, 'I didn't shit on the boat. If it wasn't for me trying to keep some kind of order and turning off the CCTV, who knows what might have happened?' They should have given me an award for bravery under fire, not sacked me. But I was never captain of Wasps again.

The moral of the story? If you're ever at a party and someone asks if you want to see a beer fountain, just say no.

2

TRAINING LIKE A LUNATIC

DEDICATION WORKS

The reason I made my debut for Wasps as a teenager was because I'd been training like a lunatic for years before then. But it took a dose of failure when I was 15 to make me realise how hard I needed to work. The night before regional trials I went to the cinema with my old mate Ted Cooper. After the film, we persuaded a bloke to buy us a six pack of Fosters, before pushing each other around an Asda car park in shopping trollies and doing a very bad job of chatting up girls in the bowling alley. When my dad turned up to collect us, he was not best pleased. We'd only had three cans of lager each but that will make you pretty drunk when you're only 15. The following day, I played like a muppet. And even though I made it through to the next stage, the coaches told me I'd slipped from being a potential England starter to nearly missing out.

Before the final England Under-16s trial, I was given lots of extra work to do. But I just didn't do it. My dad was pulling his hair out, but all I was interested in was girls and not much else. I didn't understand the concepts of commitment and proper hard work – but then who does at 15? As a result, I played badly in the final trial weekend and ended up missing out on both the main and the second-string A team. I vividly remember getting the dreaded phone call from the chief selector, saying I hadn't made it, and crying like a baby. My dad, ever the pragmatist, said, 'Look, either you can play rugby for fun from now on or you can see this as a kick up the backside and a challenge to work harder.' When you're 15, it's hard to hear that you failed at something because you didn't give it your all, and it's easy to be resentful and chuck it all in. But not making that England Under-16s team was one of the best things that happened to me.

If it wasn't for my mum and dad, I wouldn't have achieved half of what I have. They provided a loving home, gave me and my brother every opportunity in life, and almost bankrupted themselves putting us through a bloody expensive public school. They didn't always do things by the book, but they weren't stereotypically pushy parents. They just wanted me to make the most of my opportunities. My dad never missed a game when I was a kid. He'd often turn up late because his timekeeping was terrible and he was always so busy, working to pay the bills. But he'd always be there at the final whistle, when other dads weren't. And they just cared so much. I was once part of an England Under-18s team that won a tournament, only to receive nothing for it. My dad wasn't having that, so he paid for trophies to be made for the players and coaches. I would never have achieved what I have without them both.

My dad had a friend called Henry Abrahamian, who was a personal trainer and took me under his wing. I started to train with him at weekends and during school holidays before he started coming to my boarding school twice a week during term time. I'd finish my homework at 9 pm, run down to the school gym and work with him for an hour before bedtime, running up hills in the dark, sprinting up and down fields, proper *Rocky* stuff. I started going to this meathead gym in Bracknell, full of mutant bodybuilders wearing fluorescent leggings and stripy string vests. (One guy told me he was so big because he ate 15 chicken breasts a day. Being a naïve 15-year-old I believed him, and I even persuaded my mum to buy 30 chicken breasts at a time, which must have cost her a fortune. What I didn't know was that Chicken George was roided out of his mind and could have exploded at any moment.) When I first started lifting weights, I could barely lift the bar on its own. It was obviously a bit embarrassing for a teenage kid, but I conquered my self-consciousness and gradually got bigger and stronger.

Some of my behaviour became borderline obsessive. Henry got me in such good shape that people thought I was on drugs. He must have been a disciple of Chicken George as he would bring me three chickens he'd bought reduced from Tesco and I'd eat one and a half of them before bed and give the rest to other senior boys. That was the solids taken care of. As for the liquids, I was in charge of the school bar but didn't really drink. I look back now and think, 'Jesus, you had access to unlimited beer and you hardly touched a drop. A few pints here and there wouldn't have made much difference.' Even on the rare occasions I went on the piss, I'd wake up the following morning full of guilt and train all day.

One summer, Henry joined us in Bahrain and trained with me and another mate – Stuart Mackie – for a week. It's no exaggeration to say that Henry was the person most responsible for moulding me into a professional rugby player. My schoolmates probably thought I was weird, because it was cooler to get drunk and smoke in the bushes. But when I made the England Under-18s team as captain, that was the proof I needed that dedication worked. The other great spur was the fact that I thought I wasn't very talented. Having natural talent is a curse for some kids, because it tricks them into believing hard work is optional. At that England Under-16s trial, I was a streak of piss with poor fitness. But a year and a half later, I was 10 kg heavier and as fit as a butcher's dog. It was a stark and simple lesson: if you put the necessary work in, and work smart, anything is possible.

THAT'S MY BOY

On that first pre-season trip to Poland, I was desperate to find out what it meant to be a professional rugby player, even though I'd be going back to school to do my A levels at the end of it. I was now 17 and I may have bulked up, but the coaches wanted to wrap me in cotton wool. That was under-standable, because I was used to playing against kids my own age from Eton and Harrow, and now I was training with grown men and seasoned internationals, players like Lawrence Dallaglio, Phil Greening and Simon Shaw. But I kept nagging the coaches, until eventually they caved in and threw me into full-contact training and full-on fitness drills.

I'd already pissed a few players off by beating them in fitness tests and saying a few things I shouldn't. And then I made a far bigger mistake, which was making an enemy of Trevor Leota. Trevor was 5 ft 9 in, 20 stone, played for Samoa, was related to former heavyweight world title contender David Tua and probably hit harder. In my first full-contact training session, we were practising mauls and Trevor kept coming in at the side. I got all fired up and thought, 'If this bloke does that again, I'm going to bang him out.' A few minutes later, he did it again. So I hit him, fell on top of him and hit him again. Panic set in when I realised I hadn't put a dent in Trevor and he was very angry, before he countered with a short, chopping punch that split my face open. But rather than it being a negative thing, everyone seemed to love it. Warren Gatland shouted, 'Lads, did you see that? He's only 17 and he's dishing it out to Trevor!' Then Trevor came over and gave me a big hug. Gats spent the rest of the trip coming up behind me, massaging my shoulders and growling in my ear, 'That's my boy.' I earned respect, and everyone now thought I was a very fiery competitor. That wasn't true, but my team-mates thinking it did me no harm. Of course, I spent the rest of the trip not running anywhere near Trevor, as he may have hugged me but I knew given half the chance he would fold me up in a tackle like a travel map.

Gats was a clever coach. He gave his players a certain amount of freedom, but in exchange for that freedom he expected them to buy into the culture completely, work like maniacs and have a physical edge. Every Tuesday and Thursday, we'd have massive sessions, and every session was do or die for me. I'd always be in a tackle suit, putting big hits on people or grappling with someone. That was my thing, full-throttle physicality. And it never stopped being my thing, because I always had a chip on my shoulder about not being physical enough – probably because when I started training with Wasps, I was a 17-year-old schoolboy pitted against strong, hard men.

At Wasps, they encouraged competition, even needle, between players. We used to have what they called power-endurance days, which involved all the players being split into pairs and going head-to-head in a variety of exercises in the gym, before heading outside and doing shuttles, down and ups, wrestling and tug of war. When I first turned pro, they'd pit me against Lawrence Dallaglio. Gats would spice things up by telling Lawrence that I'd been telling people that he was over the hill, and telling me that Lawrence had been telling people that I was never going to make it. So me and Lawrence would have these life and death tear-ups, until after about three weeks

I let him win a single rep of wrestling. I saw a spark light up in his eyes and he let me win the next one. We still went hard at each other, but instead of engaging in insane battles, we put our egos on hold for the greater good. He even started taking me for breakfast. I'd offer to drive, but he didn't fancy travelling in my nan's Vauxhall Astra. So not only did I get to ride in his Range Rover, he always paid! Had I kept a diary, it would have read like this: 'Dear Diary, today was a glorious day, my hero Lawrence paid for poached eggs on toast ...'

BANGING PEOPLE OUT

As you can imagine, all that testosterone was bound to boil over on the training ground occasionally. One of the first training-ground fights I saw was between Lawrence and Joe Worsley, which might have scared me if Joe knew how to punch. Instead, he looked like an old woman trying to fend off a mugger with her handbag. Then there was the time I thought Josh Lewsey had killed Danny Cipriani. We were doing a defensive drill and Cips didn't fancy it. Which was not a huge shock. Instead of putting the shoulder in, he was running up and touching the attacker with his fingertips. This didn't go down well with Josh, who gave Cips a volley of abuse. Cips told Josh where to go, Josh told Cips never to speak to him like that again – before Cips spoke to him like that again. I heard a bang and when I turned around, Cips was on the floor snoring, with Josh standing over him shouting. It was like a shit version of that famous photograph of Cassius Clay towering over Sonny Liston. Josh reminded me of Nicky Santoro from the film *Casino*, in that if you fought him, you'd have to kill him. I later learned that Josh had knocked Cips cold with a sweet right hand. Cips finally came around and for the next five hours kept asking the same questions: 'What happened? What day is it?' Someone sold the story to a paper and the following week, after Cips set Josh up to score, they did a boxing celebration out on the pitch, showing they were still as always the best of friends.

Training-ground fights don't happen as much as they used to, although I tried to bring them back into fashion in Japan, when I was playing for Tokyo's Ricoh Black Rams in 2011–12. While I was always physical in training, I wasn't normally one to start anything. But during my stint playing for the Rams, we were having a particularly intense training match when this prop squared up to me, feinted to punch me and I whacked him. All hell broke loose. It was like I'd murdered someone. I had about seven meetings, with lots of different people – coaches, managers, senior players, retired players – telling me that hitting people in training isn't part of Japanese culture, and the head coach was utterly appalled. He kept saying, 'If you did that in a game, you'd get a red card and a ban.' But it wasn't a game, so I couldn't quite work out what the problem was. Someone squared up to me, I hit him and we shook hands afterwards. No-one died. As for the bloke I hit, the only mistake he made was not hitting me first, which is exactly what I told him once we hugged it out.

THE LEICESTER BORG

We had a tough culture at Wasps – even one of our scrum-halves, Pete Richards, had a cauliflower ear – but the most aggressive trainers I played with were the Leicester boys, back in the day. Those Tigers only had two modes, ON or OFF, there was no in between. And when we joined up with England, all of a sudden we were in the Leicester world. The Leicester players were like the Borg from *Star Trek*, separate organisms with a shared hive mind. They'd change together, walk out to training together, shower together, eat together, drink together. If someone had told me they shared each other's wives, I wouldn't have been the least bit surprised. To be honest, I and most other players found it a bit weird that the England coaches tolerated the Leicester clique, which is exactly what it was. Martin Corry, Julian White, Louis Deacon, George Chuter, Lewis Moody, Harry Ellis – don't get me wrong, they were all excellent players and great blokes, it's just not good for team bonding to have one club just hanging around together all the time. Things would get so bad that the non-Leicester boys would watch them from afar and do David Attenborough-style voiceovers: 'Leicester Tigers are fiercely independent creatures. And because this prop is injured, he is even more dangerous than usual. On this morning, some poor bastard is going to get filled in ...'

Whenever it's a player's first training session, he'll go at it like it's a Test match. You'll sometimes hear some of the older play-ers having a grumble as they traipse off the field at the end of the session. 'Jesus, he's a bit keen ...' In my first England train-ing session, I tackled someone, got back to my feet and stole the ball, and as I was re-setting I heard someone call me 'a fucking nause' and got punched in the face. When I looked up to see who it was, Martin Corry and Louis Deacon were staring back at me. I think it was Louis, but to be honest it would have been a hell of a risk to hit him back, let alone punch an inno-cent party. If you think the Tigers boys grouping together for a coffee was bad, imagine what would happen if you decided to fight one of them. They would have been like a pack of hyenas. However, I refused to let them bully me. The next time I tackled someone, I stole the ball again. That was my way of saying, 'Fuck you', and hopefully earning their respect.

When Leicester legend John Wells was England forwards coach, he'd turn everything into full contact, even warm-ups.

This is a man whose highlights reel as a player, discovered on YouTube, consisted of him diving into a ruck and getting shoed half to death. As far as Wellsy was concerned, if you got cut to ribbons but disrupted the other team while doing it, it was job well done. I am obviously doing him a disservice, but Wellsy was most happy when he was at the bottom of a ruck, getting kicked, while clinging onto the ball with his considerable farmer's strength.

John would put you into groups of three at the start of a rugby session and get you to play a very simple game, which was for two of you to attempt to steal the ball off the other person. But he wouldn't be happy unless you were hurting each other. He'd walk around shouting in his shrill, slightly camp Yorkshire accent, 'James! What are you doing? Twist his wrists! Bend his fingers back! Pull them as hard as you can! Break them if you have to!' Before one game against France, Wellsy wanted to know how we were going to get the ball off their prop Jean-Baptiste Poux at the back of the line-out, but he kept pronouncing his name as 'poo'.

'Right, how are we going to get poo off the ball?'

Cue lots of sniggering.

'What's so funny? Poo's on the ball! How are we gonna get poo off it?'

Wellsy looked at Tom Wood, who was in his first England camp, and said, 'Woody, how are we gonna get poo off the ball?'

'Erm ... twist his nuts off and snap his fingers?'

You could see Wellsy vibrating with sheer excitement.

'That, Woody, is the best answer I've ever had! Now, all of you, go out and show me that in training.'

I turned to Woody and said, 'What the fuck are you doing? Don't fuel the madman. Never fuel the madman. And also, you've never tried to rip anyone's balls off or snap anyone's fingers in your life. If you did, you would get banned.'

'Sorry, mate, I just got carried away.'

If you weren't bleeding at the end of a warm-up, Wellsy wasn't happy. I recall one warm-up before a game against Wales when I had to get stitches, and I'd never seen Wellsy so thrilled. As far as Wellsy was concerned, the blood was a sign that I was going to play a blinder. The Leicester boys even had a game called 'maul touch', which was the worst game ever invented and only popular at Welford Road. Everyone would be running around playing a fun game of touch and Wellsy (who always used to say to me, 'Hask, less flash, more bash!') would march over and start barking at you to set up a maul, which would often descend into a fight. And if Julian White hit you, you were lucky if your head didn't fall off the back of your shoulders. Luckily, Julian found me quite amusing, however much he hated the fact. A recurring theme of my career was people desperately wanting to hate me but finding they couldn't.

LIABILITIES

Lewis Moody was a good bloke but a liability to himself and his team-mates. Every time he made contact, he'd knock himself out or get kicked in the balls, and one or more tacklers would be writhing about on the floor in agony. Even if he had a tackle shield in his hands, he'd use it as a deadly weapon. We should have called Lewis the spine compressor instead of 'Moodos'. Lewis was an incredible player and competitor, but he only had two settings: off or absolutely mental. The same went for anyone who played for Leicester. Moodos would get very upset if everyone else was only working at the prescribed 50 per cent and start telling everyone to buck up their ideas. And if you tried to explain that we'd been told to hold back, it wouldn't make any difference. A few minutes later, he'd be trying to smoke everyone and then the lads would ramp things up to 100 per cent trying to smoke him back, which of course he absolutely loved.

Some players are dangerous simply because they're ridiculously clumsy. At Wasps, whenever James Dunne jumped in a line-out, he'd elbow someone in the face, punch someone in the neck and land on someone's foot. Pretty much every one of his team-mates suffered multiple DRIs – Dunney Related Injuries – so that there should have been a separate Dunney Related Insurance policy. Every training session, you'd get someone rolling around on the floor and shouting to the physio, 'DRI! DRI!', like a wounded soldier calling for a medic. But every player will tell you, whatever club they played for, that they had their very own Dunney, an injury trap running around like a maniac, waiting to ruin your day with his size 16 feet or massive cow head.

Peter Buxton was responsible for roughly 80 per cent of injuries at Gloucester and maybe 50 per cent of injuries in the Premiership. BRIs were a big problem. Pete would fly into a ruck at 100 mph, take out three people from his own side, three people from the other side, bounce straight up and carry on running. Players from both sides would be scattered all over the floor, groaning. Then there were players like Trevor Leota, who was so dangerous he was banned from tackling in training. He was so hard that I once saw him get off the floor after a tackle and his cauliflower ear was hanging on by a single thread (he simply had it strapped up and carried on, but it took 23 stitches to reattach after the game). Some poor kid would cut a line and Trevor would appear from nowhere and bury him. The kid would be folded up on the floor like a deckchair, struggling to breathe, and you'd hear a coach say, 'Jesus, Trev, you've done it again', and Trevor reply, 'Sorry, bro.'

THE WIGAN WAY

Rugby union may have gone professional in 1995, but some of those early pros never really stopped being amateurs in their attitudes to training. But no-one exemplified the new paid era more than Jonny Wilkinson. Jonny trained like a madman, to the extent that it was a miracle he ever turned up fit for a game. Jonny would do extra this and extra that and took things to a whole new level. By his own admission, his perfectionism wasn't always a positive thing, because it stemmed from an almost morbid fear of failure and made him extremely unhappy. But if it was good enough for Jonny, it was good enough for me.

After my first day at Wasps, my dad took me aside and said, 'Listen, son, you've never tackled properly, and you and I both know you don't like doing it. You need to work on it, or you will never make it as a professional.' It didn't go down well, but he was right. So I asked Joe Worsley for help. 'Joe, you're an unbelievable tackler, the best I've ever seen, can you teach me?' And he did. After every training session, I did 15 minutes extra tackling with Joe and Tom Rees. And I never stopped doing extras on every part of my game for the next 18 years. When me and James Wellwood went on holiday to Majorca during some time off from Wasps, we found a football pitch with a running track and trained every day until we were spewing, while everyone else was nursing a hangover. Even when I went on holiday to Las Vegas, I'd try to train every day. The lads would be walking along with some girls, the day after an all-day session, and see me through the window of the gym, sprinting on the treadmill. There's no real secret to getting better, at whatever it is. It's mainly about working your bollocks off and doing more than most other people are prepared to do.

Some of my older team-mates weren't keen on lifting weights, drinking protein shakes or taking supplements. But Warren Gatland's rugby philosophy was quite simple: be fitter, bigger and stronger than everyone else. Apparently, it stemmed from the 2002 Middlesex Sevens, when rugby league's Bradford Bulls destroyed Wasps in the final (although we did better than most Premiership teams that weekend). After that game, Gats decided to completely overhaul the Wasps set-up and lured conditioning guru Craig White back to rugby from Bolton Wanderers. Craig and his assistants, Paul Stridgeon and Mark Bitcon, all went to the same school in Wigan, as did Shaun Edwards. Between them, they instilled rugby league levels of professionalism – 'the Wigan Way' – into Wasps.

Suddenly, there were conditioning coaches everywhere, which meant players couldn't hide and had no choice but to work hard. Before Craig's arrival, the backs and the forwards would do the same weights routines, which was madness because we were all different body shapes (nowadays, ironically, everyone looks the same, and in some cases backs are bigger than forwards). But Craig introduced intricate period-ised weights and fitness programmes tailored to individuals, and taught us that good training was about intensity and rest, rather than volume. On pre-season trips to Poland, we'd have some mad scientist putting us in cryotherapy freezers, years before any other clubs were doing it. You'd be sitting in this thing, set at −170°C, shivering what was left of your bollocks off and thinking, 'This is complete madness, but I'll go along with it.' Craig was a pioneer, years ahead of his time. And because Gats and Lawrence demanded that everyone buy into his culture, Wasps stole a march on their rivals.

LIFTING COWS

When you're a young pro and keen to prove yourself, the weights room can be a very macho place. Wasps hooker Phil Greening used to say to me, 'There's no point in being able to lift a cow if you can't catch one, outrun one or outthink one.' Today, I tell kids something similar. 'Concentrate on core skills rather than spending all your time in the gym shifting weights. The reason people miss tackles isn't because they're not big enough, it's because they don't know how to tackle properly or don't have the right attitude.' But I didn't take much notice of Phil, just as kids today probably don't take much notice of me.

Because they knew players were naturally competitive, Wasps' coaches would stick players' personal bests on the wall and you'd see boys eyeing them up, maybe checking what their rival for a starting spot was lifting. They had a bell in the weights room, and you'd ring it if you set a new PB. When I first joined Wasps, I was already 100 kg. But Gats locked me and Tom Rees in the weights room for six months with Mark Bitcon (aka Big Guns), and everything changed. Written on the gym wall in big letters was Big Gun's motto, 'Get big or die trying.' I emerged weighing 110 kg, an absolute monster.

In the England set-up, Andrew Sheridan loved lifting weights, the heavier the better, stuff like 300 kg squats and 220 kg bench presses. Towards the end of my England career, Joe Marler took fellow prop Kyle Sinckler under his wing and their sessions were intense, like an episode of *World's Strongest Man*. If you ever wanted to give Kyle a bit of a lift, all you had to say was, 'Sinks, your back is looking massive', and he'd be absolutely chuffed. 'Do you really think so? Thanks, Hask, I've been working on it ...'

Manu Tuilagi would do chin-ups with an 80 kg dumbbell hanging off him. Before the 2015 World Cup, they got this

American guy in who created weights programmes based on something called force plate testing. You stood on this plate, jumped upwards, and it told you areas you were strong in and others you needed to work on. Maybe you needed to work on squats or build up your hamstrings. Manu did it and almost blew the machine up. The American guy had worked with countless NBA and NFL players but reckoned Manu was the most powerful vertical jumper he'd ever seen.

A lot of the Pacific Islanders had to be careful with weights because they got too big. I had a team-mate at Northampton, Taqele Naiyaravoro, who was told to stop doing weights altogether, after he blew up to 140 kg. He was a winger, by the way. I never got as big as that, but I prided myself on being really strong and spending a lot of time in the gym. During the 2011 World Cup, me and Tom Wood both box squatted 295 kg and I was bench pressing about 195 kg. I got a reputation as a meathead, which I was never able to shake off. But eventually I realised that Phil Greening had been right all along. Did being able to lift loads, or look great in the mirror, make you a better player? The honest answer was no, but what did was focusing on the technique of the individual areas of rugby, the core skills. Once I realised this, there was a huge sea change in my training and what I did. I moved away from gym work and focused on my mobility, carrying, tacking, passing, running lines, etc, all the elements that were actually going to make me a better player.

MELTED WHEELIE BINS

Rugby isn't as professional as it's made out to be, in many respects. For a long time, clubs were very backwards in terms of nutrition. At Wasps, I'd get advice on what to eat and what not to, but I was never given a specific nutritional plan or encouraged to track my food intake. Eventually, I went and paid for advice out of my own pocket and started weighing my food out, so I could change my body when I needed to and maximise my performance. Trying to look like a cover model is not going to make you a good player, or help you perform well in games. Some might say my commitment to eating properly was obsessive. When I was 26 or 27, I moved back in with my mum and dad for a bit. I was on a mad diet at the time – six meals a day, consisting of 200 g of a protein source, 380 g of a carbohydrate source and 30 g of fats – but all pretty bland and regimented. When I came down for breakfast every morning, there would already be chicken and potatoes boiling and salmon cooking on the grill. As I was eating, my mum and dad would be systematically filling Tupperware, like robots on a car assembly. Once filled, they would be put in my super 1980s Jane Fonda-style coolbox that I would carry around for the whole day. This was extreme, and you would often find me staring at a huge portion of cold white fish and brown rice, wishing it would disappear. Reflecting back, I can see it actually affected how I looked at food. I did get into mental shape and performed well on the field, but I realise now that food is meant to be fun and flavourful. Cold fish, boiled chicken, cold butternut squash and broccoli is no fun at all, especially not for the eighth day in a row.

The rise of professionalism and sports nutrition certainly didn't eradicate fat props and hookers. The changing room would be packed with brick shithouses but there would always be a couple of melted wheelie bins. Apparently, before the 2003 World Cup, Clive Woodward got Josh Lewsey to take his top off, pointed at him and said, 'Everyone in this squad needs to have a body like that.' Jason Leonard put his hand up and said, 'Boss, that ain't gonna happen.' Jason had an excuse – he'd been playing since the 1950s – but there's no reason for props and hookers to have guts nowadays. They need to be a certain weight, they need a low centre of gravity and they might have an excuse to have higher body fat than the rest of us, but they don't need to be blubbery. In fact, there's no reason for any professional sportsperson to be fat. The excuse that you just love your food is not valid. It's just poor nutrition.

Andrew Sheridan was one of the first props who was built like a tank, with hardly any fat on him, while my best pal and Wasps and England team-mate Paul Doran Jones had a six pack (his nickname was BLT, as in big, lean and tanned, although I suspect he made that up himself). But not everyone got the memo. One Wasps prop who shall remain nameless had probably the worst body of any professional rugby player I ever saw. It looked like a cross between a burst beanbag and a fire-damaged Portakabin. The nutritionist tried to fix it, but there's only so much a nutritionist can do when the player's excuse is that everything tastes good.

When a season finished, Trevor Leota would be in unbelievable shape. But he'd return for pre-season about 40 kg overweight and get out of breath walking from the car park to the changing room. They'd get Paul Stridgeon to live with him and try to stop him eating KFC and drinking bourbon and Coke every night, and a couple of months later he'd be one of the best hookers in the world again. But then the cycle would start from the beginning again. Even when he was in decent nick, Trevor was always a hair's breadth away from an all-dayer in the Redback in Acton. During one exhibition game between Wasps and South Africa's Sharks, the referee called Lawrence Dallaglio over and said, 'I'm worried about your hooker, I can smell Jack Daniels coming off him.' Lawrence quick as a flash replied, 'Oh, he always smells like that, that's just his aftershave,' and gave the ref a wink.

THE ROPE

Aside from one emphatic victory over the All Blacks, Stuart Lancaster's reign as England head coach will sadly and unfairly be remembered for the disastrous 2015 World Cup. But one thing I did enjoy about his stint in charge were the heated trousers we wore on the bench. You'd press a button and a minute later you'd feel like you'd pissed yourself. Other fads I came across I wasn't entirely sold on. For example, I never worked out whether ice baths worked, even though there was a time when just about every professional sportsperson in the country was using them. I recall someone shitting in the communal ice bath at Wasps, so there was at least one person in the rugby community who was even less convinced by their benefits than me.

When I joined Stade Français in Paris in 2009, the medical staff were very machine orientated. That's if they could fit you in. You'd pop along to see them and they'd be on their one-hour lunch break. And because the unions are so strong in France, you'd just have to wait. The hour would pass and they'd go straight into a 20-minute fag break, before strolling back into the treatment room stinking of Gauloises. One time, I had a dead leg and one of the lads pulled out a pair of women's tights. I was thinking, 'Jesus, I know things can get a bit fruity in Paris, but I'm not into this. Well, not on a school night.' I thought he wanted to paint me like one of his French ladies. He persuaded me to put them on, before pulling out what looked like a Henry hoover (an Henri hoover, perchance?) and vacuuming my legs. And you wonder why I spent my one day off a week travelling back to London to visit my personal physio Kevin Lidlow, out of my own pocket, before returning to Paris for training the following morning.

Talking of eccentric, Paul 'Bobby' Stridgeon, Wasps' former strength and conditioning coach, was completely off the charts for all the best reasons. Bobby is one of those unknown heroes of professional rugby, a legend of a man in every way. Anyone who has worked with him, either with Wasps, Wales or the Lions, will tell you he is an indispensable part of any team. Brian O'Driscoll once said that Bobby would be his first pick for any coaching staff, and I'd completely agree. A former GB wrestler who once took on eight Lions forwards in New Zealand, and beat them all, Bobby is one of the biggest characters in rugby, brilliant at his job, always wired off his tits on caffeine and has the biggest cock I've ever seen, which he nicknames 'The Rope'.

Bobby's party trick would be to put a full can of Red Bull on the edge of a table, pull out The Rope and use it to slap the can across the room, like he was playing a game of human pinball. He was also a master of the penis windmill and penis puppetry. If you're ever lucky enough to meet Bobby and ask him nicely, I'm sure he'd be happy to teach you everything he knows. The Rope also has magic powers, in that it can inspire people to do great things. I would be lying on my back, about to do a bench press, and Bobby would stroll past and say in his broad Wigan accent, 'Mate, you ready to lift big? Do you need Rope?'

If nervous about the lift, I'd say, 'Yes, Bob, I need Rope.'

As quick as a flash he would slap The Rope on me, to psyche me up. And you know what? Being anointed by The Rope would mean that I would go right ahead and bench press a personal best. Don't ask me how or why, some things in this world just aren't meant to be explained, but if I could pack The Rope in my kit bag for the dark times when I was searching for motivation, then I would. Sadly for me, Bobby needs it, and it wouldn't fit into any known kit bag anyway.

The Rope also healed injuries. Bobby would say to me, 'Hask, mate, how's the elbow?'

'Not great, Bobby.'

'Rope will sort it out ...'

And he'd lop The Rope out and hit my elbow with it. Strangely it worked, and I would be back training straight after.

3

PLAYING THE GAME

OUT OF MY DEPTH

My first start for Wasps was in a friendly against Montferrand (now Clermont) in France, while I was still at school. I was selected to start in the back-row, alongside Lawrence Dallaglio and against the great French flanker Olivier Magne. To call that game a baptism of fire would be an understatement. I was blowing out of my arse during the warm-up, and when Phil Greening went through his line-out moves, I didn't have a clue what he was talking about. As if that wasn't intimidating enough, just before kick-off Lawrence took me aside and said, 'If anything goes off, I want you there beside me.' I was a kid, so didn't quite understand. Forty minutes later, I knew exactly what he was talking about.

A few things stand out from that game. I vividly remember Magne running diagonally across the field and me tracking him, before he did a 20 metre, no-look reverse pass to the winger, who then scored. I didn't know that kind of trickery existed, let alone have it in my arsenal. But the game was more notable for its brutality. After Phil Greening elbowed winger Aurelien Rougerie in the throat (Rougerie later collapsed, needed three operations and successfully sued Phil for damages), a massive brawl kicked off. Just as Lawrence had told me to do, I punched the nearest bloke, who was minding his own business and happened to be a huge prop. The prop immediately punched me back, knocking the bottom bar of my brace off. I was staggering around in a daze. I could just about make out my mum, screaming and trying to get over the barrier, presumably because she wanted to stick the nut on him. The game was chaos, we got pumped and a couple of days later I was back at school.

Playing for Wasps as a teenager was obviously a thrill, but it completely ruined my schoolboy rugby. When you've spent your weekend fighting fully grown Frenchmen, going back to playing against Harrow is a bit of a comedown. I'd return to school in great shape and filled with all these professional ideals. Plus, I'd be miles bigger than most of the lads. Wasps were sending coaches down every couple of weeks, taking me through videos, telling me what I was doing right and wrong. It was intense, so that when I should have been playing my final few months of fun, carefree rugby, I was taking everything far too seriously and getting frustrated by my team-mates' relative amateurism, which as you can imagine made me popular with them. Now, when a kid tells me they want to be a professional rugby player, I tell them, 'Enjoy every minute of it. Put those chip kicks in, put those reverse passes in, do whatever you want. Because if you become a professional rugby player, you might not be able to do any of that. Unless you're as good as Olivier Magne …'

My first Premiership start was against Harlequins, on the first day of the 2003–04 season, when I was just 18. I'd trained like a lunatic and the coaches seemed to be loving what I was doing, but nothing could have prepared me for the intensity, the physicality, speed and complexity of professional rugby. That game was a complete blur. I was massively out of my depth and didn't really understand what I was supposed to be doing. I do recall Quins defending a five-metre scrum, my prop Will Green telling me we needed a big shove, me doing what I was told and our scrum disintegrating, with Will ending up on the floor and taking me with him. Their number eight Tony Diprose picked up the ball and had passed the 22 before I was back on my feet. I chased back and put a big hit on him, but he deftly offloaded the ball while in the air and Ugo Monye scored in the opposite corner about six phases later.

That was the first and last time I listened to a prop or prioritised a scrum over my defensive duties as a flanker. (For the next 18 years, every prop and scrum coach would tell me, 'Remember, your first job is to push.' I'd always smile and nod, but actually be thinking, 'Fuck pushing, my job is to make those first-up tackles.') I was taken off after about 60 minutes against Quins and we lost the game. But worse was to come. In his post-match interview live on Sky TV, our scrum-half and captain for the day Rob Howley chose to highlight the fact that I'd made quite a few mistakes and essentially lost Wasps the game. I didn't know much about being a professional rugby player, but I did know that you weren't supposed to throw a team-mate under a bus, especially if he was only 18 on debut.

I spent the rest of the season in the second team, before being promoted to the first team again for the opening game of the 2004–05 season. That was against Saracens at Twickenham, and this time I fell off a tackle, allowing them to score, and we lost a close encounter. After that game, I was exiled again. In those first couple of seasons, I made more false starts than Linford Christie. It was only in the 2005–06 season that I started to feel at home.

THE SECRET OF WASPS' SUCCESS

Superior strength and fitness were the basis of Wasps' success at that time. We beat teams up in defence, were simple and direct in attack, and we never wilted. The style of play Warren Gatland came up with at Wasps was essentially the same as he used, to great success, with Wales and the Lions. But you need more than strength and fitness to succeed at the highest levels of rugby, and Gats was no tactical mug. What a lot of people don't realise is that good coaching is usually about picking a game-plan to suit the players, rather than the other way around. And Gats's game-plan, married to Shaun Edwards's boundless emotional energy and unique defensive system, clearly worked because we won everything.

Obviously, Gats had some seriously talented players at his disposal. Four of Wasps' starting XV that won the 2004 Heineken Cup final – Lawrence Dallaglio, Josh Lewsey, Joe Worsley and Simon Shaw – were part of England's 2003 World Cup-winning squad, while another seven had either played for England or would in the future. Two of the other four players were Rob Howley, one of Wales's greatest-ever scrum-halves, and Samoa's Trevor Leota, who I've already said I thought was the best hooker in the world on his day. After Gats left for Wales and Ian McGeechan took over, not much changed in terms of personnel. Wasps' starting XV that won the 2007 Heineken Cup final included five English World Cup winners (Phil Vickery had joined from Gloucester) and 12 past, present and future England players in total, plus French great Raphaël Ibañez at hooker, Ireland scrum-half Eoin Reddan and little old me on the bench. To date that was one of the biggest high-lights of my career, and not because when I came on I ran 80 metres after a scrum turnover, to fall just five metres short of the Tigers line. (This still haunts me today: why did I not just keep looking forward, instead of looking over my shoulder? It would have been the highlight to end all highlights.) It was because that was my only H-Cup win. I thought winning things came easy, as I was spoiled at Wasps in those early years. The closest I got again to European glory was a semi-final loss against Saracens. For me, winning Europe is one of the greatest things you can do as a player. I should have celebrated it more.

Most of the players in that squad could have earned more money at other clubs because Wasps always hugely underpaid, however good you were. But players stayed because they knew they were part of something special and almost guaranteed to win things. For four or five years, we had a group of unbelievably gifted players and huge personalities. We'd go harder than any other team off the field but train harder than any other team on it. Gats gave us enough rope to hang ourselves with, because, having been a player himself, he understood the value of a good night out. That's why he loved hearing all the stories. It was that combination of fun, ruthlessness and shared suffering that bonded us so tightly and meant we played teams off the park. It felt like being part of an all-conquering family.

TEAM SPIRIT & CAPTAINCY

I've heard sportspeople say that team spirit is a myth. I don't agree. It can be paper thin and come and go, but it's definitely a thing. Some teams never have it, usually because they contain lots of conflicting personalities with different motivations who aren't controlled properly by a strong coach. They have players who aren't made to feel part of the family, who then eat the place out from the inside, until the roof comes down on everyone. If players can't talk to coaches, and vice versa, and the players don't work or trust each other, then it's all just PowerPoint presentation bullshit.

When trust within a team is wafer-thin, it will easily erode under pressure. It's like loyalty in a marriage; it might look solid from the outside, but how solid will it be when times get hard? A group with genuine team spirit is one that sticks together and stays upright through thick and thin. I've played with men and coaches who talked about team spirit but went missing when the flak started flying and the team desperately needed them to make sacrifices. I didn't come across many of those men playing for Warren Gatland's Wasps or Eddie Jones' England.

Captaincy goes hand in hand with team spirit but is nowhere near as important as the media makes out. Journalists and pundits are obsessed with this idea of the England team having a 'figurehead' and make captaincy sound like herding cats. The way they talk, you'd think that if players didn't have a captain to motivate them, they'd all be wandering around the pitch muttering, 'Why are we even here, what's the point?' That's not how rugby works. Good teams have multiple leaders. What matters most is players in key positions making the right deci-sions and getting their messages across clearly. That said, some captains are better than others, and I played under some of the very best.

Lawrence Dallaglio was a captain in the classic mould. You could draw a direct line from Lawrence to the great Willie John McBride, who instigated the 'one in, all in' policy on the 1974 Lions tour of South Africa (which basically meant that if a Lion got hit, his team-mates had to hit the nearest Springbok). Lawrence was a great talker and had presence and charisma. He looked the part – the lantern jaw, the puffed-out chest – and acted the part. Before a game, he'd shadow box in front of the mirror in the changing room. He'd crush plastic cups and toss them over his shoulder, like Superman crushing coal into diamonds. And then he'd do his big sniff, which meant he was about to start talking. 'Fucking hell, lads. It's a big day. It's gonna be a street fight with no rules, so bring your tools. We're gonna do these mugs over. Who are this fucking firm anyway?' It was more like a bad British gangster film starring Ray Winstone and Danny Dyer than *Henry V*. But it usually did the trick.

Lawrence could be more eloquent when he wanted to be, and was fully capable of the rousing Churchillian speech. Before one of the Premiership finals at Twickenham, he spoke about losing his sister (who died in the *Marchioness* boat disaster in 1989), the fact that he played to make his parents proud and how he wasn't able to look at himself in the mirror unless he knew he'd given absolutely everything. He had tears in his eyes, as did most people, and everyone bought into it. Trevor Leota, normally a quiet man, suddenly started talking about what a tough time he'd been through and how his team-mates were a replacement family. Lawrence was brilliant at capturing what everyone else was thinking, or what they should have been thinking. Like Lawrence, I wanted to make my parents proud and be able to look in the mirror knowing I'd left nothing out on the field. I didn't cry (my wife thinks I'm emotionally dead) but I was fired up inside, on a knife-edge, and we destroyed whoever it was we were playing that day.

Of course, how a captain performs on the field is far more important than anything they say in the changing room. And Lawrence always led by example and commanded total respect from his players and the opposition. He was a great number eight, had a huge personality, was physical, never took a backwards step, could be dark if he needed to be – and expected his players to get dark alongside him if required, like on my first start for Wasps against Montferrand. People always compared us, but I was never the player he was or achieved anything like he achieved, even if I had a good go at it. Lawrence had his faults but he was my idol, a massive part of my career, and I absolutely loved having him as my captain. For me to be one of his foot soldiers was, and still is, special.

But while Lawrence was everything a great captain should be, you don't have to be exactly like him to be a great captain. Dylan Hartley was probably just as good a captain as Lawrence, despite having a different style. Eddie Jones called Dylan 'the fat butcher from Rotorua', presumably because he thought he looked like a fat butcher from Rotorua (Dylan was quite happy with that as a nickname because some of Eddie's other nicknames were far less flattering). But Eddie had a huge amount of respect for Dylan, which is why he made him his captain shortly after taking over as England head coach.

Captaining England was not a nine-to-five job for Dylan. He wore that responsibility 24 hours a day, seven days a week. He set the highest standards, on and off the pitch. He was meticulous when it came to research and extra work, and ran a very tight ship. He didn't care about not being liked, so had no problems with dressing down team-mates, which is not easy to do. He trained harder than anyone – Eddie worked him to within an inch of his life, and if I'd been on his training regime it would have finished my career. He wasn't a Churchillian speaker like Lawrence, but he spoke sense, with passion and directness. He was also an intelligent captain without too big an ego, so was happy for those around him to take the lead. I couldn't have been more impressed with Dylan as a bloke and a leader. Without Dylan, that early Eddie Jones England team, coming off the back of the 2015 World Cup disaster, would not have been as successful. The combination of Eddie Jones, Steve Borthwick, Paul Gustard and Dylan Hartley was like a perfect storm that changed the face of the England senior squad, hopefully for ever.

DOING LOTS OF DAMAGE

In my first few seasons with Wasps, I was playing with and against players I'd been watching on TV for years. I even had some of their autographs. But I was never in awe of anyone. I did sometimes turn up for games, eye up opponents during the warm-up and think, 'Jesus, look at the size of that bloke. This could be interesting …' But you couldn't be scared, because you had to go in on them hard. I relished pitting myself against them, however much they'd achieved in rugby and however mean they seemed.

Henry Tuilagi was definitely one of the most intimidating men I played against in my early years. He was built like a minibus and ran with pure hate etched on his face. He'd lurk in the deep, if it's possible for a 21-stone man to lurk, and if anyone made the mistake of kicking the ball to him, he'd carry it back with one hand, as if it were nothing more than a loaf of bread, and you'd see the fear in defenders' eyes. Some defenders would think about tackling him before thinking better of it. The first couple of defenders brave enough to put their bodies on the line were usually vaporised. And then it might be my turn. All I could do was run at him equally hard, shout, 'I love you, Mum', and dive at his knees – or, as Graham Rowntree used to put it, put my head in the spokes.

Henry was pure, raw, frightening intensity. The fact that he was also quick, with great feet and hands, made him unplay-able at times. Henry's tackling wasn't bad either. You'd be running with the ball, see him in front of you … and then he'd disappear from view, because he knew you were going to arc in his direction. He wore an arm guard that seemed to be made of the same material as Wolverine's blades, and when he swung his arm and hit you, it was like being struck with a giant tuning fork because your head would start vibrating. I think it's safe to say that Henry has been enjoying his retirement. I recently saw a picture of him and his brothers, and they looked like a giant set of Russian dolls. Henry, the biggest doll, was about as wide as the rest of them put together. Manu was the smallest doll, and he weighs about 17 stone. I wish I could have tapped into some of those Tuilagi genes – that family are special.

Henry and his brothers all hail from Fogapoa in Samoa, and it was usually the Pacific Islanders who hit hardest. They were big, fast, aggressive units who could – and often did – do opponents lots of damage. My first taste of how hard Pacific Islanders could hit came when playing for England Schoolboys against New Zealand. My team-mate lobbed me a hospital pass and this kid ploughed into me so hard that we both ended up in the crowd. My bones were rattling, my teeth were chattering and I was crying, because I thought I'd never be able to catch my breath. That was the worst I've ever been winded. When I did finally pull myself together, I went hunting for revenge and cleaned my nemesis out at a breakdown, headbutting him for good measure. But this kid didn't even register it. Instead, he laughed at me and called me a cunt. At that precise moment I realised that these guys on the other side of the world were brought up to play the game tougher

Newcastle's Sinoti Sinoti wasn't a big man but he was ludicrously fast, with the best feet I ever saw. But rather than sidestep to beat a man on the outside, he was one of those blokes who would sidestep into a man to knock him over. Former All Blacks centre Sam Tuitupou, who played for Worcester, Munster and Sale, hit me harder than anyone else I ever played against. And he wasn't that big either. Munster fans nicknamed him 'Hacksaw Sam', but it was more like being hit by a swinging girder. He used to go all-out to damage you. And it's not very nice when you're off on a gallop and someone like Sam suddenly flattens you from another direction. It must be like stepping into a road without looking and being hit by a four-door saloon. Suddenly, you're cut in half, flying through the air and wondering if you're going to land safely. And when you do land, you're like a rag doll with the stuffing removed, unable to move a muscle. Not that Sam escaped from all those big hits unscathed. By the end of his career he looked like a mummy, with his shoulders strapped to his arms and his head strapped to his neck.

Then there was New Zealand's Jerry Collins, who was also born in Samoa and hit like a runaway freight train. Not that the England coaches seemed to have noticed. We were preparing for an England game against New Zealand and one of the coaches said, 'Lads, we've figured out a plan to beat New Zealand. We've seen a chink in their defence that no team has exploited before. The gap between the tail of their line-out and their 10 is big, so we're going to send someone down there.' Then he played a clip of one of New Zealand's previous games, which showed a guy running through this gap and Jerry appearing out of nowhere, closing the door on this so-called gap and absolutely melting him. When someone pointed out the obvious, the coach replied, 'But Jerry Collins won't be there when we play them, because we're going to move him around in the line-out, and pretend we are going wide ...' The room fell silent as we watched the rest of the clip, which showed the ball being moved one way and the other, while Jerry's victim was still down clutching his ribs, now being sick and clearly crying. The coach finally stopped the tape just as the poor guy was being lifted onto a stretcher. There were often weird moments like that in team meetings, when players were looking at each other and thinking, 'Is this bloke watching what we're watching?' Either they'd forgotten what rugby was like, or it was a very different game to the one they played.

As you can imagine, there were no volunteers to put their masterplan into action.

But while the Pacific Islanders hit hard, the most attritional sides as a group were almost always South African. Every time you played against a South African team, whether it was the Springboks or a Super Rugby outfit, it would be insanely physical for 80 minutes. They developed this tactic that involved a couple of players grabbing a team-mate by the collar and shorts and ramming him into you, which meant you spent most of the game at shin height, trying to take their legs out. That's why I made so many tackles, 35 if I remember correctly, when we drew 14–14 with the Springboks in Port Elizabeth in 2012. The Stormers used the same tactic, so when I played against them for the Highlanders a month or so earlier, I spent 80 minutes being rammed by a rotating combination of Siya Kolisi, Eben Etzebeth and Duane Vermeulen, 70-odd stone of pure steel.

BEING LESS NICE

It's amazing what pulling on a rugby shirt can do to a man. Former England lock Nick Kennedy was one of the nicest people you could meet. But if it all kicked off on the field, he'd be in the middle of it, trying to choke someone out. Then, after the game, he'd wander over and say, in his very posh accent, 'Oh, hello Hask. Bloody good game today.' It was the same with another England lock, Danny Grewcock. You'd go up to him after a game and say, 'Danny, you almost decapitated me and pulled my balls off.' And he'd reply, 'Oh, did I? Sorry about that, I honestly didn't mean to.' And he meant it!

I'm the most yellow-carded England player ever, which wasn't one of my ambitions as a youngster, but at least it means I'm top of something. I picked up six in 77 Tests but I was never a violent player, I just tended to get booked for little bits and pieces of gamesmanship and genuine incompetence. I never wanted to illegally hurt anyone, there were just certain players I relished having a physical contest with, on and off the ball. Michael Cheika, who coached me at Stade Français, was a great help in that respect. He used to say to me, 'Hask, you need to be less nice, get into opponents' heads, create and win those one-on-one battles.' And because Michael was so passionate, especially when it came to talking about the physical side of the game, I listened. There's nothing worse than someone going on about putting your body on the line when you know they've never made a tackle in their life. But as with Shaun Edwards, who was the most passionate coach I ever played under, Michael wasn't asking me to do anything he hadn't done in his career.

I put Michael's advice into practice in a game between Stade Français and Toulouse. Every time Thierry Dusautoir got the ball, I clobbered him. I kept pushing him over, using him to get back to my feet. In the end, he tried to elbow me, out of pure frustration. Luckily, I saw it coming and ducked, otherwise it would have taken my head off. Dusautoir was a great player, a nice guy and someone whom I really admired, but I enjoyed getting under his skin, just as Michael Cheika had taught me. If you get under an opponent's skin and they react, you're doing your job properly.

That said, I never understood how someone could be a gobby, aggressive nightmare on the pitch and a top bloke off it. England full-back Mike Brown was one of the angriest men I ever saw on a rugby pitch but mild-mannered, lovely and unassuming off it, like a bald Clark Kent. Former England captain Steve Borthwick was one of the most irritating people to play against, because he never stopped talking. When I tell people that Borthers was a trash-talker, they don't believe me.

But if you gave away a penalty, he was always the first one to wander over, ruffle your hair and try to mug you off with some horrible chat. But, again, Borthers was a tremendous bloke off the field.

I never thought I'd get on with Ireland's Johnny Sexton or Wales's Dan Biggar when we were all picked for the Lions because they're nightmares to play against – two of the biggest wind-up merchants in rugby, who both love a moan and chat to the ref. A few months before the Lions tour of New Zealand in 2017, I gave away a penalty and Johnny sprinted over and told me, in no uncertain terms, what a terrible player he thought I was. In response, I called him a 'shit cunt'. It wasn't exactly Wildean wit, and Johnny was slightly taken aback. But not as much as referee Nigel Owens, who took me to one side and said, 'James, there are children and mums watching this, and we can't have that language.' Quick as a flash, I responded, 'It was my mum who taught me it, Nige.' Nigel was not amused, or at least he pretended not to be. But both Johnny and Dan, who admittedly thought I was going to be a nightmare too, were as good as gold on tour and became good mates. Every now and again, I'll get a message from Johnny that simply reads, 'Oi, shit cunt', accompanied by a smile emoji.

Canadian flanker Jamie Cudmore was another lovely bloke who turned into a maniac on a rugby pitch. In fact, he's the second-most yellow-carded player in international history, with seven in 43 Tests. One time, Jamie was holding onto me in a scrum and I punched him in the side of the head, which didn't go down too well. The ball was played away from the scrum and ended up on the wing, where Jamie was waiting for me. But because I was at the bottom of a pile of bodies and he couldn't get to me, he punched my Wasps team-mate Tim Payne instead, sparking a huge brawl. When I did make it back to my feet, Jamie promptly pinned me up against the advertising hoarding, and some irate Wasps fan in the crowd leant over and hit Jamie on the head with his programme three or four times. I was quite surprised Jamie didn't nut him. But thank God for that game old fella, because he diverted Jamie's attention and I was able to slip away unscathed. Out of all the players I played against, there was probably always a real physical edge between Jamie and myself, especially in my Stade Français days. The battles between Stade and Clermont were big, as were the back-row battles between us. You would get a fist in the head at one breakdown, then dish out an elbow in a tackle, then you would get a stamp, and so it went on between us. Yet the beauty of rugby is we never talked about it; it was always straight business and all left on the field.

Everyone wanted to fill Pat Sanderson in, including some of his own team-mates. After one game between Wasps and Worcester, we both got cited for eye-gouging each other at the same time, which had to be a first. Luckily, it got thrown out, because we both said it never happened, which it hadn't. Tonga's Chris Hala'ufia was about as ruthless as they come, and his highlights reel of destruction makes you wince. He stamped on my hamstring once, when he was playing for London Irish, and I thought he'd burst my leg open. I got my revenge when they attempted a line-out move and I cut him in half. Then I went and spoilt it by overdoing my celebration. Even Andy Goode got in on the act. It was only when my exuberance had died down that I realised how reckless our celebrations had been; we'd laughed in the face of one of rugby's most devastating operators, a former policeman in Tonga (imagine how hard you have to be to deal with out of control Tongans), who would now be seeking terrible revenge. Luckily, he got taken off a few minutes later. At the final whistle, I sought him out in the stands and apologised – for the celebration, not the tackle. He took it in good spirits, but I could see in his eyes that I was now near the top of his very long hit list.

One of the beauties of our game is that rugby players are very good at knowing when the competition starts and stops. It's a game, not life. That said, it makes me cringe a bit when I hear people going on about rugby being a gentleman's sport, whereas football is for louts and cheats. They're incomparable. Football is the biggest sport in the world, played in every country and by every demographic, while rugby is a niche sport played hardly anywhere. I believe rugby has a lot to learn from football in terms of promotion, accessibility and professionalism, though I think football could still learn a few things from rugby in the areas of discipline and respect. Rugby is a far more violent game than football, but there isn't the same contempt for authority, even if you think the officials are doing a shit job. Play-acting and dissent have crept into rugby, but officials are quite hot on it. And in rugby, you're held accountable for behaving like a dick by team-mates and coaches, as well as by fans and the media.

If a rugby player claimed he was tripped and appealed for a penalty, his coach would say to him at Monday's meeting, 'What the hell do you think you were doing? We don't want any of that shit at this club.' This stinging rebuke would be followed by endless replays of the pathetic act for all to enjoy, in slow-motion and from multiple angles. All the while, the player's team-mates would be doubled over with laughter and devising some horrific nickname for the diving fanny. Imagine a coach embarrassing Neymar like that in front of his team-mates. The club would get a strongly worded letter from his agent that afternoon and Neymar, or the coach, would be gone soon enough.

THUGGERY

You probably don't believe me, but I never had a reputation for being a pain in the arse on the pitch. Just off it. I could, however, be easy to wind up on the right day, like during a game against Harlequins when Joe Marler pulled my scrum cap off, hid it up his top and squirted water at me. I love Joe, but he's got a black belt in being a pain in the arse, and I wasn't having that. Also, I hadn't played for eight weeks and had a lot of pent-up aggression. So when Joe decided to take the piss, assuming that I would do nothing as we are genuine mates, I went a bit mad, threw him to the floor and for good measure put the old Vulcan death grip on him. Then, as the referee was fumbling for his yellow card, I made the mistake of telling him what Joe had done to wind me up. As I was trudging off to the sin bin, all the Quins players were shouting in high-pitched voices, 'Sir! Sir! He squirted water at me!' In my defence, Danny Care squirted water at me again on my way off, but I wasn't going to retaliate because he probably would have done me. You could lose an eye if you took on an irate DC. He might be small but he can be vicious when backed into a corner, like a nasty but good-looking little rodent with loads of teeth.

As you've probably noticed, what with all the water squirting, rugby thuggery ain't what it used to be. Eye-gouging seems to have been eradicated, because of the number of cameras and length of bans associated with it. But back in the day, it was quite common. In a game between Wasps and Sale, Sébastien Chabal stuck his fingers in my eyes, and when I grabbed his arm he stared at me blankly and trotted off, as if nothing had happened. Northampton's Neil Best got 18 weeks for gouging me in 2008, which I thought was harsh but about right because he used my head as a bowling ball and almost pulled one of my eyes out. Even today, I'll wake up in a dry, air-conditioned room and that eye will be hurting and blurred. Weirdly, Neil has never forgiven me for getting him banned (that's how he sees it) and, at least according to the Northampton lads, 12 years after the event I'm still on his kill list – he actually has, I am told, a notebook of names who are going to get it.

Back in the day, if someone eye-gouged you, you were well within your rights to hit them. But punch-ups are also a thing of the past, because if you connect, regardless of the provocation, you're sent off and banned for weeks, which doesn't tend to go down well with your coach or team-mates. So instead of punch-ups, you get players doing the fake tough-guy stuff, which involves lots of pushing and pulling and swearing, or what is commonly known as handbags. Most teams still have one handy bloke up their sleeve, just in case. What most people remember about the 30-man brawl between London Irish and Gloucester a few years back was Jim Hamilton and David Paice being sent off for starting the whole thing. But if you watch it back, you'll see London Irish's Samoan number eight Ofisa Treviranus picking people off on the fringes, like Sugar Ray Leonard. But most of the time it's all a bit pathetic, to the extent that I normally didn't even bother making the effort to trot over and get involved. My dad would say, 'Why did you not run in and help when it all kicked off?' And I'd reply, 'Because I can't do anything. What's the point?'

In my early days, I'd come off the pitch and the whole of my back would be red, raw from where people had been rucking me out the way – or legalised stamping, which is basically what it was. If you fell the wrong side of a ruck or lay on the ball, you could expect a nice helping of shoe pie. But stamping on opponents, whether it's their back or their face (which I saw happen), tip-tackling, knee-dropping to the head, have all decreased in frequency. That's mainly because instead of one bloke filming a game from the halfway line with a magic lantern, there are now 50 different camera views and another bloke sitting in a box, watching replays of every single incident. If a player wants to be a purveyor of the dark arts nowadays, he has to be a lot more cunning with it – stuff like landing in the 'wrong' place or 'using' opposing players to get back on his feet.

But the modern game is more about hurting opponents with raw physicality, which basically means hitting hard, whether you're the carrier or the tackler. One of the best at causing carnage legitimately was my Wasps team-mate Raphaël Ibañez, who would run into a breakdown, almost kill three or four players and emerge without a scratch on him. You would have to replay the incident time and time again to see what he'd actually done. When Raphaël wreaked havoc, it was almost a work of art.

TALISMAN PLAYERS

When it comes to analysing the opposition, you can overthink things. Most of the time, it's a case of playing what's in front of you and being aware of specific threats. But you might make exceptions for fly-halves, because their decision-making is so important to a team, and certain wingers and back-rows. When I was with England, we'd call the special talents in opposing teams 'talisman players'. They were the players we'd spend most time analysing, so if we were playing against Italy, for example, we'd basically have clips of Sergio Parisse on loop, because if he had an outstanding game, they had a chance.

I'd always study players I wanted to learn from, people like Jerry Collins, South Africa's Schalk Burger and Duane Vermeulen, Australia's Michael Hooper, George Smith and

David Pocock, Ireland's Sean O'Brien, Italy's Sergio Parisse and France's Thierry Dusautoir and Louis Picamoles. I'd watch how they picked up the ball from the back of a scrum, which hand they held it in and how they defended line-out moves. I didn't just study back-row players. Australia's Israel Folau has some bigoted views, but if I could have any rugby player's ability, I'd choose his. His physique, his running technique, his speed, his power, how high he can jump. The man's a freak. I would also look at other sports to get inspiration to see if I could improve any areas of my game by even a couple of per cent. I loved watching guys like Ray Lewis or J. J. Watt from the NFL, dissecting their aggression, mindset, tackle technique and training routines. I would then take what I saw and add it to my own routine. I would even look at MMA stars and wrestlers to see if could learn things to improve my tackling and fitness.

But the player I spent most time watching was New Zealand's Richie McCaw. In terms of back-rows, he was the best I played against. He read the game so well and knew exactly where to be and what to do. The way he saw things that were about to unfold was like a chess player. He'd go into a breakdown and choose exactly the right thing to do, out of a possible six or seven options. That would be either to clear the man out, steal the ball, help a mate steal the ball, fall the wrong side to delay the opposition 9 by half a second, go into the breakdown to force the opposition to commit players, not go into the break-down completely and wait for the opposition to clear out and then attack the exposed ball, or wait at the side to get the 9 when he passed or ran. The thing that set Richie apart was he played his own game within the game. He was selfish, but by being selfish he helped his team. Too many players, myself included, played what we were coached, not what was happening. Just watch old footage of his running lines and see how he just put himself exactly where the action was at all times. He was also great on the ball as a carrier, a world-class tackler and obviously one of the world's best scavengers. If he went into a breakdown to compete for the ball, nine times out of ten he would come out with it.

Let's also recognise that Richie cheated well, which is a skill in itself and something I never mastered, hence all the yellow cards. I think Richie got something like two in 140-odd caps. I'd get the England analysis guys to send me footage of Richie and watch it on the way to a game, whoever I was playing for or against. It would give me clarity over what I needed to do in the upcoming game, and the ways I could impose myself. I probably developed my game more from watching hours and hours of him play, than I ever did from coaching. There is no coincidence that my form rose to a level and stayed there after following and adopting what Richie McCaw did. Sadly, I was never the player he was, but it was not for lack of trying. After games between England and New Zealand, and during my time in New Zealand with the Highlanders, I got to know Richie quite well. I am not sure he ever realised I was a fanboy. I'd email him from time to time, and being the secret rugby nause that I am I'd ask for advice or specific drills to help improve my breakdown work. He'd just ignore me and pretend that I never sent the email or asked the question. Half of me thinks he thought I was taking the piss, as I don't come across as a rugby keeno, but the other half thinks his competitive spirit that made him the world's best meant he'd never help an Englishman or any enemy back-row. Or perhaps he just didn't like me, which as we all know is not uncommon.

Another genius I played against was Ireland's Brian O'Driscoll. In one game between Wasps and Leinster, Brian got the ball, ran at Tom Voyce, chipped the ball over him, ran around him, volleyed the ball over someone else, ran around him, caught it and scored. I was standing there thinking, 'I might as well give this game up.' That's the kind of player he was, so good he was exasperating. The maddening thing about extra-special players is that they don't really know how they do what they do. Before the 2007 World Cup, Jason Robinson spent a couple of hours trying to teach the forwards about footwork. Jason had two of the best feet in the history of rugby but trying to pass that talent on to others, especially an England forward pack, was an impossible task. While Jason was demonstrating what to do, Martin Corry, Julian White and Phil Vickery, who had the turning circles of cruise ships, were falling all over the place, like grannies on roller skates. Jason was getting more and more frustrated – 'Lads, it's not hard! You send the opposition player one way and step the other way. Just do what I'm doing!' He would then send the defender completely the wrong way and easily skip around him. We all tried to do what he did and got nowhere, in fact I almost broke my ankle – in the end he lost his shit and just walked off. It was a fool's errand, like trying to teach hippos to tap dance. As for my greatest team-mates, the list is a long one. I played with Ben and Aaron Smith, both World Cup winners, for the Highlanders; Sergio Parisse for Stade Français; Ma'a Nonu, another World Cup winner, for Ricoh Black Rams; and countless wonderful talents for Wasps. But the team-mate I'm probably asked most about is Danny Cipriani, usually couched in terms of, 'What's he actually like?' and 'Why didn't he achieve more?'

Cips has great natural ability, works tirelessly on his skills and reads the game so well. And he showed what he could do when he was loved at Gloucester, for whom he was the best fly-half in England leading up to the 2019 World Cup. But he's been hamstrung by a number of things, not least people's perceptions of him. The media haven't been kind to him, which means the public have got the wrong end of the stick. Just because you shag a few famous women, that doesn't make you a bad person, and Cips is actually a lovely, caring bloke whom I really admire and respect. As such, he needs coaches to make an effort to understand him. That hasn't always happened. Instead of putting an arm around him and explaining that they'd give him a bit of leeway if he was prepared to compromise, for the good of the team, some coaches saw him as an unsolvable problem and didn't try.

On the other hand, Cips was sometimes his own worst enemy. I always thought he had an individual sportsman's mentality in a team sport. Don't get me wrong, he wanted the best for himself and the team, and if all his team-mates had the same attention to detail, the team would be amazing. But some people don't, and he sometimes found that difficult to cope with. By his own admission, Cips is not very good at playing the game, by which I mean politics rather than rugby. To get on in any walk of life, sometimes you've got to do what you're told, even if you don't think it's the right thing. You've got to pick your battles. Cips thought he knew what was best for himself, and he probably did, but didn't always take it very well if coaches disagreed and wanted him to work on aspects of his game that he didn't think were as important. As a player, you've got to understand that coming across as too self-sufficient can be problematic for a coach, and if you do so you'll end up scuppering yourself.

4

PAIN

PLAYING THROUGH INJURY

Rugby has got a lot of things right and also has an awful lot of problems, but the most pressing concern, for anyone who loves the game and professes to be concerned about the people who play it, is player welfare. People don't realise the hell rugby players put their bodies through. We take great risks and suffer terrible injuries. Look at what happened to my old England Under-21s team-mate Matt Hampson – one minute I was watching him have a punch-up in training, the next he'd dislocated his neck and severed his spinal cord. In France in 2018, three players died of head injuries in a five-month period. So many players end up with degenerative diseases and are broken by the time they're 40. They talk about becoming forgetful, finding lights too bright, noises too loud, suffering from vertigo. I meet old rugby players at functions, lads in their fifties and sixties, and their thumbs will swivel 360 degrees when you shake their hands, their legs will look like they've been put on the wrong way round and they'll be walking downstairs backwards while clinging on to the rail. And these are people who played the game when it was nothing like as physical as it is now.

I had it relatively easy. Well, easier than some. I wake up in pain every day, and can't run anymore, but it could be worse. I only had four operations during my career: I had a huge piece of floating bone removed from my ankle; a patellar tendon scrape on my knee; toe reconstruction surgery; and surgery to fuse a finger because it kept popping out. The finger would pop out when someone shook my hand and even when I was asleep. On the Lions tour I had to have it strapped 90 per cent of the time, even when not training. I just about found some strapping that worked and kept it in place. That was until I ran into Welsh rugby legend Scott Quinnell. Scott and I have always got on and he was pleased to see me – he shook my hand with one of his bear paws and, as he squeezed, my finger popped out again. He didn't notice and I spent the next hour trying to get it back in, but it wouldn't go because of all the strapping. Chloe would watch me make a tackle during a game, get up, put my finger back in and run off to the next ruck. I knew it was time to get it fixed when I went on holiday after the tour and it kept popping out whenever I was asleep or went to switch the light off.

Doctors have told me that if you scanned a normal person's body and they had the injuries of an average professional rugby player, they'd be sent straight to A&E. But rugby players can't be getting things fixed all the time, because they have games to play, so they put things off until they absolutely have to. Plus, many insurance companies won't pay out on pre-existing injuries – including concussion – which is why players are often reluctant to have scans. It's always a battle to get any medical insurance company to pay. They charge you all these premiums, but lads have to wait months and months to get a payout. It's more than likely they will get nothing. I only got my ankle seen to because I was running on it in training and suddenly couldn't turn properly. I sent an email to the medical team and was in London being operated on the next day. It was very business-like. The piece of floating bone the surgeon removed had been there for about 12 years and was way bigger than he thought it was. Sadly, like most surgery, it was not quite the quick fix I had hoped for.

I was in pain for so much of my career that it became normal. I'd wake up every morning in pain. Everything would be sore – my neck, my shoulders, my back, my hips, my ankles, my feet, my toes. Then I'd limp downstairs, make breakfast, limp out to the car and drive to training. I just had to get on with it. I had no choice, because playing rugby – and therefore being in pain – was what I was paid to do. Hardly any players are 100 per cent fit. Maybe some kid on debut, but never again. I was never a pill-smasher, but many times in the past I got my ankles and toes jabbed with anaesthetic or anti-inflammatories to numb them so I could play, or post-surgery to deal with pain. I am sure there is some ethical dilemma in there somewhere.

A lot of lads trained and played on anti-inflammatories. Before one international, I was in so much pain but unwilling to go and tell anyone that I ended up giving myself an anti-inflammatory injection in the buttock in the changing-room toilets. It was 100 per cent legal, and only a Voltarol jab, but it felt very wrong. I didn't want to be sticking needles in my arse, and I probably should not have played that day, but the desire to represent your club or country burns very bright. You don't want to let someone else have that shirt.

Unless it was a small injury, I struggled to function in pain or when I was under the weather. Lots of players can fight through sickness or pain, but the nature of the back-row position makes it very hard not to go at it 100 per cent, and flankers can't really hide out on the wing. Many times through my career I tried to force it, and I always ended up playing badly and ultimately damaging my reputation – because fans and journalists don't know players are in pain and are medicating to get through 80 minutes. They just think you've suddenly become a bit shit, and will helpfully either write it in the papers or message you on social media to tell you as much.

There are still coaches who prefer to leave it up to players to decide whether they're going to play or not. They'll say, 'How do you feel? Do you want to play?', to which most players will reply, 'Yeah, I feel fine, I'll give it a go.'

I found that lots of coaches would give the player the benefit of the doubt a few times around, but for example at Wasps, Dai Young and I had many frank discussions about me playing when injured or not well. In the end he would pull me out of the game, as we both agreed that I had tried to play many times before and just not performed. That's why it's always important to be able to communicate honestly and openly, and I was lucky to have that relationship with Dai and my other head coaches. It's hard when both parties want you to play, but you have to decide what's best for the team.

One coach whom I had worked with during some age-group rugby with England, who went on to coach in the Premiership for many years, had a famous saying: 'What's wrong, chief? Nothing a bit of pills and tape won't fix.' His solution to any problem was to get some soup (I am not sure what magic properties soup has, but you could say the same about the mystical powers of Bobby's huge penis) and pills down a stricken player's neck and just strap up the injury. Sadly, quite a few players adopted that mantra and ended up falling to bits.

I think in the past too many coaches took advantage of good, loyal people who desperately wanted to do what was best for the team. No player wants to be seen as weak, not putting their body through the wringer when everyone else is. It's a macho thing, a guilt thing, similar to not wanting to be sitting in a field hospital when your mates are going over the top. That's why every rugby team should have a strong doctor, someone willing to say to the head coach, 'I don't care what he says and whether you want him to play, he's not playing, and that's the end of it.' I think this is one of the most important things missing from many teams. The medical team are always going to be under pressure, but you need people who are prepared to stand up and do what's right. Yes-men are a huge problem on both sides of the story. If the decision is 50:50 and the player has no chance of making it worse, that's one thing, but unless it's an actual World Cup final, caution is a much better option.

At least if a player was injured in France, their club would be quick to take action. When I played for Stade, if there were any concerns about my health or general injuries, I would be sent off for a scan. At other clubs I have played for and from speaking to players in this country, if you got an injury and they'd run out of medical budget for MRI scans, you simply wouldn't get it seen to. Players would be hobbling around with knocks and tears. I am not saying this happened in the case of poor Jack Willis as it's not my story to tell, and I would be the last one to ever point fingers. But Jack ended up playing the 2018 Premiership play-off semi-final against Saracens with an undiagnosed broken ankle. Sadly, on top of that he did the opposite knee in the game, and ended up in a wheelchair with both legs in the air, needed months of surgery and rehab, and missed most of the following season. You can scrimp and save on the medical budget, it's always going to be a huge drain, but players need that care and attention. I believe it's better to get a scan and have nothing show up, than not doing anything and just guessing what the problem might be.

KNOCKOUTS

I was only knocked out once in my career – 35 seconds into my comeback game for Wasps in 2017, having been out for eight months after toe surgery – but as I have been told many times by people, especially by my good friend and personal physio Kevin Lidlow, being knocked unconscious is not the only kind of concussion. It's something I have always believed. I have suffered plenty of what you might call cerebral events. I'd hit someone in a tackle and my tongue would go numb on one side, or I'd get up and start running one way and end up going in the opposite direction. Or I'd suddenly forget all the line-out calls – but that also happened on a normal day, to be honest.

When I started playing professional rugby, players being taken off for concussion was rare. It's almost as if concussion started in rugby in 2014 in the eyes of the media and the medical world and went from there. However, that is clearly just rubbish; players must have been getting concussed all over the place and it's just that nothing was done about it. I remember having to tell physios that players had been knocked out and to do something about it. Players would be asking where they were, what the score was, what had happened. I would always just get them off the field. Now, players are pulled off instantly, every incident replayed and replayed. There are even people in the stands with iPads watching the game just for these head-knock moments. Rugby is going in the right direction with regards to head injuries. New laws and protocols are being introduced. But people who think you can eradicate head injuries from rugby are deluded. You can tell players not to tackle high until you're blue in the face, and make punishments harsher, but it's a complex collision sport played at great speed, and players make mistakes. Trying to make contact sports danger- or risk-free is like having a pencil without any lead – pointless.

Believe it or not, sometimes you can almost decapitate an opponent and not even know you have caused a major incident. In a game between Wasps and Harlequins in 2018, I thought I'd made a perfectly good tackle on Wales centre Jamie Roberts. I honestly didn't know where I'd hit him, and it was only when I heard the groan of the crowd and spun around that I saw he'd been knocked out cold. When I saw the replay, I was mortified and knew immediately that it was a red card, which is why I stayed by his side and made sure he was okay before leaving the field. For the tackle itself, I simply ran up too fast and just didn't adjust in time. I didn't go low enough. My mobility was never great, but on that day I was about as supple as the Tin Man from *The Wizard of Oz*. My shoulder connected with his jaw, and even though I would claim that not hitting Jamie Roberts's huge jaw is easier said than done, it was a terribly mistimed hit. I would say, though, that outraged fans and journalists have to understand that super-slow-motion replays make things look deliberate when they're not. They remove context and don't take into account slight miscalculations by the tackler and sudden, last-second movements by the ball carrier. When you watch a reply over and over again, you lose intention from the equation. You just see outcomes. I think that the ref should see replays, and the fourth official, but they should not be replayed over and over again for the crowd to pass judgement.

I'm not going to be one of those people who says rugby has 'gone soft', and I can understand why they're trying to make the game safer, but common sense has gone out of the window when it comes to certain aspects of the game. Of course, clear head shots need to be punished, but some of the other stuff is far more nuanced than people would have you believe. Kids should be taught to tackle low; that for me is one of the biggest issues. Proper technique is not often taught, and the kids do not drill it enough. Tackling is not for everyone. All you have to do is watch kids' rugby, and you'll see maybe 1 out of 10 will go low. As a player it takes a lot to hit someone low around the legs who is moving fast.

The problem is the second tackler can't go low as well, because it's his job either to stop the offload, hold the player up or add an impact to stop momentum. Rugby at the moment is all about getting from A to B as quickly as possible with as much brute force as possible while facing super-organised defences, with a minimum 14 players on their feet following a breakdown. Purists talk about running into space, but there is no space, unless you go forward first with big men that require more than one tackler, so at the six or seventh phase of play you might have some space to play in as the defence runs out of numbers.

Then you have to factor in what happens when the ball carrier is crouching and the tackler is a lot taller than him. And tackling without the arms is a tricky one. Replays can make it look as though a player never intended to wrap his arms. But sometimes if you look at the same tackle in real time, you'll see the tackler made contact with his shoulder and the ball carrier went flying before the tackler was able to wrap his arms. Suddenly, people are calling for players to be sent off for making perfectly legitimate tackles that would have won a player a bottle of champagne from his coach 15 years ago. And officials are too scared to say, 'Actually, I've had a look and there was nothing wrong with it.' Trial by the media, traditional and social, can shake even the firmest resolve.

There is also the issue of how you carry the ball these days. You are told not to lead with elbows and arms, but there is limited space and a real emphasis on making the gain line. It's a minefield and a good captain will try to point out problems to a referee. During the 2019 World Cup game between Wales and Australia, Wales's Rhys Patchell ran up to tackle Samu Kerevi, the Aussie centre, with the terrible bolt-upright technique that most number 10s have (unless, of course, you're Jonny Wilkinson), the Australian ball carrier put his arms up to protect himself and Rhys got bumped off. However, the Australian was penalised for running dangerously. While the video was being reviewed, Wallabies captain Michael Hooper explained Patchell's terrible tackle technique to the referee and the referee agreed and waved play on. Without that dialogue, the ball carrier could have been looking at a yellow card.

BEGGARS BELIEF

It doesn't help that rugby's law-makers don't really consult with players. A couple of people in suits would turn up on the first day of pre-season and take us through the various new laws and what was expected of us. Things that I'd only just mastered would suddenly be outlawed. It made me feel like I had no control over my trade. Some sports science person would give us a PowerPoint presentation on how we were now supposed to tackle, and I'd be thinking, 'This person has never played professional rugby, yet they're telling us how to tackle.' They were always fiddling with the rules, but I was hardly ever asked for any input and I don't know many, if any, players who were. I know a lot players feel the same way. For example, on *House of Rugby* we discussed the re-appointment of Bill Beamount as International Rugby Board president and what it means to players. The answer in short is nothing. We have nothing to do with the IRB: we don't get asked for our input on anything, and all decisions, having been made over coffee and biscuits in shiny boardrooms far away, are just passed on to the players.

I don't remember a single player saying, 'We need to get rid of grass pitches and start playing on 4G ones.' But 4G pitches have been foisted on us. Everyone hates 4G pitches. And now the stats are showing they cause more serious injuries than grass pitches because there's no give in them. And on the rare occasions the IRB did ask for input, they ignored us. A few years back, they asked players if it would be a good idea to extend the season, and everyone said no, it would be a very bad idea. A few months later, they announced they were extending the season. It beggars belief.

That is why there are calls to take power into the players' hands and set up an addition to the Rugby Players' Association called the Rugby Players' Epoch (RPE). This would mean that players actually have a say. The issue is sportsmen and women are selfish and self-interested, but you have to be to achieve anything. That means, however, that unless it directly affects you, you never really pay much attention to what is going on. Players will say something about not wanting X and Y, then not bother with it. Then when we get shafted there is outrage. Every club has players who force these issues and try to rally the troops, but more often than not these things are seen as distractions to doing our job, which is winning games, so everyone just brushes them under the carpet, not wanting to deflect from the day work. We all knew clubs were cheating the salary caps for years and said as much. No-one wanted 4G pitches. No-one wanted a season extension. The 25 per cent players' pay cuts during the coronavirus lockdown, despite being the right thing to do, were just enforced without any proper discussion. All we have ever wanted is to be involved in the process and spoken to like adults. Hopefully, the players will understand that without them there is no game, and that authority is just an illusion. If they don't want something, then they can stop it.

To put it simply, the season is too long and we play too many games. Players love playing games, but we have so many rubbish, little add-on tournaments that no-one actually cares about, which just extend the season. The odd thing is these bolt-on tournaments actually pay more in prize money than winning the Premiership or Europe, meaning that some clubs will enter with their second team, and if they get to the latter stages they then roll out the big guns. Most of these games are not televised and are played in front of tiny crowds. No player wants that. I think you should get rid of them and encourage the sponsorship money to be put into clubs, the Premiership and Europe. So your season looks like the following: 10- or 12-team Premiership and one proper European Cup.

On top of this, the real problem is the amount of training and the lack of rest and rehabilitation. There are too many coaches stuck in the dark ages, doing things the way they've always been done, because they're too afraid of doing things differently. The prevailing mentality in rugby is that you should do as much as you can possibly do because players and coaches are scared that other teams might be doing more. Players are still flogged to within an inch of their lives in pre-season. Coaches think that if their players aren't beating each other up twice a week in training, they're not going to beat up the opposition on a Saturday. If that is the case, then surely it's far more of a mental problem than a physical one. How much time do teams spend working on the mental side of the game? Answer: almost none. Administrators and coaches have to consider whether players need to be doing so much full-contact training. In American football, the NFL monitors how much full-contact training teams are doing. And while players are bigger in the NFL on average, they're only going at it for a few seconds at a time, over short seasons, while we're going at it for 80 minutes and our seasons are far longer.

Towards the end of my career, I started working with a Kiwi exercise guru called Travis Allan. He made me realise that training as hard as I was wasn't really helping me. He said to me, 'James, why are you turning up for games sore and tired? No-one wins awards by training too hard.' Some weeks, I was lifting weights two evenings, seeing the sprint coach Margot Wells three times, and wrestling one evening, on top of a normal training load. I did all sorts of mad classes, including reverse treadmill-running, which involved me wearing a harness with some nutcase shouting at me as I sprinted, to help build up speed. I would hire personal trainers and do weights at five in the morning before I went into Wasps, just to help me get the best out of injury rehab. I never left my career and its success in anyone's hands but my own. I did everything I possibly could, usually out of my own pocket, to put myself in the best possible shape to be the best player I could be. I truly believe this is all we get, one life, and you need to give it your all. But it got to the point where I'd be turning up for games knackered. Somewhere along the line, I'd forgotten what training was meant to be for, but Travis reminded me that it should be about making yourself as fit and healthy as you need to be to perform for the team at the weekend. I cut out anything that wasn't going to help me be fresh and ready to perform. Travis's advice was so simple, but it led to me playing some of the best rugby I ever played.

BIGGER, STRONGER, FITTER, FASTER

Rugby players should get a couple of weeks off over Christmas, but that's not going to happen. They used to do that in France, then they got them playing again when they realised how big the crowds would be for local derbies. The game seems to be getting more and more physical, even since I stopped playing in 2019. I thought it was just because I was getting old, but now I don't think so. Backs are as big as forwards and some of the kids coming out of the academy ranks are mutants, 20-year-old wingers who are 16 or 17 stone. These kids are graduating from very professional school programmes and being picked up earlier and earlier by clubs. From a young age, they're locked in the gym and pumped full of the right kind of food, so that when they make their professional debuts they're already as big as the veterans.

Something will have to change because they aren't just getting bigger, they're getting stronger, fitter and faster. My suggestion would be around substitutions in games. It helps no-one that you can bring on a whole set of fresh players half-way through a game. It leads to tired bodies against fresh bodies and all that comes with that. The game never takes a dip. It might be a different story if players had to last longer. You might not see props coming in at 130 kg and playing just 45 minutes, before they are replaced by another behemoth.

As a result of the unrelenting, brutal physicality of modern rugby, I'd walk into training on a Monday and players would be shuffling about in the changing room like old men. The most common conversation would go as follows.

'How you feeling?'

'Fucked, mate.'

My Wasps and England team-mate Simon Shaw would play out of his skin on a Saturday then be in so much trouble on Sunday that he and the medics would be talking that it might be time to retire. He would then get put back together in the treatment room on Monday, spend all of Tuesday trying to get his body moving again, take Wednesday off, go for a light jog on Thursday, trot out for the team run on Friday, and play out of his skin again on Saturday. On Sunday, he'd be talking about retiring again. And repeat. Either he was the biggest scammer in the history of rugby or his body was dust. Knowing Shawsey as I do, he was no scammer, just a very smart operator but let's face it, he also loved a team run session – and who doesn't, as they are by far and away the best day of the week. The fact that he rested all the training week and avoided training for the sake of training meant he was fresh to perform again. Whichever way you believe it was, his life was a really bad version of Craig David's '7 Days'.

Even after retiring, I was still waking up in pain. And then I decided to become a Mixed Martial Arts fighter. That made me wonder if I'd become addicted to suffering. I'd ask myself, 'Do I need to be in pain? If I'm not in pain, am I no longer *me*?' Pain had become an integral part of my identity. I do sometimes wonder how I'll be bearing up in 10 years' time, and I'll surely pay the price for all those hits. I try not to worry about it, though, and just hope science will catch up and make it easier to cope with. In the meantime, I'll look after myself as best I can. I stay fit and eat well. I still see nutritionists, get my bloods done, look at what supplements may help. Kevin my physio joked that once I was done with rugby, like most of his sporting clients I would disappear into the ether, but sadly for him and luckily for me, I am seeing him just as much as ever to stay on top of things. I guess retired rugby players are like vintage cars: they need more care and attention to keep them going. But I do worry about retired players who aren't as upbeat as me and less able to handle the pain. A lot of Rolls-Royces I played with and against will end up as rusty old wrecks.

THE MIND

The thing that has been neglected most in rugby and pro sport in my opinion is the mind, which is the most powerful tool we've got and has a massive influence on the success or failure of an individual. I started seeing a psychologist, the brilliant Dr Jill Owen, when I was 17. If it weren't for Jill, I'd never have achieved what I did. When I first started seeing her, my confidence was at rock bottom. Even though I was getting opportunities at Wasps, I never thought I played well and always fretted that I wasn't good enough. But Jill taught me resilience and helped make me the best version of myself I could be. I paid for Jill's services out of my own pocket – and she actually gave me quadruple that amount of time for free – because I didn't think my club would take me seriously. If I'd told a coach or senior player at Wasps that I was struggling mentally, I don't think they would have taken the piss; they just would have been confused and tagged me as weak.

Jill had me scribbling down thoughts in a notebook and encouraged me to listen to music before games. The notes were simple, key focus points for my game, little trigger words that helped me remember my role, motivated me and got me into the right mindset.

Music creates positive reactions in us. We all know that one song that makes us feel like partying, or working harder, or calling a loved one. Once you harness that, it means you can get yourself in the right frame of mind emotionally to run through walls. I'd be the only player on the coach wearing headphones, whereas most players would be sitting in silence or staring out the window. Remember, this was the time before smartphones. Nowadays, you are odd if you don't have head-phones on. The fact that I was the only one nodding along to music used to upset some of the senior players. Someone would rap me on the head and say, 'Take those off and pay attention.' Or they'd say, 'What are you writing? Get your head out of your book and concentrate.' I was told to listen to the captain, that I didn't need all this nonsense. I watched it really unsettle other players. When I got an iPod, I started writing my notes on that instead, so that people thought I was scrolling through my tunes rather than reading my notes back. Later on, when technology got better and the first video iPod came out, I would have a highlights reel that I would get the club's tech guy to create, and watch it on the coach and pre-match. No-one knew. I would always just agree with whatever people wanted of me, and then just go and do my own thing. That's really been the story of my life.

Throughout my career the clubs had psychologists, and so too did England, but players didn't want to use them. Maybe they thought that talking about your feelings wasn't manly. You could tell some coaches weren't sold on psychologists and only brought them in because it looked like the right thing to do. Players pick up on that kind of thing. You have to make speaking about the mental side of the game the norm and psychologists central to the programme. If they're hovering outside the team circle, that creates suspicion.

I truly believe that a lot of players think seeing a psychologist means lying down on a chaise longue, talking about your childhood and crying for an hour. Before I started seeing a psychologist, that's exactly what I thought it was all about. I think some of my coaches thought the same. When I opened up to a few England coaches, they freaked out and started treating me differently. I told them that just saying I was crap wasn't helping. I said that highlighting the positives and pointing out things I needed to work on would be more useful. I asked them to give me practical solutions, like training drills, to help me fix things. But they just thought I was overthinking everything. That's not ideal when you're desperate to get better. Then when Eddie Jones became England head coach, he, Steve Borthwick and Paul Gustard got where I was coming from straightaway. They understood that the reason I was too hard on myself was simply because I wanted to improve, and they came up with practical solutions to help me do just that.

In the past, coaches thought that because I'd spoken to them about my mental health, I was mentally frail and seeking attention. They didn't understand that the opposite was true, that employing a psychologist and acknowledging my struggles made me stronger and more self-sufficient. Coaches and teammates also couldn't understand how I could be so upbeat yet apparently so soft in the head. When I discovered that certain players had been struggling with their mental health and told them that they could have reached out to me, they said that they didn't think I'd take them seriously. How ironic is that? The man who seemed to need a psychologist least was one of the few that used one.

At both club and international level, coaches would rarely make a connection between poor performance on the pitch and players' mental states. If we played badly on Saturday, at Monday's meeting we'd all dissect the game and decide that the reason we played poorly was because we hadn't trained hard enough in the week. It didn't matter what had gone on, that was almost always the conclusion. It's the equivalent of telling a depressed person to cheer up. Instead, people should have been asking, 'Why did we start too slow? Why did we miss so many tackles? Why did we make so many poor decisions?' Often, the answers had nothing to do with how hard we had or hadn't trained, it was to do with where our heads were. But that was hardly ever talked about. Poor decision-making under pressure was common, or doing the same thing over and over again in a game and expecting a different outcome.

It's very easy to sit in the stand and see what's going on. That's why I smile when fans say they know exactly what's going wrong, and why don't we just sort it out. The fact is, changing a game-plan mid-match is like trying to turn a super-tanker on the open seas. It takes time and is far from easy. You have players blowing out their arses, trying to implement a game-plan they have drilled all week, which is now not working. Is it not working because of poor execution or because it's a flawed plan? Then you have to get 15 players to all realise it's not going right, put their emotional egos on hold, keep a razor-sharp focus and then go in a different direction. It's hard to tell what the problems are on the field, so players try harder, not realising that is not the solution. The only team I have seen be able to do this consistently is New Zealand. Often, trying to fix on-field problems has nothing to do with working harder or doing what you are doing better. There is more to it than that, much more. The only coach I have ever worked with who looked into this was Eddie Jones. He would do specific scenario training, putting all the key decision-makers around a table with a load of foot soldiers and going through problems the team would face. Steve Borthwick would set challenges to the team. For example, you are five points down, you have a penalty, the line-out maul is not working, kicking is no good, what do you do? How do you do it? What do you say to the team, what do you say to certain players, how do you address the ref? We would do this once a week. It sounds simple, but it started to transfer to the on-field decisions. Players knew how to adjust and what to change. For example, when we played in the Grand Slam decider in Paris in 2016, we had talked all week that if there were any injuries in this game it was the team that came out the other side with more momentum who would win, especially against France. We ran through a few scenarios, one being what would happen if our captain

Dylan Hartley went down. What would we do? Who would take the lead, who would address the team, what would be the next action if we had the ball?

Lo and behold, with 25 minutes to go in the game, Dylan knocks himself out. We had talked about me calling everyone in, then Owen Farrell would calm everyone as stand-in captain, George Ford would let everyone know what the plan was. Owen would make sure everyone was on the same page, reinforce the importance of momentum and then speak to the line-out forwards to make sure that for the new hooker coming on, we would call a simple line-out throw to get him in the game. (It's amazing how many times a fresh hooker is brought on and made to throw straight to the back of the line-out, which is a much higher-risk option.)

The game-plan worked perfectly, and we won the Grand Slam. All of the above is down to preparation and having mental clarity. It's not rocket science, but only Eddie understood what was needed in the heat of the battle.

Rugby players should think of their minds in the same way as they think of their bodies. But while players will go out and buy the most expensive training gear and the best supplements, happily pay for physios and nutritionists, and spend hundreds of hours making their muscles bigger in the gym, they won't even speak to a psychologist. That simply makes no sense.

5

SCANDAL

ROLE MODEL?

I never intended to be a role model. I don't think anyone does. But sportspeople are role models whether we like it or not, simply by being in the public eye. However, there are ways of lessening the pressure on yourself. If you pretend to be purer than white and you're not, that's a recipe for disaster. Look at Tiger Woods. He could have just been honest, or more importantly one of his close advisors should have flagged to him the risks in what he was doing. They should have encouraged him to stay single, shag everything that moved and no-one would have cared. He could have carried on being a Nike athlete, earning hundreds of millions and being universally feted. Instead, he pretended or tried his best to live the archetypal American dream, of God and family values, which probably meant even more money for him and was perhaps what he wanted but just couldn't stick to. Being that talented, that famous, and with their own personal obstacles to overcome, often forces a person's pent-up pressure to seek escape down certain paths: drugs, alcohol and sex being top of the list. When Tiger Woods did inevitably get caught cheating and all the other bits that went with it, his fall from grace was horrendous.

Lots of sportspeople are happy to play different, less authentic versions of themselves in order to win endorsement deals and the like, but I can't be someone I'm not. I've missed out on a lot of opportunities because I'm deemed to be too controversial, a bit of a loose cannon, someone who could say the wrong thing at any moment. I lost a deal with Land Rover after me and my wife Chloe did a Valentine's Day interview with *Fabulous* magazine in which she spoke about our sex life. She was in a latex dress, I was in leather trousers and they used Chloe's quote about us having sex every day as the headline. It was a bit risqué, but very far from being porn, and frankly tame in comparison to some of the stuff I have done or posed for. But the Land Rover people told me it wasn't the sort of image they wanted to portray and ditched me after 12 years. They did this all via an email, which I found the hardest, as I had always gone above and beyond for them. In my email response I said to them, do they think people who drive Land Rovers don't have sex? I also pointed out that people who drive Land Rovers don't buy the *Sun* newspaper. This all fell on deaf ears, so I was out, not being seen as palatable enough.

Sports journalists and rugby fans could never understand how I could be interested in things outside of rugby, have a bit of a subversive personality and still be 100 per cent committed to the game. Although, I have to admit, mistakes were made. Like the time, unbeknown to me, my dad, ever the marketeer, got someone to build me a personal website. Back then, hardly any sportspeople had websites – maybe Tiger Woods and Michael Jordan – and I was only 18. It didn't take long for my team-mates to find out. To say the general reaction was a shock to me would be an understatement. Soon, every man and his dog were taking the piss. The website included a fans' forum, on which team-mates would post abusive messages. They'd pretend to be Warren Gatland or Shaun Edwards, call me every name under the sun and tell me not to bother turning up for training because they thought I was a wanker. Word soon spread to other clubs, and opposition players started digging me out. I remember playing in the Middlesex Sevens and accidentally headbutting someone. He looked at me and said, 'Fuck off, you dot com piece of shit!' At the time, people thought that anyone who had a personal website was a complete weirdo or narcissist on a level only matched by Donald Trump, and 'Dot Com' – or 'Dot Cunt' – soon became my nickname.

I asked my dad to take the website down, but he wouldn't have it. He just couldn't understand why I was being ridiculed. As far as he was concerned, it was a business opportunity. He'd say, 'Son, these people don't understand. Or they're jealous. This is the future, this is how you make money, everyone will have a website soon.' So the website stayed up and the bullying from team-mates was merciless. Meanwhile, I had fans telling me I was too shit to have a website and that I should hang myself. One day, my Wasp team-mate Peter Scrivener found me in the changing room, having a moment. He put his arm around me and told me everything was going to be okay, because he thought he was going to find me swinging from the changing-room ceiling. The piss-taking went on for years. Even when I started playing for England, team-mates would bring it up. It made me determined, though, to be my own man, as you can weather most things and some things are worth sticking with. It was a good early lesson that the Haskell way wasn't always the best way, and that sometimes you do have to worry about what other people think, or worry about the majority of what people think. I apply the rule that if more than 90 per cent of those people agree it's wrong, then it's wrong. If it's a few critics, just ignore them. But, despite all the grief I got, my dad did it out of the goodness of his heart, as he always did. He also ended up being proved right, as I made money out of having a website, and nowadays almost every player has a personal website or at least a presence on social media.

My image wasn't helped by a disgruntled ex-coach, who got the hump when I didn't re-sign for Wasps and put it out there that I was much more interested in being a brand than a rugby player. A few pundits ran with it and the nickname 'Brand Haskell' has followed me around ever since. It suggests I'm a money-grabber, a whore for a pound note. More recently, people had a pop at me when we sold our wedding photos to *Hello!* magazine. But if that money helps us pay for other things in our lives, why would we turn it down? In fact I challenge anyone to turn good money down, just because they take a moral view. It's more often those who rally against taking money who would be the last to be ever offered money for anything – perhaps to play Russian roulette with a machine gun, but that's it.

People think that unless a sportsperson is holier than thou, doesn't do anything other than play sport and sits at home crying whenever they lose a game, their focus is off. That's why so many sportspeople seem so distant from the public, clam up and give robotic answers in interviews, because they're scared that if they let people see what they're really like, they'll be judged. Life would have been far simpler if I'd been more like most of my old team-mates – uncomplicated and humble – but that's just not me. I'd like to be remembered as someone who showed that you can be incredibly professional but also a lot of fun – a bit of a joker in the changing room but the ultimate competitor on the pitch. That should have been the sub-title of this book.

Sometimes I think I should have played 'the game' a bit more. Then I think, 'Nah.' That's why I have the *The Good,*

The Bad and The Rugby podcast, because I can be myself, have fun, swear, tell bawdy stories and have strong opinions. I couldn't stand having to constantly bite my tongue because someone somewhere might be offended. It's great that everyone is more sensitive and understanding nowadays, but the downside is that people get offended by pretty much everything. The mindset of most people in 2020 is, 'I am offended, change my mind.'

When Australia's Israel Folau took to Instagram to say that 'hell awaits' drunks, homosexuals, adulterers, liars, fornicators, thieves, atheists and idolaters (they all sound like the guests at my next house party, if I'm honest), I thought I had a duty to speak out and condemn his views. Folau can do what he wants in the privacy of his own home, whether painting pictures of gay people burning in hell or throwing darts at pictures of famous alcoholics. But as a sportsperson with a high profile, Folau is a role model, whether he likes it or not, and has to watch what he says. He's also a rugby player, from my world, and if anyone is made to feel unwelcome in my sport, that's literally my business.

What I didn't appreciate before filming a YouTube video on the subject was just how upset people get if you question someone's religious beliefs. I got called every name under the sun, received death threats, was told I was going to hell and that I needed to learn more about Jesus. (I replied that I knew all about Jesus. Wasn't he a little bit like Harry Potter, in that they both do magic, well except Harry doesn't allow three million children under five to die from disease every year, claiming it's just him 'working in mysterious ways'? That didn't go down well.) People even complained to the RFU, trying to get me fired. These were people claiming to be Christians, yet the level of hatred was off the scale. When Chloe read some of the abuse, she was genuinely scared for my safety.

I was also called a liberal leftie, a Marxist and a virtue signaller, which was a new one on me. I also had people saying to me, 'Where were you when gangs of Muslim men were raping girls in Rochdale?' or 'Where were you when ISIS were blowing people up in Manchester?' It turns out you can't ever go against religion of any kind. For people who preach turning the other cheek and understanding, they are the most aggressive, hard-line, unforgiving bastards you will ever come across. But there are already too many people giving opinions on things they don't fully understand. And I wasn't aware that if you had a strong opinion on one thing, you had to have an opinion on everything. Who knew?

SEX, TRIES AND VIDEOTAPE

Sometimes when I do DJ sets at universities, the student rugby team will rock up wearing their kit, which is odd for a night out on the tiles but a sweet homage to me. They almost look gutted when I am not in full kit. Occasionally, they'll even come dressed directly as me. The attention to detail can be extraordinary. The other day, I spotted a guy in the crowd wearing full England kit, red scrum cap, strapping and boots while waving a video camera around. That was clearly a reference to the so-called porno movie I made at school. That catastrophic error I made when I was only a teenager still haunts me as a 35-year-old man. Drunk, sweaty students will collar me and say, while covering me in phlegm, 'Did you make a porno at school?' I usually just roll my eyes. I should have given my side of the story at the time. But I was only a kid and advised not to. Maybe now is the time to put the record straight for good.

When I was in my final year at Wellington College, my best mate Paul Doran-Jones, or Doz, was sleeping with a female sixth former. One fateful day he said to me, 'I've got this girl coming over later, do you have a video camera?' Being a dumb teenager, and because me and Doz had such a dangerous friendship, with almost no filters, I thought it sounded like the best idea in the world. So I replied, 'No, Doz, I don't. But I bet I can find one …' I persuaded another schoolmate to lend me his video camera, and because I always wanted to be a show-man, instead of handing the camera over and leaving, I recorded what you might call a pre-match interview with Doz, about what to expect from the upcoming blockbuster. Interview in the can, I hid the camera in a cupboard and got the hell out of Dodge.

I popped back to my boarding house for some toast and when I returned a few hours later, I saw Doz and this girl leaving his room. So I sneaked in, grabbed the video camera and took a look. It was grainy and blurry and hardly graphic (remember this was 2003 and technology was not the best). But what I remember most about it – and what is forever scorched into my eyeballs – are Doz's green grandpa grits. No pristine white Calvin Klein's for Doz; it looked like he'd robbed a care home's odds and ends bin. But because it was a boarding school and there were lots of bored kids milling around, word spread like wildfire. 'Doz and Hask have made a porno!' And as soon as the girls got wind, they were in his face asking questions. Doz denied everything but the girls didn't believe him, so one afternoon while he was out, they broke into his room, found the tape and nicked it.

Meanwhile, I decided it would be a good idea to tell my mum when she took me out of school for a doctor's appointment. Not because I felt guilty, but because we had a cool relationship and I thought she might find it funny. But instead of high-fiving me and dissolving into hysterical laughter, my mum said, 'You did what? You know that's illegal?' She was shitting herself, and told me off accordingly. After she flagged our huge stupidity, I was now also crapping my pants (the expression not seeing the wood for the trees really springs to mind). And things went downhill from there. As soon as I got back to school, a panicked Doz informed me that the tape had been nicked. And the following day, we discovered that the girls had watched the tape, which sealed both of our fates because of the 'pre-match interview'.

A few days later, I was working behind the sixth-form bar, where the students would have one or two sensible drinks at the weekend, supervised by a teacher. Doz was leaning on the bar, chatting to me, while some friends of Doz's unwitting co-star were sitting around a table looking deadly serious and staring at a lone pint of beer. A lad came up to Doz and said, 'See that pint they're staring at? One of them is going to pour it over your head.' What Doz should have done is shrugged and taken the hit. But our whopping male egos took over. I handed him a big jug full of dregs and told him to be ready for the inevitable attack.

As soon as the teacher made the mistake of popping out, one of the girls (who was nothing to do with the video but just an aggrieved friend) grabbed the pint and the room went deathly quiet. But just as she was about to empty it over Doz's head, he grabbed the jug of dregs, spun around and launched it in her face. The poor girl was drenched. And she hadn't even have time to get her shot off. I can picture her now, frozen to the spot, shocked and sobbing, still holding a full pint of beer. And then it all went off. A wine glass smashed into Doz's head, the girl finally pulled herself together and let fly with the beer, and some of the lads decided to join in. It ended up in a huge 50 person drink-throwing, glass-smashing, table-tipping war. When the teacher came running back in, like a sheriff through the swing doors of a Wild West saloon, there were wounded drinkers on the deck, tables and chairs overturned and beer, claret and smashed glass everywhere. Unsurprisingly, the teacher was rather keen to hear an explanation. At which point I appeared from below the bar polishing a glass like an insouciant French barman in a World War II film whose Nazi patrons had just been machine-gunned to death by some Resistance hitmen in a passing car. I didn't have a drop of alcohol or blood on me and casually said, 'I don't know what you mean, Sir. I didn't see a thing.'

I thought I'd done a decent job of covering the incident up, but a couple of days later there was an unusually loud bang on my door at 6.30 am. I usually got on well with my housemaster – he'd even bring me a cup of tea most mornings, to get me out of bed – but on this occasion he marched straight in, pocketed my mobile phone and said, 'Mr Haskell, the headmaster needs to see you.' When I entered the headmaster's office, it was like *Dragon's Den*. There was the headmaster himself, the deputy headmaster, the head of sixth form, the school bursar, and finally my housemaster, all fanned out behind the desk.

When the interrogation started, I had no idea what they did or didn't know or if they had seen the video or not. I knew the melee in the school bar had led to questions being asked, but I didn't know if the girl in the video had said anything. After the precision raid on Doz's room and the loss of the tape, it was anyone's guess what was happening. So I just denied, denied, denied. Until, that is, they hinted that they had seen the video. I thought that's it, the girl has shown them the tape, and I did a U-turn and confessed to everything. Honesty being the best policy, or so I am told.

When it was Doz's turn for a grilling, he decided to deny everything, not knowing that I'd thrown him under the bus just 20 minutes earlier. I had no way of telling him that I had sung like a canary. So while I got suspended, Doz got expelled for good. It transpired that the headmaster hadn't seen the video but knew enough to bluff us. The girl who was in it had destroyed and binned it the moment she watched it. In fact, she hadn't told any staff members about it. Instead, one of her mates had stitched us up, which meant that the video girl got suspended as well, for having sex at school.

A few weeks later, the Wasps kitman called me out of the blue. He told me he'd just had the *Mirror* on the phone, that they had somehow got hold of the sex tape story, were ready to publish and wanted to confirm that they had a correct photo of me for their story. I knew things were serious when I woke up the next morning to find my dad still at home. He was never not in the office by 8.30 am. And at 10.30, the shit hit the fan. I walked into the kitchen and my dad picked up a copy of the *Mirror* and held it up for me to see. My face was on the front page, eyes blacked out like a rapist and under the headline: 'PORN DORM'. The story was grist to the mill for the left-wing *Mirror*, whose feature included the cost of boarding at Wellington, the estimated price of my mum and dad's house, my favourite food (oysters) and the fact that the school had a nine-hole golf course, as if that had anything to do with anything. They also said that I was hiding in the cupboard, like a depraved contortionist, which is the part of the story that everyone remembers.

I was still trying to come to terms with the fact that my first appearance on the front page of a national newspaper was not down to me winning the World Cup but was instead down to me making a grubby porno video, when the ravenous press pack started to flock. For the next few days, there were cars cramming the lane outside my mum and dad's house – at one point there must have been 15 cars blocking the road – with reporters climbing over fences and posting notes through the letterbox. 'We need you to tell your story!' I'd been advised not to say anything, in the hope it would soon go away, but it ran and ran. The *Express* made Wellington College sound like the last days of Rome, while a feminist columnist called us 'public school animals'. After I'd done my A levels (I sat them in the headmaster's office, with Doz sitting opposite me), I joined up with Wasps. And apart from the chief executive, who just wanted a quick chat about what had gone on, everyone seemed cool. So it was easy for me to forget about it and move on. I had embarked on a whole new adventure, and could focus on making an impression. Doz went over to Dublin to study medicinal chemistry at Trinity College, hoping he would escape the media. We both moved on quickly, but that wasn't the case for the rest of my family.

My dad struggled with it, and my brother found it hard because he was still at Wellington and I'd shamed the name of his school. He was subjected to bullying by pupils and staff alike for my actions. While my dad was able to put a brave face on, my poor mum has never got over the humiliation. She thought I could do no wrong and couldn't get her head around how I could be involved with something like that. It doesn't help that the story refuses to die. I'm very sorry for what I did. Filming anyone without their consent is absolutely not on. But apologies don't matter to the media. Hence the headlines when I was first picked for England: the *Evening Standard* called me a 'peeping Tom'; the *Sun* went with 'SEX, TRIES AND VIDEOTAPEs'; another went with 'LET'S GET READY FOR THE SEX NATIONS'. What should have been a proud moment was somewhat soured, and my mum was mortified. When Doz made his England debut, there were journalists referring to 'the old pair being back together' in their articles. And then when I went on *I'm a Celebrity* ... some of the same headlines got reheated, as if they were new and had just happened.

I don't deserve to be known as a sick porno cupboard voyeur. But clearly some people think differently. We keep having to remove references to the episode from my Wikipedia page, because some prick keeps putting them back on there. It's like a silent war of attrition, some nerd versus me. People desperately want to believe that I was hiding in the cupboard with my scrum cap on, holding the video camera in one hand, knocking one out with the other, while watching my mate have sex. They honestly think I still have a copy of the video and that if they ask, I'll whip out my phone and show them. For other people, the lies are more amusing than the truth, which is why they can get upset if I tell them it didn't happen as they've been told. However, the old saying is true: if you make your bed you have to lie in it.

NEW BALLS PLEASE

But while I do have moments when I think, 'My life would have been a lot easier if I hadn't done this or that,' mostly I try to be philosophical. Or pig-headed, whichever way you want to look at it. You can't worry too much about things you can't control. I've made errors of judgement, like most people. Unfortunately, my errors of judgement appear in the newspapers. But I know that fundamentally I'm a good person and I've done more good things than bad. And while I'm not trying to play the victim, I've had some bad things done to me. Like the time my ex-girlfriend cheated on me with an investment banker and part-time tennis instructor (don't worry, it was the same person).

When I discovered what was going on, I was obviously a little bit irritated. So I sent this guy some messages on Facebook, which from my past experiences I knew might come back to bite me, but I thought, fuck it. The messages said something along the lines of, 'If you carry on shagging my missus, the only tennis you'll be playing is on your Nintendo Wii.' It was only tongue in cheek, but I thought it made my point nicely. As sure as night follows day, those messages ended up in the *Sun*. And the following week, they ran another story with photos of them kissing in a park (which weren't staged at all) under the headline, 'NEW BALLS PLEASE'. I'd been seeing this girl for a few years and it was difficult to read. Thankfully, most of the lads were pretty good about it, apart from England attack coach Brian Smith and one player who was getting a lot of stick about the new veneers on his teeth. (He had only done the upper set, and left the bottom fangs untouched, so the lower lot looked like they'd been thrown into his mouth from a distance. Why would you not get the full set?) After a bit of stick from me in one of our usual cutting exchanges, where I may have said something like, your teeth look like a bucket of smashed crabs, he ended up hitting me with, 'At least my missus didn't shag her tennis coach, you cunt.' That was a bit much. Talk about going from zero to turbo. If he'd said, 'Anyone for tennis?' I might have found it funny. After going straight to nukes there are not a lot of places you can go. I thought about hitting him but smiled weakly and walked away instead, as we were mates and team-mates.

What I eventually learned from all the scandal I was involved in was to take matters into my own hands if a situation looked like it was going to take on a life of its own and spiral out of control. I regretted not saying anything when the sex video story hit the newspapers. I regretted not standing up for myself more forcefully when the Rugby Football Union, the RFU, hung me out to dry during the 2011 World Cup, more of which later. So when the story about the Wasps boat party broke, and people were trying to blackmail us and club officials were panicking, I made it clear that I wasn't going to take the rap for it. Yes, I was present. But I didn't shit on the boat. And I told him to clean it up! I was in charge of 40 supposed adults and I tried to control them as best as I could. So I told my bosses, 'If you try to pin this on me, I will come out and tell the truth.'

I realised too late in my rugby career that the world is divided into people who toe the party line, whatever they're being told to do, and those who stick to their principles, to hell with the consequences. Toeing the party line might make life easier, because some people in authority find the truth inconvenient and infuriating, but sticking to your principles means you can look at yourself in the mirror and say, 'You stood up for what you believed in.' I'd much rather spend the rest of my life saying what I think, rather than what people want to hear, even after what happened to me in my final days at Wasps.

ACRIMONY AND BITTERNESS

Despite plenty of success on the field during my first decade with Wasps, their finances and very existence had always seemed precarious. So when the club was bought by Derek Richardson in 2013, he was deservedly received as a hero. We'd almost been relegated from the Premiership the previous year, which might have finished us off, and now this rich Irish businessman had stepped in and secured the club's future. Without him there would have been no more Wasps. His decision to relocate the club from High Wycombe to Coventry was less well received. But if the new bosses said moving to Coventry was the only way to secure the club's future, I was going to support them 100 per cent, despite the fans' misgivings and cries of betrayal.

I was even happy to be a poster boy for the move. After one game, I got wind that Derek and the chief executive Nick

Eastwood were on the verge of being mobbed by angry fans, so I walked into this room at our old stadium Adams Park, grabbed the microphone and got up on stage. All these fans were going on about the club's great history and how they'd stop supporting Wasps if we moved, and I told them how I thought it was: that the club would fold if we stayed at Adams Park and that the players wanted to move for the sake of their livelihoods, because the fans' ticket money wasn't enough to pay our wages. They came back with all the usual stuff that fans believe, that if we don't support you, there is no club. Sadly, that is not true. We made no money out of Adams Park, and with average crowds around the four thousand mark, the money generated wasn't enough to pay for the lads' lunches. And I told them that if they couldn't continue to support us in Coventry, that's the way it had to be.

We wanted the fans to come with us. There were even coaches laid on to get them to and from the amazing Ricoh Arena. We valued them, but Wasps was never a club about location. We trained in London and played in High Wycombe. We didn't really have a community like, say, a Northampton or Bath. We would fill Twickenham with eighty thousand on finals' day, but not even 6 per cent of them would come to regular Premiership games. Wasps was all about the people, not where we played. The argument put forward by impassioned fans and old Wasps coaches, that we should drop down several leagues rather than move, was stupid and frankly the ramblings of the uninformed. I diverted the heat from Derek and Nick, and said that the Wasps train was sadly leaving the station; if the fans wanted to be on it, great, but if they could not come then we thanked them but the move was happening. I then spent the remaining weeks doing interview after interview with all forms of media promoting the move and its virtues.

It wasn't long before I was wondering if I'd been duped. There had been a lot of talk about building an all-singing, all-dancing training facility in Coventry – our current training-ground pitch in Acton looked like a particularly war-torn part of Syria, hence the reasons so many were keen on the move. Instead we ended up training at a grassroots club called Broadstreet. Don't get me wrong, I've got nothing against grassroots rugby. Grassroots rugby is great, the cornerstone of the sport. But I wasn't a grassroots rugby player, I was a professional rugby player who expected to train in a professional environment. Broadstreet had a nice clubhouse but the physio room was a Portakabin and the weights room was a Portakabin. The rear pitch had no drainage and the first-team pitch had holes all over it. When we complained to the management of Wasps, they looked surprised and said everything was great. It was a bit like that scene in *The Lego Movie* where they keep playing the song 'Everything Is Awesome' to cover up for the fact that it's actually hell. *Everything is awesome ... everything is cool when you're part of a team ... everything is awesome, when you're living out a dream.* But everything was not awesome. Far from it.

It soon became clear that sharing the clubhouse was going to be a problem. We came in for training one Monday morning and the place had been wrecked, because they'd had a big wedding in there and no-one had cleaned up. The windows had been smashed and the floor was covered in broken glass and puke. Another time, we turned up the morning after a funeral and the scene was even worse. I couldn't work out if that counted as a good or a bad send-off. Then, when the rain came, the pitch cut up like a bog. It was so bad that we had to get a full-time groundsman on it all day every day. The poor bloke was out there trying to brush water off and smooth over huge holes, for hour upon hour. He got nowhere, and being ruthless we told him as much. It got so bad that we had to stop using it and train on AstroTurf or indoors at Coventry University instead. Sometimes, we couldn't train at all. When we decided to use Broadstreet's first-team pitch, it was not much better, and ripe for a sprained ankle or worse. They also hated us using it as we were destroying their hallowed turf.

The changing rooms were always covered in mud and rubbish, from all the kids' rugby over the weekend or Broadstreet's midweek training sessions. The showers were cold. The generator would cut off because the fuel bill hadn't been paid. One day, a couple of lads from the company who owned it turned up in a lorry and head coach Dai Young had to persuade them not to take it away. It was like a shit version of the Tiananmen Square standoff, these two lads trying to load it on a lorry and Dai Young standing in front of them saying no. Luckily, Dai – being 150 kg and the size of a tank – won the argument, so they gave up and left. Sometimes in the winter months, when the fuel ran out again, we'd have to do morning weight training in the dark and the freezing cold. Which as you can imagine is not ideal for a professional team, plus dangerous. If the power went overnight, the ice machines would flood the physio room. Oh, and someone shat in the ice bath we had installed.

If we were playing on a Sunday, we'd have the team run on Saturday morning. Before our first Sunday game, I turned up and there were kids all around the changing room. I had to get some extra kit out of my locker and all the kids were asking if they could have it and bombarding me with questions. 'Who is your favourite player?' 'What's the best team you've played against?' 'Who is the hardest player at Wasps?'

Then an adult came in, in a real panic, and said to me, 'You can't be in a changing room with kids, please leave.' I obviously asked why being in a room with kids was a problem and the answer came back, 'What happens if you expose yourself?' I was raging. For one, I was a professional rugby player just wanting to get changed for training. Two, as if I was going to expose myself to a load of kids!

Another time, the lads were in the changing room when this random woman and three kids walked in, bold as brass, and started taking their clothes off. The lads all made themselves scarce, because no-one wanted to be in a room with a woman and three kids – especially with no clothes on – and when the team manager asked the woman what she thought she was doing, she said they came in once a week for a shower. It gets worse. Another time, this bloke strolled in wearing a McDonald's sponsored bib and started praying to photos of old players on the wall. Obviously, my nutter alarm went off, so I continued to watch him very closely. When he clocked me looking at him, he started praying to me. Next thing I know, he was helping himself to the powdered supplements, literally scooping handfuls into his mouth. Eventually, he was persuaded to leave, but however funny it was, it was also worrying. God knows where this bloke's hands had been – down his trousers, up his arse, serving up Big Mac Meals, all as bad as each other – and he also posed very real anti-doping concerns.

The pitch at the Ricoh Arena, which we shared with Coventry City FC, was terrible. And after they re-laid it, it was somehow even worse. As the season went on, it compressed to something like concrete and the grass wouldn't grow, so the lads had nasty cuts and abrasions all over their arms and legs. To add insult to injury, every time we had an away game and left our cars at Broadstreet, they'd get robbed. The criminals around Coventry could not be accused of lacking ingenuity. They just looked at our Wasps playing schedule on the internet and turned up on every away game for what was like an open house. One bloke was caught on CCTV smoking a spliff in Matt Mullan's car, that's how concerned he was about getting caught. Something like 12 cars got broken into in the space of a few weeks, until they finally hired a security guard.

Every six months or so, someone would pop in and tell us to be patient, that they were working on this miracle training facility and that spades would be in the ground soon. But we waited and waited, and nothing happened. That led to a few players adding clauses to their contracts stating that unless the training facilities were improved, they would be allowed to leave.

Meanwhile, the owner was putting pressure on Dai Young to get us to do more corporate appearances, including at property conferences that clearly had nothing to do with rugby. But because we weren't getting the answers we wanted – and not receiving image rights payments, which were a big chunk of our salaries – players kept refusing. Now the owner was getting the hump, because he was used to getting his way. And disobedient players weren't his only headache. By 2018, he was owed almost £20 million by Wasps' controlling company, which was £56 million in debt.

Then one day, a few of the suits called a meeting and announced that the training ground they'd been going on about for the last four years wasn't going to be built. That's when we all lost patience. We were sick of the broken promises, sick of the shit pitches, sick of the lights going out, sick of showering in cold water, sick of the way the players and coaches were being treated, sick of sharing the changing room with nutters off the street and sick of not getting paid. So Dai Young called the senior players in for a meeting to discuss what we wanted to do. Dai was just as frustrated as us. Instead of being a director of rugby, he was spending a lot of his time fighting off-field battles. We talked and talked and eventually

I said, 'Look, we've got the power here. Why don't we just go on strike? Then they'll have to meet us and maybe they'll listen or at least just hear us out.'

Dai was understandably apprehensive about being seen to lead a mutiny and said, 'Don't do that yet.' It was only when we asked for a meeting with the bosses and got no reply that Dai said to me, in a regretful tone, 'Go for it, take the lads on strike, it's the only option left.' So I got the boys together and suggested we no longer fulfil any commercial and media commitments, until the bosses agreed to sit down with us and talk. We also compiled a dossier of grievances, which looked like a *Wisden Almanack*. It included every piece of evidence bar a photo of the shit in the ice bath, as we didn't want to muddy the water further (excuse the pun). But when the team manager presented the dossier and accompanying letter stating all the problems to the bosses, instead of saying, 'Bloody hell, the players are upset, we'd better do something about it,' they said, 'Right, you're all in breach of contract. We will not be dictated to. And who's the ringleader? Whoever organised this is going to get sacked.'

The players' situation wasn't helped by Lawrence Dallaglio, who was a paid Wasps board member and also working as a pundit for BT Sport, when he told viewers that we were out of order and that if players submitted their invoices late, they should expect to be paid late. The fact was, I hadn't been paid my image rights for 18 months, and it had nothing to do with me not submitting invoices on time. I texted him, saying, 'Lawrence, the stuff you're saying is making life harder for the players. I'm talking to you as my old captain and my mate, not Lawrence Dallaglio off the TV or as a Wasps board member. The lads are really unhappy, they're not getting paid, the club is in trouble and you're telling people that everything is okay.' Lawrence didn't believe me, or it wasn't convenient for him to believe me, and it was very disappointing that he chose to take the owner's side against ours.

We then had a meeting with the RPA, told them what was going on and that we were on strike. They were worried that the bosses would start firing younger players – and I could understand why some of the kids were twitchy – but the senior players insisted that if that happened, we'd all quit in protest. The RPA seemed more worried about us being in breach of contract than the validity of our complaints, so I said to them, 'Lads, are you going to help us or not? Because if not, we'll get someone else to represent us.' That seemed to do the trick, and they were very supportive once they realised we weren't messing around and meant business.

But the owner still wasn't budging, because now he had it in his head that he was being held to ransom. So there was a Mexican stand-off, with the owner refusing to meet us unless we withdrew our threat to go on strike and us refusing to withdraw our threat to go on strike unless he agreed to meet us. Eventually we ceded a little ground – it was always going to be us who blinked first, because a few of the lads were beginning to be leaned on and panic – and the owner suddenly announced that he'd come and meet the senior players.

Weirdly, after all that posturing, the meeting went really well. Everyone spoke openly and the owner explained at length how the rugby club was his focus and not, as his then CEO had been quoted as saying in a Midlands newspaper, an add-on to a property development company. The owner even got a bit tearful at this meeting, apologised for not doing things properly and promised to make changes. We were quite buoyed by the proceedings, but nothing changed. And when rumours started circulating about Elliot Daly, Joe Launchbury and one or two other high-profile players wanting to leave, I started filming all the stuff that was wrong with the Broadstreet training ground and putting the videos on Instagram – partly as a joke, but partly as a protest. Broadstreet's secretary wasn't happy about that, calling me out on Twitter and proclaiming Broadstreet's facilities as the envy of most Premiership clubs. I think he must have been on the same stuff as that guy in the McDonald's apron. The secretary also made sure that the *Coventry Telegraph* knew all about it and said I was no longer welcome at the club. Well, every cloud …

But those Instagram videos also pissed off the owner because the story got snapped up by the *Daily Mail* and he thought I'd sold it. I think a player did sell it, but it wasn't me. And when we finally spoke on the phone and he started to chew me out for criticising the club, asking why I felt the need to record things and refer to Broadstreet as a grassroots nightmare, I told him he wouldn't like what I had to say and we should just leave it. I had two weeks to run on my contract, so let's part in a civil way, I said, but he insisted on hearing me out. So I switched from guns to missiles and let him have it. I told him he'd ripped the heart out of Wasps, that he bought players in who didn't care about the club, that he'd treated the players like idiots, that the facilities were shit, and that he'd made promises he couldn't keep (which was not a problem in itself, but he needed to be honest with the lads and tell them that the club didn't want to spend the money or didn't have it, instead of saying we couldn't have a training ground as Premiership rugby were talking about a full-time second-team league and we needed a training ground that would be viable in 50 years – that was one excuse we got). All the players wanted was to be treated as adults, not an afterthought to be fobbed off with nonsense. He had clearly never been spoken to like that in his life, and when I had finished, all he could stutter back was, 'I'm going to have to check my position,' when he probably meant, 'I'm going to speak to our lawyers to see if we can get rid of you.' And that was pretty much that.

A couple of weeks later was the Wasps end-of-season dinner. I was stuck on a table at the back, by the bins. When they asked me up on stage with another player, I was asked one question by the compere, he gave me a framed shirt and that was it. I must have been up there for 30 seconds. That hurt. I couldn't tell you what I think I should have got as a send-off, but it wasn't that. I'd given 12 years of my career to the club. I was their youngest-ever player, a former captain, helped them win Premiership titles and Heineken Cups. I shed vats of blood, sweat and tears for Wasps. And it ended in acrimony, bitterness and a perfunctory goodbye. When I sat back down I said to my wife, 'I guess that's it.'

Chloe was absolutely furious. She'd seen how they'd treated me when I was captain, making me the scapegoat for the boat party that went horribly wrong. She'd seen how they'd try to screw me in contract negotiations, always trying to fob me off with less because of my age, rather than rewarding my experience. Apart from when they lured me back for my second stint at the club, every deal I did came with an offer of a pay cut. She'd seen how I'd fought tooth and nail for my team-mates after the move to Coventry. And now she could see I was putting on a front and was utterly heartbroken. We didn't stay long before slipping out the back with Danny Cipriani, a loyal mate who couldn't believe the way I'd been treated either. That was 2018, and I've not been invited back to Wasps since.

When the new season started and I'd moved to Northampton, I got quite a few messages from my old Wasps team-mates, telling me the club wasn't the same without me. I'm told that one of the reasons Elliot Daly gave for leaving the club was the way they treated me. That was nice to hear, although I wouldn't have been much use to my old mates on the field, given my injuries. Dai Young was an interesting case. We'd always got on and I enjoyed working with him. But he was ruthless when it came to contract negotiations. He'd say stuff like, 'Look, you're getting older. Don't tell me you're better than you were last year.' But after I left, he texted me four or five times, saying how quiet it was without me and that he wished I'd stayed. He also told the media that I was one of his favourite players to have coached, despite having initial misgivings about me. I'd heard that plenty of times before. It was nice to hear, but it was too little, too late. That said, it wasn't his decision alone and I don't blame him. We still speak now, and however hard he tries not to laugh, I always get a smile out of the big man. Dai is a great man and coach. The simple fact is the club I loved wanted me out. They didn't even suggest a new contract, let alone a pay cut. And that's just business.

I'd long understood that professional sport was ruthless. Players are commodities. They join a club – some with fanfare, most without – and give everything for the cause. Many don't have what it takes and don't last long. Some are forced to retire early because of injuries, some of them life changing. Most of those lucky enough to have long careers spend the rest of their lives in constant pain. Not many players have fairytale endings, like Richie McCaw lifting the World Cup for New Zealand. I had many wonderful years with Wasps and gave them so much, but as is often the case with love affairs, it ended in heartbreak. I suppose it was some consolation to know that I wasn't unique and that they treated me exactly how I thought they would, given who was cutting the checks at the end. But it still upsets me. These business types care so much about the image of their brands, yet they treat their employees with breezy contempt. But shit happens in life, and you've just got to deal with it.

6

CHANGING ROOMS

STYLE

My wife always says to me, 'No wonder rugby players have all got self-confidence issues, you're all so horrible to each other all the time.' She's right. When I was in the jungle for *I'm a Celebrity* ..., if I'd behaved like I do with my rugby mates, I would have been turfed out after a few hours. Being part of a rugby team is a ruthless existence. One bad haircut, one bad shirt, one pair of dodgy shoes – one misstep in any direction – and you're labelled for life. But I adored that environment. I was glad to take it and even gladder to dish it out.

I've heard it said that I'm the world's worst-dressed teammate. Admittedly, my shoe game is terrible. Under Armour used to send me these size 13 trainers with inch-thick soles, and the joke was that they should have come with a prescription. Sadly, I was the one who had asked for those specific shoes, as my toe and ankle issues meant practicality over fashion. And it's true that pictures of me wearing black brogues, boot-cut jeans and a hoodie have appeared in certain newspapers. But they will have been taken while I was staying at my wife's for a few days and dressing from the boot of my car. My fashion game needs work, there's no avoiding it. But there are far worse dressers than me, of that I am certain.

Weirdly, Michael Cheika owns a fashion label, but when I worked with him at Stade Français, all he seemed to own was one well-worn T-shirt. Shaun Edwards, however, has to be the most eccentric dresser I've ever met. Whatever else he was wearing, he always finished his outfit with a black bomber jacket (with a picture of the boxer Steve Collins on the back rather than Castrol GTX), a flat cap and white trainers. Wedding: blue suit and trainers. Funeral: black suit and trainers. Black tie function: tuxedo and trainers. I said to him once, having summoned up the courage, 'Shaun, why do you wear trainers with everything?' And he replied, 'Mate, this one time I was on a night out and I was wearing smart black shoes with slippery soles. I got into a fight, slipped over and got filled in. I've worn trainers ever since, so that I'm always ready.' Who on earth makes sure they're ready for a tear-up at a funeral? Who has that kind of mindset? Shaun Edwards, that's who. Talking of trainers, Eddie Jones has a trainer fetish. He's like an Australian Imelda Marcos, must have a whole wing of his house devoted to them. He's also a trainer snob. If you're wearing a bad pair of trainers, he will take you down. God alone knows what he made of my trainer game. I'm guessing not a lot.

When I first started playing, flashes of sartorial individuality were frowned upon by many of the old guard, the kind of people who thought a Barbour jacket in blue, rather than the traditional green, was unnecessarily ostentatious. I was one of the first forwards in the Premiership to wear white boots, having tested the water with silver. There were a few sly digs, but my captain Lawrence Dallaglio and coaches Warren Gatland and Shaun Edwards liked players to express their individuality. In fact, I'd go as far as to say that if I hadn't come through at Wasps, who valued a player's personality as much as their commitment to playing hard, I might not have had a career in rugby. If I'd come through at Leicester, I'd have hanged myself after half a season, because they didn't tolerate anything that veered from their orthodoxy. And if I hadn't topped myself, I'm sure one of the Leicester old guard would have helped me on my way. I am pretty certain Martin Johnson wouldn't have put up with my bombastic personality.

Never mind a Ferrari, a Leicester player owning a beige Volvo V60 would have marked them out as a maverick. When their flying winger Tom Varndell turned up for an away game at Wasps with a pair of purple boots, his coach Richard Cockerill told him he wasn't allowed to play unless he coloured them with a black felt-tip pen, which he spent most of the warm-up doing. The attitude from the old guard was, 'We'll not be having any of that individuality at Welford Road.'

PAMPERING

Apparently, the Leicester orthodoxy extended to pubic hair. As the twenty-first century got into its stride, being metrosexual – moisturising, fake tan and the manscaping of pubes – became perfectly acceptable, even among forwards (apart from the props). But apparently not at Leicester. I once walked into an England changing room and was greeted by the sight of Martin Corry naked, with what looked like Bob Marley's head attached to his crotch. I hadn't known him long, so didn't know what to say. I was all trimmed up, so that my old fella looked like the last chicken in the shop, and here was Martin looking like the bloke from *The Joy of Sex*. When I'd got over my shock, I stammered, 'Are you not going to … how have you allowed that to happen?'

'Don't you worry about me, James. I'm married.'

'Oh. Right. Well, that's an interesting look you've got going on there.'

The atmosphere was so tough at Leicester that when a player left for another club, he'd often veer in the opposite direction. Like someone escaping a cult. Andy Goode spent about 10 years at Leicester, on and off, but by the time he joined Wasps in 2013, he was a fully signed-up member of the manscaping club. Like most grooming pros, myself included, he'd veet his sack, back and crack. How do I know this? Because every time I walked into the changing room, by some quirk of timing, Goodey would be bent over with his cheeks splayed. I'd put my arms over my eyes and fall to my knees, as if I'd looked into the Eye of Sauron. He'd say, 'Stop looking at my arse!' And I'd reply, 'Goodey, you're pulling it apart, you sick fuck! Stop it!' Goodey, a great team-mate and friend, was not afraid of taking stick. He couldn't be, because he was one of the world's first sportsmen to sport a skullet – bald on top, mullet at the back – which he proudly rocked for the last 10 years of his career. Then, six months after retiring, Goodey suddenly reappeared as a broadcaster with a full head of hair. He'd been waiting all those years to make his move, because he knew that if he'd got a weave while he was still playing, the abuse would have trumped the skullet-baiting 100 times over. Goodey, I think you look amazing, and as my lid disintegrates I may follow the path you have scorched.

I'm not going to lie to you, I liked a bit of pampering. On a Friday before an England game, I'd do the team run at Twickenham, nip down to Richmond, have a sunbed and a nice massage, grab a Nando's and maybe watch a film at the cinema, before heading back to camp, trimming my leg hair and packing my bag for the game. Then my partner would arrive at the hotel and we'd chill out for the evening. Some people swore by no sex before games, but towards the end, I had sex on the day of a game and won man of the match, so that rule went fully out the window for me.

Before the 2011 Six Nations game against Ireland, I was suffering from dry skin. My pillow looked like a flapjack. So my then girlfriend leant me some moisturiser, which I duly slathered all over my body, not knowing it was tinted – with sparkles in it. When I got on the coach to go to the match day walkthrough, I got a few funny looks. By the time I got off, I looked like Dale Winton and everyone was in hysterics. And I was getting browner and more sparkly all the time. No-one believed I'd done it by mistake. They thought it a case of 'Classic Haskell' always doing anything for attention. Later that day we got hammered by the Irish, and I got blamed for upsetting the team's carefully cultivated togetherness and focus.

I should clarify that when I say I trimmed my leg hair, I don't mean going at it with a Bic, like Wales's Gavin Henson. Gavin was very pioneering with his shaving, and not in a good way. In fact, it was very niche and very odd. Playing against Gavin was like playing against a mannequin. A mannequin who was very good at rugby, but a mannequin all the same. Of course, some players don't have a choice. At Wasps, Phil Greening and Italian hooker Carlo Festuccia didn't have a single hair between them. It was like sharing a changing room with a couple of highly evolved dolphins.

HYGIENE

As for front-row players, most of them still haven't mastered basic hygiene. Even the young ones will get in the shower, stand under the water and move the mud around, without bothering to use soap. But at least they make a token effort. With some players I never saw them shower the whole time I played with them. As for others, they wouldn't get fully naked. Like children. There are a few basic rules to live by as a rugby player: never trust a team-mate who never attends team socials; never trust a team-mate who doesn't front up in contact sessions; and never trust a man who showers with his pants on. If you do all three, you're persona non grata. Even two out of three is deeply suspect.

There was a Newcastle player, a prop, who had a double first from Oxford or Cambridge, but not enough room in that big brain of his for thoughts of cleanliness. After a game, he'd eat food with his hands and stuff it in his pockets for later, like Dan Aykroyd with the salmon in *Trading Places*. He behaved like a student and stunk like a tramp. It transpired he had some woman on the side who lived in Jersey. After a game, he'd drive to Newcastle airport and jump on a plane, still with mud all over him and his strapping on, turn up at this woman's house, and she'd lovingly remove his strapping and bathe him. That was his one bath of the week, the weird, kinky bastard.

Props are very odd people. A strange breed. Almost like a sub-species of human. Or different creatures completely. Very aggressive, like trolls. Prop is easily the worst position on the field, closely followed by hooker. Why would you want to do that for a living? The only reason I can think of for anyone wanting to be a prop is that they're fat and weird, so they can't do anything else. A bit harsh, I know. I played with quite a few props who could scrummage and nothing else. If the ball came anywhere near them, they'd panic. I'd look at them and think, 'How the fuck have you become a professional sportsman?' The worst part was, they'd often be the best-paid player in the team, because decent tight-head props are like hen's teeth.

If you'd asked an Irish prop I used to play with at Wasps if he had any shower gel, he'd sound all offended and reply, 'I certainly do not!' It was as if you'd asked him if he'd ever had sex with his mum. I won't reveal his name, but those who played with me will know who it is instantly. I shared a room with him once (once was quite enough, thank you) and it was honking. When he paid a visit to the bathroom for a shower, which was a shock on its own, I grabbed his can of Lynx Voodoo, stuck a pin in it, chucked it in his bag – like a gas grenade – and zipped it up. Big mistake. Now the place smelled like one of those perfumed dog poo bags or a shit in a flower-bed, so that I ended up gagging into my pillow. Mind you, and in the interest of balance, it wasn't just forwards who whiffed a bit. The boys used to call Mark Denney, a centre by trade, Clifford, after the Listerine dragon. Every Secret Santa, he'd get a pile of toothpaste, mouthwash and chewing gum. It was overkill, but I'd argue he needed telling.

ROOMIES

Props weren't the only room-mates with irritating habits. On the 2017 Lions tour, Sean O'Brien would open gift packs from my wife and eat all the Ferrero Rocher (you never know when you're going to meet an ambassador on a Lions tour). When I confronted him, he'd say, 'What's your problem? Room treats, Hask, room treats …' To be fair, I did have more considerate roomies on that tour. On the stopover in Australia, I roomed with Sean's fellow Irishman Tadhg Furlong. I barely knew him – one of the strangest things about being a professional rugby player is sharing hotel rooms with strange men – but when I walked into the room, he looked at me and said, 'Hello, Hask. You look like you need a hug.' I did! So he gave me one, and it was lovely. That night when we went to sleep, we were like *The Waltons*.

'Goodnight, Hask.'

'Goodnight, Tadhg.'

Northampton and England lock Courtney Lawes wasn't quite as sweet-natured as Tadhg. Lawsey would crank the heating up to about 200°C and walk around bollock naked. He had (and still has, presumably) such a gigantic penis that when he walked past the lampshade, the room would go dark. It was like a solar eclipse. He'd have three laptops on at the same time, which we called his sub-station, causing the lights to dim as there was such a drain on the hotel's electricity. It looked like he was in the control room at NASA, overseeing the launch of a rocket. In fact, one screen was for films, one was for gaming, and one was for Pornhub/match analysis. On top of that, because he was so tall and couldn't keep weight on, Lawsey would constantly be munching on Crunchy Nut Cornflakes or Hobnobs, washed down with lashings of Ribena. And room service would be knocking on the door every half an hour, delivering club sandwiches or cheese omelettes. Putting all of this to one side, Courts was a great roommate, and always good for having a laugh and a moan with.

In England camps, Wasps' Tim Payne used to room with Harlequins' Nick Easter. They were both lovely guys, but with very negative vibes, so it was like Morrissey and the Cure's Robert Smith sharing a room, or the two Berts from *Sesame Street*. Rooming etiquette said that if you had to go for a piss in the middle of the night, you couldn't turn any lights on or flush the toilet. But because the bathroom was on Payner's side of the room, after a while Nick thought, 'Fuck it', and started pissing in the kettle. Payner used to drink upwards of six cups of green tea a day, and only found out after Nick retired, or so the story goes.

TOILETS

The suspect hygiene of Wasps' prop paled into insignificance next to a nameless Stade Français team-mate who also played for France. One day, this guy came into training with a huge lump on his head, looking like a Klingon out of *Star Trek*. The player left training soon after, and got so ill that the club had to call for an outside doctor to visit him at his house, where he was found to be living in unsanitary conditions. Apparently, there were Coke cans, crisp packets, McDonald's bags, pizza boxes and God knows what else strewn all over the floor. How bad does it have to be for a doctor to report you for living in squalor? That's what happens to hoarders and old people who can't look after themselves, not someone who plays for one of the biggest rugby teams in France.

I don't think the team-mate in question stooped as low as shitting in his living room, but French players were big on toilet humour and would sometimes take it to extremes. Before one game for Stade, someone shat in Pierre Rabadan's boot and he put it on. Pierre was a bloody club legend – why would anyone do that to him? At Wasps, Raphaël Ibañez got involved in a tit-for-tat with Phil Vickery, which ended with Raphaël 'hiding' a toilet seat in Phil's bag. Phil was walking around with that toilet seat in his bag for weeks before he noticed. Raphaël had plenty of previous. If you started a war with him, it was bound to get dirty and he'd always win. Apparently, he once shat on a towel and hid it at the bottom of Clément Poitrenaud's suitcase as an act of revenge. This caused a huge stink in the French squad, as no-one knew who it was, and Clément was refusing to train or play. I'm told that another team-mate Damien Traille came over all Hercule Poirot – 'I know it's you, Raphaël, and I will prove it' – but was never able to finger his chief suspect.

When Fabien Pelous reached 100 caps for France, he was awarded an engraved silver salver, which Raphaël decided to shit on. Pelous only discovered this foul deed the following morning, by which time Raphaël's toxic evacuation had burnt right through to the pewter. What makes that story even stranger is the fact that Raphaël was captain.

Inevitably, toilets provide the stage for a whole host of rugby club mishaps, bordering on crimes. Every team has a phantom player who blows the toilets up every time he sits down on the throne. The culprit having sneaked out unseen, you'd survey the wreckage, like someone standing in a crater after a bombing raid, and think, 'How on earth has this happened? And why? What an awful world we live in.' Sometimes, the only logical explanation would be that whoever did the terrible deed had swung upside down from the cistern and shat vaguely in the direction of the toilet bowl, out of a second arsehole located in the middle of his back.

Then there would be the inquest – text messages flying around, a dedicated WhatsApp group – so we could get to the bottom of which depraved animal among us had bombed trap one. Some players were more brazen. A classic of the genre was barging into a team-mate's hotel room and doing a shit in their toilet, so that you or your room-mate didn't have to put up with the smell. The more deviant player would do a reverse cowboy, facing the cistern, so that the shit missed the water, stuck fast to the pan and the victim couldn't flush it away. But the very worst I heard was when someone did what he triumphantly labelled a 'top deck', which involved him shitting in some poor team-mate's cistern. How he managed it I will never manage to work out. What I do know is that every time the victim flushed it wasn't pretty.

BOOTS

Wasps scrum-half Joe Simpson used to put eggs in my boots, the little bastard. Luckily, they weren't raw. Unluckily, they were so hard boiled that I once almost broke my ankle trying to put my boot on. I resisted taking revenge, because once you get drawn into tit-for-tat pranking it can so easily get out of hand and become all-consuming. Especially against Joe – he had way too much time on his hands. He once caused a riot on a Facebook housing forum, just to get revenge on a team-mate who lived in that housing complex. He pretended to be an angry elder resident who lived there too (not hard when he looked 55 on a good day). He said that this player was having illegal raves, and dumping rubbish in the courtyard and parking in the wrong parking spaces. The player was vilified, but Joe eventually got caught out.

One opportunity I couldn't pass up to prank someone was when Andy Goode bought his wife some Louboutin shoes and made the rookie mistake of leaving them unattended in the changing room. For probably about two seconds. I removed the shoes from the box and replaced them with some old rugby boots, before Goodey took the box home and wrapped it up for his wife's birthday. The following day, Goodey suddenly popped up in a WhatsApp group. 'Right, which one of you wankers nicked my wife's Louboutin shoes? She's unwrapped her birthday present to find a pair of muddy size 12 Adidas boots. I will give whoever stole them the opportunity to drop them off at my wife's workplace, otherwise I'm going to call the police.'

He wasn't joking either. So I had to drive back to Acton, sneak into the changing room and dig out these Louboutin shoes, before driving to Mayfair, where Goodey's wife worked at some private members' club, and leaving them with the receptionist. I thought I'd got away with it, but Detective Inspector Goode managed to get hold of the CCTV footage from the members' club, and posted the footage on WhatsApp. He saw the funny side. Eventually. The biggest mistake Goodey made was not buying his missus an angle grinder, like another old Wasps team-mate John Yapp. I probably wouldn't have nicked that. Yappy was a Welsh prop and part-time builder whose missus and child would sit in his van while he was training. After a session, I'd ask Yappy if he fancied a coffee and he'd reply, 'Can't stop, Hask, family's locked in the van ...'

CARS

Many changing room gags involved either stealing or hiding something, not much different to what we were doing at school. Wasps hooker Ben Gotting spent two weeks walking around with a 15 kg dumbbell in his bag. Wasps and England team-mate Elliot Daly, who adored a prank, once cleared my bag out, wrapped everything in clingfilm and stapled it to the ceiling. There was also lots of sneaking into hotel rooms and turning them upside down, while there isn't a rugby player in history who hasn't had his keys nicked and his car moved. One of the finest sights in rugby is a team-mate storming into a changing room with a look of blind panic on his face, ranting and raving about his car being stolen. Not that many players had a car worth stealing.

While it's perfectly normal for a young footballer to drive a Ferrari or a Bentley, you'll hardly ever see a car like that in the car park of a rugby club's training ground. Worcester scrum-half François Hougard drives a Lamborghini Aventador, but he's got loads of other business interests and that kind of extravagance is very unusual for rugby players, even today. My first car was a Fiat Panda 4x4 Alpine edition. It was 800 cc and sounded like a lawnmower, until you hit 60 mph, when you felt like you were in a Space Shuttle about to take off. I progressed to my nan's old Vauxhall Astra – if that car could have talked it would have screamed – and that was when I was on the verge of the England team. Lawrence Dallaglio and some of the other senior lads drove Range Rovers, Audis and Mercs, but some of the younger players' cars were comically bad. Peter Elder, who was a slightly odd bloke full-stop, drove a purple minivan that his mum and dad bought for him. It looked like a popemobile and was pure fanny repellent. It wasn't just embarrassing to be seen in the thing with Peter, it was embarrassing to be seen in the same car park as the wretched vehicle.

Since I'm on the subject of cars and girls, I should tell you the tale of a former Wasps team-mate of mine, whom I was going to name, but when I told him, he massively panicked and called me pleading to change it. So, for the purposes of this story let's call him Bruce. This is the story of Bruce Smithington and his chauffeur. Bruce and another Wasps team-mate used to go to Las Vegas every year and reinvent themselves for however long they were there. They'd book a table in a night-club, order a load of vodka, Rémy Martin and champagne and tell the women who came flocking that they were property moguls or casino owners or something to do with saving wild-life. Bruce was the fussiest man in the world when it came to women – she could be the most beautiful woman in the world but if she had a wonky toe, he wouldn't be interested. But one night, he fell head over heels in love with this American girl, who must have been perfect in every single way.

Bruce and this girl had a whirlwind romance, and when it was time to say goodbye, he said to her, 'I've had an amazing time, why don't you visit me in London?' He only said it for appearances' sake, but this girl immediately said yes. When Bruce got back home, I overheard him telling some of the lads about his predicament, namely that this girl who was arriving in a couple of days thought he was a wealthy property developer, not someone who played a sport she'd never heard of living in a small flat in Kingston. So I said to him, 'Tell you what, I'll pretend to be your chauffeur and take you out on the town.'

Bruce didn't actually think I was going to do it, but I was deadly serious. I nipped home, phoned my mate who had a garage and asked if he had any flash cars I could borrow for an afternoon. I wanted an old Roller, but the Bentley he offered me was good enough. The next port of call was a joke shop, from which I procured a policeman's peaked hat. Once I'd removed the badge, it looked no different from a chauffeur's cap. I also rigged my laptop up to a camera, which I stuck on the dashboard, so I could film the whole charade and play it at the next team meeting. Back then, I was so committed to pranks and such, I even asked my mum and dad if they'd move into the guest house for the weekend, so Bruce and this girl could stay in the main house. My mum and dad, who were always happy to help a friend of mine in need and liked a bit of mischief, were up for it, but Bruce politely declined.

When Bruce emerged from his apartment with this beautiful American girl on his arm, I was waiting for them, dressed in my suit and chauffeur's cap and polishing the Bentley. Rather than James, I'd asked Bruce to call me 'Bitterman' – no idea how that name came to me – and when we saw each other, we both slipped into our roles quite seamlessly.

'Afternoon, Bitterman, how are you?'

'Very good, Mr Smithington What a pleasant evening. Delighted to meet you, madam.'

Minutes later, we were on our way to Mayfair, because Bruce had arranged to have afternoon tea at the Ritz. Because I was still a teenager and hadn't been driving long, I was relying on one of those first-generation TomToms and spent about half an hour trying to get out of Kingston. I was hitting dead ends, doing U-turns and frantically pressing buttons on the TomTom, and every now and again I'd look in the mirror and see this girl flashing me quizzical looks. Then she asked me about the camera, which I explained was a security measure, 'because Mr Smithington is a wealthy man.'

Once I'd worked out which direction I was supposed to be travelling in, me and Bruce fell into some magnificent ad-libbing.

'How's the family, Bitterman?'

'Very good, Sir, thank you for asking. Mrs Bitterman asked me to say thank you for the Christmas bonus, that was far too generous of you.'

'My pleasure, Bitterman, it's the least I could do.'

When the girl commented on my size, Bruce replied, 'He's not just my driver, he's also close protection.'

When Bruce remembered the camera, he really started warming to his role.

'So, Bitterman, how's our old friend Dallaglio?'

'Funny you should ask, Sir. I've been spending a lot of time with Mr Dallaglio. And, while I don't mean to be indiscreet, he's been doing an awful lot of partying. Different events every night, Sir. Which is quite impressive when you consider how old and decrepit he is. If I may be so bold …

'I have also had Mr Lewsey in the car, I often drop him and his boyfriend off for dinner.' (There was an amazing tabloid story that suggested for some reason that Josh, who was married at the time, had been dating the singer Will Young. Which was manna from heaven to the lads.)

When I finally located the Ritz, I parked right out in front, jumped out of the car, helped the girl out and she said to me, 'Thank you so much, Bitterman, it was wonderful to meet you.' Meanwhile, Bruce has ostentatiously dropped a £20 note into my top pocket. With that, I tipped my cap, climbed back in the car and left them to it, before giggling all the way back to the garage.

As for Bruce's date, it sounded like the most stressful in

history. Because booking a table for afternoon tea at the Ritz isn't easy, he'd made up a load of bollocks about him intending to propose to his girlfriend, which swung it for him. But he spent the entire meal looking over the girl's head, because he was terrified that the violinist, who was hovering near their table and had the look of a sprinter waiting for the sound of the starting pistol, would burst into a celebratory rendition at any moment. Meanwhile, various waiters kept fussing over the couple and winking at Bruce.

At one point, Bruce bent over to do his shoelace up, forgetting what he had suggested might happen when he got down on one knee to the hotel staff, the room went quiet and a waiter appeared with a bottle of champagne ready to pop it. Bruce, realising what had happened, leapt back to his feet and strode off to the toilet in one motion, his American lady friend looking more bewildered by the second. When he came out again, he was intercepted by the maître d', who whispered in his ear.

'Monsieur, is everything okay?'

'Sorry about that, but I've actually decided it's not the right time …'

The stress levels for Bruce became unbearable after that. He dared not make eye contact with anyone, while his lady friend noticed the sweat on his brow and the nervous twitching. With no other way out, Bruce was forced to improvise, saying that one of the prawn sandwiches he had eaten was not sitting well, and he and his 'bride-to-be' made a quick exit.

Sadly, there never was any footage of the car journey because the camera wasn't connected to the laptop properly. As for Bruce and his girl, I assume he discovered an unusual mole on her back and sent her packing.

MOANING

Some guys are always the victim of the lads' pranks, including England wing Jonny May. Jonny is a lovely guy and incredibly meticulous and committed, a man at times like Forrest Gump, running so fast after a ball, or with ball in hand to score a try, that he forgot how to stop, or that the pitch was going to end at some point, or that there may be obstacles in the way. I've seen him run full pelt into golf buggies, going through the plexiglass and into the hoardings, doing a full flip into the seats. Team-mates would genuinely have to shout, 'Stop, Jonny, stop!' He is also one of the most professional players going; he stretches for at least an hour before and after every training session. But Jonny is on another planet, what we would affectionally name a space cadet. He operates on such another plane of thought that I don't think he knows where he is half the time. If you tell him something, good or bad, the chances are that he'll shrug and reply, 'It's just news,' and walk off. There was the time years ago when he thought he was possessed by the spirit of a chicken. This went on for several months, to his Gloucester team-mates' annoyance. They even locked him in a cage when the clucking and squawking became too much. There was some sort of exorcism and the chicken spirit was released and Jonny became normal Jonny again. Well, normal in the loosest sense of the word. You'd often hear Jonny wandering around the changing room, sighing and muttering, 'Has anyone seen my notebook? Has anyone seen my trainers?' And usually Joe Marler, with whom Jonny has a love-hate relationship, would have nicked them. Someone once stole Jonny's orthoses (those things you put in your shoes to help your posture) and he developed a foot condition that put him out of action for a couple of weeks. Jonny's never forgiven whoever it was (Marler, again) and has probably got a case for bullying in the workplace. I have always liked Jonny a lot and have always refrained from getting in on the pranks against him. If you start that nonsense it never ends, and before you know it there is turd in your cistern and someone has soaked your bed.

Wasps was a very accepting club in many ways, but only if you accepted that if you rocked up with a dodgy haircut, shit clothes, big nose, limited hygiene, a set of teeth like burnt fence posts and anything that wasn't 100 per cent agreeable to every member of the squad, you were going to get buried, like it or not. But as time went on, players became a bit more reserved and lacking in edge. We had a long-standing training-ground game called 'Three Gs', which stood for 'Three Genuines'. In short, the rules were that if you were caught out lying, you'd have to pay a fine. We had a dice of misfortune, and each number meant a different fine. If you rolled a one, you had to drive the entire length of the M25 at rush hour taking photos of specific landmarks; a two meant you had to shave your head; a three meant you had to buy 100 coffees for everyone; a four meant you had to clean the changing rooms; a five meant you had to wash the lads' cars; a six meant you had to do the washing-up in the canteen. But ignoring fines started to become the norm. Players knew that if they ignored a fine, there would normally be no sanction, because what used to be seen as self-policing and drilling discipline, toughness and maturity into young players was now perceived by some as bullying.

One morning after I'd been made captain, Christian Wade bowled in late for about the twentieth time, and still owed 200 cups of coffee in fines, before someone pointed out that Phil Swainston, one of our props, had lost on a Three G but was refusing to have his head shaved. And I completely lost it. 'This is bullshit! No-one's paying any fines! Where's the discipline gone? Phil, we're shaving your head!' I grabbed my gumshield and asked a couple of lads to help me pin Phil down, while the rest of them were standing back and looking at me like I'd gone mad. But Phil didn't go down without a fight. He was kicking out and pulling hooks off walls, until I finally had to say, 'Phil, if we let go of you and you try anything, that's not gonna go down well.'

We let go of him, he squared up to me and I whacked him. Everyone was open-mouthed, no doubt thinking, 'Is Hask having a breakdown?' A couple of minutes later, Phil was having his head shaved, while shaking with anger. I must have been having a bad day, because that really wasn't me. And I felt bad about it, especially when Phil's missus told my girl-friend what I'd done. Apparently, Phil's missus wanted to hit me herself. On the plus side, from that day on, if someone was asked to do a fine, they did it. Even Wadey, who rocked up a few days later wearing a sheepish grin and carrying 200 cups of coffee and a side of cakes.

Luckily for Phil and his missus, at Wasps we even tolerated moaning on an industrial scale. In fact, it was encouraged. We weren't unique in that respect – all sportspeople seem to do is sit around saying, 'This is bollocks' – but we were bloody good at it. We called it having a 'sappuccino', which consisted of a load of us sitting round and slagging everything off, from the coaches, the facilities, our team-mates, our team-mate's part-ners, to the kit, the kitman, the ball boys, the food, the cooks, the lack of Drifters in the vending machine. Just because a player was sappy didn't mean he was bad for morale. When I describe people as negative in this book, I don't mean it as a bad thing. I just mean they are negative funny, like that miser-able robot from *The Hitchhiker's Guide to the Galaxy*. Tim Payne was one of the best yet most negative people I ever met, but he gave everything on the pitch and for his team-mates. Having a moan can lift the spirits, because players can get a lot off their chests and it can be very funny to listen to. Although not many players went as public with their sappiness as Wasps wing Paul Sackey. When interviewed for the club programme and asked for his likes, Paul simply replied, 'Chilling.' And when asked for his dislikes, he simply replied, 'Rugby.'

SKIMMING

While moaning was fine, one thing that was certain to demoralise a team was the act of vandalism known as 'skimming'. Forget eye-gouging, skimming is the darkest art in all of rugby union. Let me explain. Because rugby players spend most of their time watching what they eat, they get very, very excited at the prospect of a bit of stodge. With Wasps, like most rugby teams out there, we'd normally be put up in a shitty hotel before a game and always have crumble and custard. That would be the culinary highlight of the week, something that everyone in the squad looked forward to. But the dastardly skimmer could destroy a squad's equilibrium with one wicked thrust of his spoon. A skimmer is a man who skims all the crunchy goodness off the top of a crumble – the crumble, if you will – and leaves only fruit (or the pastry off the top of a pie, just leaving the filling). If a skimmer served himself before you, it was enough to put you off your game. Some weeks, I'd stare at the sad fruit in the tray and my bottom lip would quiver. Others would be angry and shout, 'Who's been fuckin' skimming?' Lots of lads were skimmers, but Joe Simpson was skimmer-in-chief. His bowl would always be 90 per cent crumble and 10 per cent fruit. He was such an inveterate skimmer that we even started calling him Joe Skimpson, or Skimmo for short. Skimmo always denied it, but he would, because his dark addiction to skimming created serious issues for the team.

For some reason, the hotel staff always used to put the custard vat next to the soup vat, and I once witnessed Wasps' head coach Dai Young ladle custard into his soup bowl, sit down, take a mouthful and look confused, before salt and peppering it, finishing the lot and going up for a second helping. In the England hotel, custard was considered a bit unsophisticated. So instead, the culinary highlight was chicken goujons and chocolate brownies at 4 o'clock on a Friday afternoon. But one Friday, the new nutritionist, in a moment of sheer madness, served up something different and there was a minor uprising, like in a prison when the food is inedible. The lads were actually waiting for him when he came back in on the Sunday night and said he could fuck off if there were not goujons and brownies there next time. The poor bloke was in fear of his life, and while he never made the same mistake again, I'm not sure he ever fully regained our trust.

RONNIE

One player it was impossible to get one over was England hooker Mark 'Ronnie' Regan. I knew Ronnie was going to be an interesting character after my first England training session. When it started raining, Ronnie picked up what he thought was a waterproof top, inspected it closely and put one arm into it. I could see him thinking, 'This doesn't seem right, but I'm going with it,' and a minute later he was wearing a pair of waterproof trousers on his head.

Ronnie's reputation as a player was greatly enhanced by a quote from South Africa captain and hooker John Smit. Smit said that Ronnie had spoken to him more in one game than his wife had spoken to him in 10 years, which the England coaches took to mean that he was a master of psychological warfare. In truth, Ronnie was just really, really irritating, as

John confirmed on my *House of Rugby* podcast. He wasn't what I would describe as the sharpest tool, but his chat, delivered in the buzziest Bristol burr, was incessant, which meant he could never really be beaten. He was one of the most unintentionally funny men I ever played with.

Before the 2007 World Cup, we trained with the Special Boat Service. When we turned up, the SBS guys were looking at us and thinking, 'These boys are prima donna arseholes. We're gonna give them hell.' But it didn't take them long to work out that we were all honest, hardworking blokes and not much different to them. On the first night, we played some weird drinking game in the soldiers' mess, involving a tree trunk, a hammer and some nails. There was lots of booze, lots of impromptu scrummaging and lots of fun.

On day one, we had to do a canoe race, which involved groups of five carrying canoes on our heads. The idea was that only four of us would be carrying the canoe at any one time, which meant swapping someone in and out every few minutes. But because Ronnie was in such bad nick – which is a problem when you're training with one of the finest military units in the world – and constantly having to sprint to catch us up, he'd last about 10 seconds under the canoe, before spluttering, 'Hask! Hask! Swap out!' After a mile or so, Ronnie was trailing behind us, blowing out of his arse and not helping in the slightest. But when we came up behind Tom Palmer and his group, their canoe suddenly swung round and flew off their heads, scattering them like ninepins and knocking one of them out. As Team Palmer were trying to work out what had gone on, Ronnie drew up beside me and whispered in my ear, between great lungfuls of air, 'Espionage, Hask. Espionage ...' It turned out that Ronnie had flicked their water bailer, which was hanging from their canoe on a long piece of string, round a fence post, thus stopping their progress in spectacular fashion. To be honest, what staggered me most wasn't Ronnie's wicked plan, it was that Ronnie knew a word as long as 'espionage'.

As we were approaching the end, Ronnie drew up beside me again and spluttered, 'Here, Hask, swap out!' Being a junior player, I did as I was told, Ronnie took over and then suddenly sped up, so that when he passed the finish line, dropped the canoe and fell to his knees, head coach Brian Ashton felt moved to pat him on the back and say, 'Well done, Ronnie, great effort.' Meanwhile, I was half-dead on my back, muttering to myself, 'Are you fucking kidding me, he did fuck all!' Right on cue, Brian looked at me and said, with a sad, disappointed face, 'You're going to have to work on your fitness, Haskell ...'

Later, they had us climbing up and down these tiny ladders, which required us to rely on our feet rather than our arms. Ronnie got halfway up and died, so that he was hanging off the rung and almost crying. He was basically stuck, and while we were all on the floor doubled over with laughter, some poor SBS instructor was trying and failing to pull Ronnie up to safety.

Then there's the classic Ronnie Regan 2007 World Cup final story. In the changing room before the game, skipper Phil Vickery got the lads in a huddle, and just as he was about to deliver his motivational speech, Ronnie piped up with, 'Err, lads, we didn't have the best start to the tournament, but we've got better and better, and tonight we'll rise like a pheasant from the flames.' The lads, who a few seconds earlier had been fired up and focused, were now trying not to laugh. One of them finally said, 'Ronnie, it's a phoenix from the flames.' And Ronnie replied, 'Err, I knew it began with an "f" ...'

Ronnie retired in 2009, but a few months later, before the Six Nations, one of the lads phoned him up from the England training camp and pretended to be coach John Wells, while the rest of us listened in.

'Ronnie, we have a problem. Everyone's gone down with hay fever and we need you to play against Wales.'

'Err, Wellsy, I'm not surprised. I've watched the scrums and the lads aren't doing well. Obviously, you've tried the rest and come back for the best.'

'Exactly, Ronnie! We'll see you on Tuesday.'

Unfortunately, Graham Rowntree found out about the cruel prank and called Ronnie just as he was about to leave his house and head to training.

'Erm, Ronnie. Sorry, there's been some confusion …'

OVERSTEPPING THE MARK

While the ability to give and take abuse is a key part of a rugby player's armoury, there are limits to what people are allowed to do and say. Generally speaking, if you worked hard and played hard at Wasps, you were tolerated. And teams were self-policed by veterans. But looking back, I had far too much to say for myself when I was new to the team. In fact, I was such a nause, a lot of older players wanted to punch me. One day Paul Volley, a flanker who had been at Wasps since the 1980s, was getting into me over something on the training field and I said to him, 'Fuck off, Voles, you can watch me in your retirement.' He went nuts, and I immediately realised I'd overstepped the mark. After training, I sought him out in the car park and apologised profusely.

When my ex-girlfriend sold that story to a newspaper, about her shagging the investment banker-cum-tennis instructor, I was training with England. And the day the story was published, attack coach Brian Smith walked into the changing room and said, 'Hask, mate, you're in the papers for all the wrong reasons again!' Then, after the session was over, Brian shouted to the players to run over to him. 'Last one in gets a go on Haskell's missus! Like everyone else has!' Everyone looked at me because they thought I might lose my rag. But I managed to keep my cool and not say anything. I always felt that I was on thin ice with England, and knocking out our attack coach was probably not a good idea.

The following week, Brian walked onto the training pitch, wandered over to me and Chris Robshaw and said, 'Right, drop-goal competition, last one to get one over gets a go on Haskell's missus.' Robbo was open-mouthed and looked super-awkward. And this time I replied, 'No, Brian. If I get this over, I get to do your wife up the arse.' I kicked it over and he completely lost it. 'That's out of order! That's my wife you're talking about, mate!' But that wasn't the end of it. That weekend, I went shooting and managed to take down this huge black rabbit. And before the next training session, I saw Brian's boot bag unattended, popped the black rabbit inside and zipped it up again. When he put his hand in and pulled it out, he started screaming like a little girl in front of all the lads. But it wasn't as satisfying as I'd expected, so I broke into his hotel room and put another dead rabbit in his bed. To this day, he doesn't know it was me. He should think himself lucky I couldn't afford a racehorse.

7

ENGLAND

CHECKING OUT EARLY

People think that when a player first gets picked for England, it comes with enormous fanfare. I think some people imagine that an old man wearing red and gold livery walks solemnly onto the training field, kneels in front of the debutant and presents him with his England kit, folded neatly on a tasselled velvet cushion. What happened to me was that I was driving out of Wasps' training ground, and Tom Palmer leaned out of the window and shouted, 'Oi! Haskell, you bellend! Have you checked your email? You're in the England team!'

When I was 21, my email address was something along the lines of topshagger1@hotmail.com. It was strictly for mates, not the suits at the RFU. But when I got home and checked my emails, there it was: a short message, in among the emails of naked women and cats falling off washing machines, beginning with the line, 'Dear Squad, you have been selected for training with England … report on Sunday at Bath Spa Hotel.' This was early 2007, and there was a World Cup in the autumn. England had just been smashed by Ireland in the third game of the Six Nations at Croke Park, but we had France next and were still in the running for the title. It was all tremendously exciting.

I rolled down to Bath in my nan's Vauxhall Astra and Brian Ashton, the head coach, met me in reception. He said to me, 'Congratulations, James, I'm really excited to have you in the squad. This is how it works: we're going to have a big double session on Monday, another big session on Tuesday afternoon and we'll name the match day squad on Tuesday evening. We haven't made our minds up yet, I want you to have a really big week.' When Brian was done, I checked in at reception.

'Mr Haskell, welcome to Bath Spa,' the receptionist greeted me. 'I see you're only staying for the two nights.'

'Sorry? What do you mean?'

'It says here you're checking out on Tuesday.'

'Oh. Okay, if that's what it says …'

So much for 'we haven't made our minds up.'

Nick Easter got injured against France, so I was brought back in for the final game of the tournament against Wales. And this time, I made it past Tuesday and Brian picked me to start alongside my Wasps team-mates Joe Worsley and Tom 'Robot' Rees, making it the first time a club back-row had started a game for England. I could have played for Wales, through my nan, and once got picked for Wales Under-18s. I'd played in the England trial on the Saturday, the Wales trial on the Sunday and got named in both squads. I'd even been sent all the Welsh kit, but I had to call the Wales coach and tell him I'd decided to play for England ('I can't believe it. England? You serious, boy?'). In truth, it wasn't a difficult decision. Other than my nan, there wasn't much Welsh about me, and playing for England was all I'd ever wanted to do.

DESPERATELY ADDICTED

The coach ride to Cardiff's Millennium Stadium was an eye-opener. I'd never even been out in Cardiff, so didn't know that the city resembled the opening-day sale at Primark on match days. As the team coach weaved through the throng of locals, everyone was giving us wanker or V signs. The aggression, bordering on hatred, on people's faces was something to behold. One sweet-looking, silver-haired grandma waved at me and when I waved back, she grinned and gave me the middle finger. Then, just as we were turning into the stadium, this guy stepped out of the crowd and headbutted the coach, splitting his forehead open, before being bundled away by security. I was sitting there thinking, 'Oh, my God, if this is what it's like off the field, what's it going to be like when we're on it?'

When I walked into the changing room, my two shirts – one for the start, the other for the second half – were sitting above my locker. There was no ceremony, I just put one on and that was that: I was an England player at last. I had spent a lot of time wondering how I'd feel when the time came to run out for the anthems. Would I feel nervous or upset? Would I want to be anywhere else but there? But when I ran onto the pitch, I couldn't stop smiling. Brian Ashton had let them close the roof, meaning the noise almost tore my head off. But it was the best high you could possibly imagine – better than any drug. All I could think was, 'This is what you've wanted all this time and all the sacrifices were worth it.'

That was the most insane atmosphere I ever played in. Maybe the mind plays tricks, because I'd never experienced anything like it before, but I can't think of another game that surpassed it in terms of pure, terrifying noise. People always used to ask me, 'Could you hear me cheering?' I always said yes, but I almost never could. But that day, I recall being five metres from the Welsh try-line, about five points behind, seeing individual faces in the crowd – eyes like saucers, mouths screaming – and hearing individual words. And it felt like someone or something was pushing down on my head and shoulders. It was so oppressive, and the crowd really made a difference that day. We lost that game and finished third in the table. But I acquitted myself well, and once you've had the taste, you become desperately addicted.

PATRIOTISM

When I played in junior England teams, the coaches always made a point of telling us how much our opponents hated us, whether it was the Scots, the Welsh, the Irish or whoever. By telling us that they hated us, we were supposed to hate them. But it just wasn't in me to hate anyone. It would even crop up in club rugby. I remember Shaun Edwards giving a team-talk before a Wasps game against Leinster. 'Right, lads, I'm not being funny, but everyone goes on about the Irish being so friendly, they are so nice, but they're not. They'll lull you into a false sense of security and make you feel comfortable, then suddenly they'll cosh you over the head and stuff you into the back of a van.' I knew what he was trying to say – the Leinster fans pre-match would be all like, 'Don't beat us by too much today, lads,' or 'Be kind to the boys, will ya,' but as soon as the whistle went, both they and their team wanted to kill you. You would hear the same fans screaming, 'Fucking smash'em, lads!' and if you lost they would let you know it. Suggesting that we should hate a team or a nation didn't resonate with me personally. I just didn't like losing to anyone, that was all that I ever hated, and that was the end of it.

It was only when I started playing international rugby that I sensed that the hatred coming from opposing fans was real.

And players from opposing teams were very good at owning that hatred. But because it's less acceptable nowadays to come straight out and say you hate the English because of their hundreds of years of empire building – as Will Carling pointed out before the Grand Slam decider against Scotland in 1990, he wasn't at the Battle of Culloden – they say we're arrogant instead. It's just a convenient device.

I understand why people have a deep, visceral dislike of the English. That will happen if you go around conquering countries all over the globe. I get it – our identity was being hated, their identity was hating us. But arrogance? I just don't buy it. When I played for England, I felt we were often too apologetic. In fact, we were on the receiving end of much more arrogance than we ever dished out. When we lost to Scotland at Murrayfield in 2018, the behaviour of their players was appalling. They cleverly filmed each other ripping their shirts off, drinking and screaming, changing the words to 'Flower of Scotland' so that they called King Edward's army 'cunts'. I was listening to this and seething. I thought, 'If we behaved that way, we'd be crucified. We'd be all over the front pages, there would be an RFU inquest. We'd be accused of some kind of hate crime.' But because it was the 'plucky Scots', it got brushed under the carpet.

Obviously, the more a team appeared to hate us, the more I enjoyed it if we beat them. But I was jealous of the strength of Celtic identity. I am patriotic because I love my country, but not in the same way as the Irish, the Scots and the Welsh. When I first started playing for England, I'd kiss the red rose on my shirt. But I never felt the same kind of passionate love for my country as the Celts seemed to. I don't think many English players did. I'm pretty sure even Lawrence Dallaglio's tears were for show – as soon as the band struck up 'God Save the Queen' and he saw the red light appear on top of the camera, he'd squeeze a few out, right on cue. (I'm probably doing Lawrence a disservice, but never let the truth get in the way of a good story.)

For me, it was more about being perceived as the best player in my position in England, wanting to play my best and win. I didn't take to the field thinking, 'I am a proud Englishman, and I am going to smash these pathetic little Celts underfoot.' But whenever I played in Dublin, Cardiff and Edinburgh, I'd be able to feel the patriotism, which manifested itself in hostility. I always wished Twickenham was more like that, an intimidating fortress. Instead, it was a lot of mainly posh people singing about chariots.

English people almost aren't allowed to be patriotic in the way the Celts are, because lots of English symbolism – the flag, the anthem – has been co-opted by the far right. If you see a St George's flag hanging from someone's window, you automatically think they're a member of the BNP, or at least they're very angry about immigrants. One year, I attended a St George's Day roast, which consisted of people giving speeches about what it means to be English and singing 'God Save the Queen', 'Land of Hope and Glory' and 'Jerusalem'. It was all very nice, until one bloke on my table turned to me and said, 'Tell you how I'd like to finish the evening off, by hiring four or five minibuses, driving down to Southall and beating a load of Pakis up.' It's because of people like that idiot that so many feel unable to embrace their national identity.

When Eddie Jones came in as England head coach, people started accusing him of arrogance. But Eddie was all about having confidence in what we were doing, which isn't the same as arrogance. Under Eddie, we actually went out of our way not to come across as arrogant, especially when Dylan Hartley was captain. It didn't matter that whenever a team beat us, they celebrated as if they'd just won the World Cup. There was never any showboating or whooping or hollering or flexing of muscles from England, unless we won some silverware. Even when we whitewashed Australia in Australia, we kept a lid on our celebrations. There were probably Australian players and fans who thought we were arrogant for not celebrating enough.

2007: FALSE DAWN

I don't think it's too melodramatic to say that if my career were measured by World Cups, it would be considered a catastrophe wrapped in a shitshow inside an omnishambles. I thought I was going to the 2007 World Cup in France, only to discover I'd been given a bum steer by Lawrence Dallaglio. The squad was in Bath, preparing for a warm-up game, when I got a phone call from Lawrence, who invited me up to his hotel room for afternoon tea, which I had to order. Lawrence was injured and hadn't been training, so I entered his room to find him reclining on his bed in a fluffy dressing gown, like some ailing monarch. He told me to pour the tea and take a seat, before getting down to business.

'Hask, I've been speaking to Brian and we've decided to take you to the World Cup.'

'Right. I didn't realise you were picking the team, but that sounds great.'

Lawrence then took me through his, and what I thought was Brian Ashton's, rationale for taking me – why I was being picked and other players weren't, what I had to offer that other players didn't – and I left his room in a state of high excitement, having completely forgotten about the 50 quid I'd just spent on afternoon tea. A few weeks later, the squad was announced and I wasn't in it. I didn't know why Lawrence had said what he said and why I wasn't picked. I was just so confused. I even thought it might have something to do with the song I sung on the coach after my England debut. I went with Tenacious D's 'Fuck Her Gently', and after I bellowed the line, 'You don't always have to fuck her hard,' Brian Ashton got up and shouted, 'Oh, do sit down, you silly boy.' I am sure, however, there was a lot more to it than that.

2011: A GIANT SKIDMARK

There was nothing I could have done to make England's 2019 World Cup squad, because my body finally packed up and I was forced to retire before the tournament. But that didn't make it any less gutting. Because unlike in 2007, by 2019 I had lots of World Cup memories I wanted to make up for.

The disarray that was the 2011 World Cup could be a whole book on its own. In terms of genre, it would be a mix of horror, dark comedy and misery memoir. And to think our preparations started out so well. We'd had a really good tour of Australia in 2010, beating the Wallabies in Sydney, before beating them again at Twickenham. When we won the 2011 Six Nations, it looked like we might be on to something. But things started to go downhill pretty much the minute we arrived at Pennyhill Park for our pre-World Cup training camp.

At the first meeting, head coach Martin Johnson informed the squad that we'd be doing eight sessions a day, starting at 6.30 am and finishing at 9 pm. The lads were aghast. But when scrum coach Graham Rowntree heard me muttering my misgivings, he was an even less happy man than normal.

'If you're going to be complaining on day one, you can fuck off!'

'But Graham, eight sessions a day?'

'What the fuck's wrong with you? Are you soft or something?'

'Okay, Graham, whatever you say ...'

That camp was chaos from day one and most of the goodwill that had begun to be built up in Australia, which was a really enjoyable tour, soon started to evaporate. Some of the coaches, most of them old Leicester team-mates – Johnno, Graham, forwards coach John Wells and all the other lads in fat camp – would have mountain bike rides around the park, and we'd see them having life and death races to the finish, because they didn't play anymore but were still ultra-competitive. But life was far less fun for the players. Every morning, we'd have 'get up and go' sessions, which sounds like something from *Hi-de-Hi!* But instead of doing star jumps and touching our toes for five minutes, before taking part in a knobbly-knees contest, we were split into groups and made to work on weaknesses (apart from Nick Easter, who hoodwinked each of the coaches into thinking he was always working in another group, when he was actually in bed).

We had full-contact sessions from day one and spent most of the first week working on a forwards' move called 'pig's bobble'. We practised that move every day for months and never used it once at the World Cup. We also had mandatory wrestling, which Matt Stevens thought he'd be brilliant at, because when he was banned for two years for a drugs violation, he spent a lot of his time competing in jujitsu and actually won some gold medals. However, he kept getting thrown out the ring and throwing his toys out of the pram. It was only when Ben Youngs chipped his kneecap, which put his World Cup in doubt, that the wrestling was ditched, well for the backs at any rate. The forwards still spent many an hour running full pelt into each other in tackle suits, on the padded matting. Which of course made all the difference, or so the coaches thought. It just made everyone run harder.

It doesn't matter how hard the coaches make you work in a training camp, players will always fill their downtime with mischief. I brought my rifle and shot rabbits on the golf course after dinner. I didn't ask permission, and I'm sure they wouldn't have given it to me, but I viewed it as pest control, and therefore doing the greenkeeper a favour. One night, I took Tom Wood out with me – it was the first time he'd held a gun and you could see his eyes light up. It wasn't long before he was getting a shotgun licence, bow hunting and whittling his own arrows. We'd find him in his room tying knots, sharpening knives and carving wedding arches. We even started calling him Wilderness Wood.

The rabbit-related problems began when lads started bringing air guns in, so that every afternoon, during 'nap time', you'd hear a chorus of shooting. You'd look up and see the barrels of guns pointing out of windows and hear shots hitting targets stuck to trees at the back of the hotel – and this was a five-star hotel with lots of visitors apart from us – until one day, we were all called into an emergency meeting.

Johnno stormed in and roared, 'Lads, what the fuck's been going on?'

Silence.

'I've been told some of you have been firing guns. Please tell me no-one has brought a firearm onto the property?'

Some idiot tried to deny it.

'Bollocks! I know you have, because apparently a family was out for a walk and came across a dead fox wrapped around a tree with a paper target stuck on its face!'

Lots of stifled laughter and uncomfortable shifting in seats.

'If any of you has got a gun, I suggest you get rid of it!'

After the meeting was adjourned, you could see all these lads running towards the car park with guns under their coats, as if they were fleeing the scene of the St Valentine's Day Massacre. Meanwhile, Johnno was probably staring out of a window, shaking his head and tutting very loudly.

Johnno had hired this management consultant called Gerard Murphy, who was supposed to improve communication between players and management, which to be fair he actually did for a period but ended up being nicknamed 'The Buffer'. The first time Gerard stood up and started talking we all started laughing, which wasn't a good sign. In his high-pitched Aussie accent, he said, 'You're not gonna make things fucking better with humour!' He subjected the players to psychological testing and assigned each of us an identity based on a questionnaire. Each identity comprised a colour and a bird, so that Mike Tindall was a green dove, Andrew Sheridan a blue owl and Chris Ashton a yellow peacock. I was of course a peacock too. That squad was pretty ruthless and cynical and a lot of the players weren't open to what they saw as psychobabble. It was particularly weird given that Johnno had been given the job because of his no-nonsense, straight-talking personality. In Gerard's defence he did make a lot of progress and things were awesome by the Australian tour, but all the hard work and improved coach–player relationships vaporised pretty quickly when the pressure came on.

Gerard would have us doing these exercises that involved someone sitting at the front of the group and being told by the others what they should keep doing, start doing and work on. When Steve Borthwick was still captain, he was dragged out front for the first of these sessions. The poor bloke was like a lamb to the slaughter. Prop Davey Wilson said, 'Keep being professional and really hardworking and good at line-outs, stop saying what you think the coaches want you to say, and work on not wearing shit sports trainers and jeans like Steve Jobs.' I am not sure Davey's group quite got the hang of what Gerard wanted. When it came to John Wells's turn in the spotlight, everyone just told him to stop being so negative, but he was having none of it.

'No! That's just how I am!'

'That's not really how this is supposed to work, Wellsy.'

'Sorry, nope, I won't be changing ...'

If the training camp was at times problematic, the actual World Cup was a farce from the moment we touched down in New Zealand. We were fined for having too many Nike ticks on our bags and wearing branded headphones. I'd tapped up a personal sponsor and sorted a load of coats for the lads, because our official suppliers had forgotten New Zealand can get quite cold in spring. But the RFU told me they were going to fine me for it. During our one-night stopover in Auckland, a few of the lads lost their entire tour fees in the hotel casino. Another couple of lads had a row that culminated in one of them doing a shit on a towel and putting it in the other one's sink. I was wandering down the corridor and saw this lad walking towards me carrying a towel covered in a team-mate's business and wearing a dangerous look of vengeance. I couldn't help thinking, 'This is a less than auspicious start to a World Cup campaign ...'

Our sponsors O2 had asked the RFU if I could film a behind-the-scenes diary, which even I didn't think was a particularly good idea. No-one told me what I could or couldn't film, and I knew they'd edit it, so I just carried on being my slightly risqué self. When we arrived in Dunedin, which is where we were based for the pool stages, Dylan Hartley bought an ancient Vauxhall Victor for a few hundred dollars, we christened it the 'V Banger' and I started filming me, Dylan, Chris Ashton and Ben Foden driving around and having a few laughs. Dunedin makes Bangor look like Las Vegas, we were lads in our twenties and our hotel wasn't the greatest – it was rustic, to put it mildly – so it was nice having something to break the monotony. And that was when we learned what fire pussy was, so our days weren't completely wasted.

Before our first game against Argentina, Tom Croft got sent a load of Cadbury chocolate bars but when the package arrived it was immediately intercepted by the nutritionist and fitness coaches. Meanwhile, one of the players had nicked a walkie-talkie from hotel security. So we'd pile into someone's room and mess about with it for hours, telling whoever was on the other end that we weren't handing the walkie-talkie back until they delivered the chocolate and killed Dave Barton. Barton was sort of the team's anti-hero: a lovely guy but just not overly popular with the lads and someone who got a lot of stick. One afternoon, our captain Lewis Moody suddenly came on the line and started shouting at us.

'Lads! Give the fucking walkie-talkie back!'

'Shut up, you RFU puppet! And stop swearing!'

We called Lewis 'The Puppet' because it seemed like Johnno had his hand up his arse and was working his mouth (and that's what we told him any chance we got).

One afternoon, Dylan Hartley, Chris Ashton and I were in Dylan's room doing some filming of us talking about the insane student houses we had seen, when the door opened and a maid let herself in, which we were slightly taken aback by. She asked where the missing walkie-talkie was, we told her we didn't have it, it started crackling as Dave Barton on the other end was protesting about being potentially shot and she tracked it down to the wardrobe. That's when I made the fateful and inappropriate mistake of saying, 'You still haven't given us the chocolate or killed Dave Barton. And you haven't given us an Aussie kiss, which is a French kiss but down under.' (It was a line that one of the lads had come out with a couple of hours earlier and I couldn't help parroting.) The maid replied, 'What does that mean?' Chris Ashton said, 'A BJ,' and me and Dylan told him to stop being so rude. He apologised straightaway. This gives you an idea where our heads were at. If we thought any line had been crossed we immediately corrected ourselves. As she went to leave, I said, 'Before you go, you need to say goodbye to the V Bangers on camera.' (I had not turned the camera off and we had filmed the entire exchange, something she later appeared to have forgotten.) She asked what that meant, we explained it was the name of our stupid car gang and we were getting as many people as possible to say goodbye to the V Bangers, she happily did what we asked, and left. I had no inkling that a 60-second exchange would have such far-reaching ramifications for so many people.

Nike, the England kit sponsors at the time, had this cunning plan to make us play our first game in black shirts, which went down like a shit in an ice bath in New Zealand. The shirts went missing at Auckland Airport and they had to send a replacement batch over. And because the numbers had been ironed on by some random T-shirt shop in Dunedin, they all fell off while we were playing against Argentina.

We beat Argentina 13–9, but I was caught on camera calling one of their players 'a fucking eye-gouging cunt'. The ITV commentators had to apologise for my language and after the game, Johnno took me to one side.

'We need you to play down the eye-gouging thing. Just say you overreacted. We don't need the hassle.'

'But it was an eye-gouge.'

'Just do it.'

When I was interviewed by the media and then the citing panel, I had to tell them I hadn't been eye-gouged and had overreacted. So now people thought I was a snitch and a fanny. On the bright side, we'd got the win. It wasn't pretty, Jonny Wilkinson was having problems with the balls and couldn't hit a barn door with a bazooka, but I'd had a decent game. More threats of fines for players wearing branded gumshields – 'a breach of team kit specifications', according to the authoritarian International Rugby Board – couldn't dampen our mood, and we headed to Queenstown for a couple of days' R&R in pretty good spirits.

I'd signed up for a load of activities – ziplining, bungee jumping, white-water rafting and what not – and when we arrived in Queenstown, I was called in to see Johnno and Will Chignell, England's media chief. They informed me that Sky Sports and a Getty photographer were going to join us and cover the outing, which I thought was a terrible idea. I thought the lads should be able to enjoy their downtime without the media being around, but Johnno and Will were having none of it and told me to do as I was told. So I sloped off to my hotel room and spent the evening Skyping my then girlfriend – I was never one for a big night out during a tournament – while some of the lads headed to a nightclub called Altitude.

It just so happened that their visit coincided with Altitude's 'Mad Midget Weekender', which meant revellers could combine their drinking with a spot of dwarf tossing, if they so fancied. Niche, I'd agree, but it's not as if the dwarves had been hunted down, caught in a net, bundled into the back of a van and held against their will. The story I heard was that the dwarves, who were rugby fans, spent the night bantering and play-fighting with the lads, but nothing more sinister than that. The lads had a bit too much to drink and got a bit too loose – and it's probably true that none of it should have happened in the middle of a World Cup – but there was not a single dwarf tossed by an England player. Unfortunately, the nightclub posted pictures of lads rolling about on the floor with dwarves on their Facebook page and a bouncer sold CCTV footage to a journalist. When the story appeared in the *Sun*, the dwarf-tossing played second fiddle to a stitch-up of Mike Tindall, who had apparently spent the evening 'flirting with a gorgeous blonde'. Utter bollocks.

What irritated me about that controversy was that the Irish and Welsh squads went on the piss in the same nightclub. In fact, both squads were out far more than the English during that tournament. Apparently, the Irish boys were in and out of Altitude for two days (the bar had to close and re-stock to just to accommodate them), and one of their star players had to be carried out at about 8 am. But the media narrative was that England were a bunch of entitled, arrogant wankers, while the Irish and Welsh lads were plucky, fun-loving underdogs just taking a break from the rigours of the tournament. After Sam Warburton did an interview saying he hadn't had a drink for six months (Sam has probably only had about one pint ever), the media translated that into, 'Wales are doing well because of their iron discipline,' even though it turns out the rest of the Wales squad were not so conscientious. If you have ever been part of a Warren Gatland/Shaun Edwards team, which I have on a large number of occasions, you'll know that having a drink is encouraged by the top management at the right time. Trust me, there were plenty of right times for a team that made the World Cup semi-finals.

The morning after the Altitude debacle, I was fresh as a daisy. So off I went for my helicopter ride, ziplining, bungee jumping and white-water rafting. It was great to get away from it all, we all had fantastic fun and were completely oblivious to the coming media storm. As we had a film crew and photographer tracking our every move, of course we played up to them. Creating what we thought were funny memories, we were in fact building our own downfall frame by frame. The moment we got back to the hotel, I could sense something was badly wrong. I was collared by Dave Barton in the lobby and told that I needed to report to Johnno as soon as possible. Dave was a panicker at the best of times, and so the fact that he was white as a sheet and sweating like a lunatic didn't bode well. When I walked into the room, Johnno was sitting there with the England media manager Will Chignell and the team's legal adviser, Richard Smith QC. They were not in party mood. Johnno got straight to the point, telling me that a hotel maid had accused me, Dylan and Chris of making lewd and inappropriate comments to her. The story we were told by Johnno, and which was later verified by several players, was that after the Argentina game, while I was in bed at the hotel, the maid had gone out to one of the bars where some of the England players were having a post-game beer. She was in great spirits and mingling with the lads, doing shots and chatting away, but had ended up getting extremely drunk and later in the night fallen over and knocked herself out. When her mother came to see her in hospital the next morning and asked her why she was such a mess and had gotten so drunk, she said to her mother that she was traumatised because she had been sexually assaulted by some England players a day or so before. The mother went straight to our team police-liaison who was from Dunedin, and hence a formal complaint to the coaches was made. The maid herself at the time had not actually made a complaint, but rather an irate mother had done it for her. This was actually similar to the lads who were stitched up in New Zealand some years before. Back then one of the boys had slept with a girl, and when she got home her boyfriend asked where the hell she had been, and instead of admitting the truth she said she had been raped. The boyfriend went to the police and complained. All hell broke loose, until her story fell down faster than her knickers had.

Johnno asked me for my version of events and I told him the truth: I'd said something I shouldn't have, Chris had followed suit, before Dylan and I had told him to shut up and we'd all apologised to the maid. And that was that. Or so I thought. I said we had a video of the event but only Johnno watched it (which later came back to haunt us). When he finished, Johnno started going on about how upset he'd be if we spoke to his daughter like that (which was a bit out of context as she was fourteen or thereabouts at the time) and how the three of us should never have allowed ourselves to be in a room with a woman, three on one, as it was her word against ours. I pointed out she had let herself in, being a hotel maid with a key, but that was brushed off. I began to get a sinking feeling in the pit of my stomach. This was going to go turbo and fast.

I understood why they were twitchy, because as I mentioned above, a few England players had been accused of raping a woman in Auckland three years earlier, although they were later cleared but not before having their names dragged through the mud, and for some their careers ended. But when Johnno ordered us to apologise to the maid, I didn't think that was a good idea. I explained again that the maid had let herself into the room, that we had the whole exchange on video and that an apology would make it look as though we were guilty of something far more grievous than an inappropriate comment. The RFU bigwigs were already in full panic mode, however, and someone came up with the bright idea of me, Dylan and Chris meeting the maid, apologising and presenting her with some flowers. I thought it was a bullshit idea and told them so, but I didn't have a choice. The best we could agree upon was we would not say sorry, but say that we understood she'd had a tough time ending up in hospital and hopefully the flowers might make her feel better.

A few days later, Will Chignell went out and bought $100-worth of flowers (which he billed to us), and the hotel manager led me, Dylan and Chris through a maze of corridors, deposited us in some far-flung room in the hotel, said the maid would be along in a minute, made his excuses and left. So we were standing in the middle of this room in awkward silence, because I decided it might be bugged or rigged with a hidden camera, and after about 10 minutes we started to wonder whether we should make our escape. But just as we were about to leave, the maid came in, which meant we were alone in a room with her again. Three on one. The very thing the coaches had told us off for letting happen, and what we all got found guilty of in the investigation by Rob Andrew, the RFU's Elite Rugby Director. They had walked us like Christians into the arena to meet our death. One of the lads started to apologise and she stopped him, and started to apologise to us, saying something along the lines of, 'I'm sorry for causing you guys any trouble, but your team stole my walkie-talkie a few times and I was getting stick from my colleagues, it was embarrassing.' When I told her we were sorry she'd had a tough time of it and gave her the flowers, she started complaining that she'd been banned from working on our team floor. There was no mention of sexual activities or of feeling hurt by what we said. The fact she had not been allowed to work on a floor with access to all the lads seemed to be what she was most upset about. One of the last things she said before leaving was, 'Make sure your team-mates know they can still talk to me. I don't want it to be awkward.' We stood there, taken aback by this whole saga. But I knew we had not heard the end of it. There is no way we should have been left on our own with her again. It was her word against ours, and we knew how that had gone before.

Meanwhile, all the stuff about dwarf-tossing and Mike Tindall had burst into flames and spread like wildfire, and the Sky footage of our Queenstown 'jolly' had been used as evidence that we were behaving as if we were on a stag-do rather than representing our country in a World Cup (when the Welsh lads went quad biking, which was way more dangerous than anything we did, the media said they were just 'letting their hair down'). It didn't help that Nick Easter had to pull out of the game against Georgia because of a back injury, which people assumed he suffered while bungee jumping.

On top of all that, Richard Smith had to write a letter on my behalf to the IRB, in response to one they sent me asking why I had used foul language in a game that had then been broadcast live on ITV to millions of viewers. They also wanted to know why I had said I had been eye-gouged but then changed my mind. Then our kicking coach Dave Alred and conditioning coach Paul Stridgeon were banned for one game after being found guilty of switching balls against Romania because Jonny Wilkinson was suddenly unable to kick straight. (I wouldn't have minded, but we didn't even need to kick the goals – we scored ten tries.) And as if all that wasn't enough, some of the lads went hunting, tried to smuggle a deer's head into Chris Ashton's room, got stopped by security and dumped it in the car park instead. A couple of kids found it and lost their shit, the hotel manager told Johnno and he went mental. This was not what he had signed up for.

Three games in, and having beaten Argentina, Georgia and Romania, I still had an acute sense that the incident with the maid hadn't been put to bed. Hotel staff weren't talking to me, the press officers were rushing around with grave looks on their faces and the coaches seemed off with me in training. Then, a couple of days before the final pool game against Scotland, I was informed that my presence was required at another meeting. Every day felt like the 'Night of the Long Knives' – people knocking on doors late at night, some being frogmarched down corridors, others being grilled in empty rooms. It got to the stage where I expected to be hooded and handcuffed.

It was at this point that things got really dark. We were told that the maid had ramped up her allegations against us, and instead of taking our flowers as a nice gesture it had inflamed the situation, and that we now stood accused of serious sexual harassment. Not only that, but the RFU had been negotiating a settlement figure with the maid's lawyer, without our knowledge or permission. What made it worse was our team manager at the time was having the conversations with the lawyer, and neither made any notes nor recorded it. The maid's story now included the claim that she'd been jostled and sandwiched between us during her 'ordeal' in Dylan's hotel room, and that our subsequent meeting had left her 'hurt and humiliated', because she hadn't received a fulsome enough apology and I was rude and smiled at her with an inane grin, which was all she saw when she closed her eyes, or words to that effect. She claimed I said, 'The flowers are lovely, but not as lovely as you are.' If only we'd had a witness or perhaps a member of our staff with us, because you know what happens when it's three on one and it's her word against ours. Who are you going to believe, three entitled meatheads or a little innocent woman?

The RFU offered to pay the maid's legal fees as a gesture of goodwill, only for the lawyer to return the following day and inform them that if they didn't pay her client $30,000, she'd sell the story to a British tabloid.

The RFU's handling of the situation was shambolic. I was furious that they'd put us in a room alone with the maid again. I was furious that they'd been negotiating a payout without telling us. I was furious when they told us we had to pay the maid $30,000. When I told them that I wasn't going to budge, that the woman was a chancer and that if we paid her it would look like an admission of guilt, they replied that a Kiwi lawyer had advised them that the maid had a solid human rights case against us. When we asked if they were ordering us to pay, they replied, 'You need to do what's best for the team.' It was at this point that my incredible agent Duncan Sandlant hired us a lawyer of our own.

Our lawyer, from a firm in Auckland, immediately realised that the claim against us was bollocks. As for a human rights case, that was even more crap. The only human rights violation case in New Zealand at the time had been from a boss to an employee, which consisted of systematic abuse, and she was only awarded $10,000. He played the management team the video footage, which clearly showed we were telling the truth and that the maid's version of events did not reflect the reality. Our lawyer thought it was madness that the RFU had chosen to believe the maid's version of events and they had started negotiating with her lawyer without anyone but Johnno even watching the video. How can you act without the facts, let alone advise your players what to do? They'd had three weeks to watch the video and get to grips with what was going on, but they did nothing except throw us to the dogs. The RFU didn't seem to care about the truth or our welfare, they just wanted to make it all go away.

Before the final pool game against Scotland, my girlfriend and Mum and Dad flew in. My girlfriend was a bit of an emotional wreck and didn't trust me at the best of times. So however many times I told her that we hadn't done anything serious, she just couldn't understand why we'd been alone in a room with a woman. Her grilling me just like the management team had grilled me was the last thing I needed. She said that there was no smoke without fire, that it wouldn't be still going on if we hadn't done anything. When I showed her the video she changed her tune. When I told my dad what was going on, he was outraged by the RFU's handling of the situation and immediately started mucking in. He now says it was his worst-ever holiday and the most depressing year of his life.

After the win against Scotland, which set up a quarter-final against France, we ended up in another late-night meeting. At no point in that meeting were we told that Johnno would be making a public announcement that me, Dylan and Chris had been disciplined. But, lo and behold, that's exactly what Johnno did the very next day. What we *were* told was that the maid, perhaps because she was starting to worry that we weren't going to pay her, had sold her story to the *Mirror*, who published it the next day. The article was bad, but not as bad as it could have been. The redacted article did claim that we'd 'lured' the maid into the room and 'humiliated her', before offering her a 'half-hearted' apology. She also claimed that she wouldn't have gone after us for money if only we'd written her a card saying sorry. A card, she said, would have provided 'closure'.

Now, the media were calling us the most shameful England team ever. Not only were we not playing very well, we were also a bunch of arrogant, foul-mouthed, rule-flouting, beer-swilling dwarf-tossers, who would rather be bungee jumping, sexually assaulting maids or chopping deer heads off than doing the Red Rose proud. After losing to France in the quarter-finals, we were being called the worst English touring party of any kind, on a par with conquerors and plunderers of the Imperial age and eighteenth-century slave traders.

And then, as if we needed another turd on top of a very shit cake, Manu Tuilagi decided to get pissed and jump off a ferry. I was below deck, spending some quiet time with my girlfriend after a spot of wine tasting on Waiheke Island, while the Leicester boys (the Borg) were having a few drinks upstairs. I was staring out at the harbour, making awkward chat with my girlfriend, who was pretending not to hate me, and we were approaching the ferry pier when this shadowy streak flew past the window, followed by a huge splash. A few seconds later, the alarm started going off. 'WARNING! MAN OVERBOARD! WARNING! MAN OVERBOARD!' I hurried upstairs and was greeted by the sight of Manu swimming to shore. I'm told that someone had said, 'I bet you won't jump in,' and Manu had replied, 'Hold my beer,' before stripping off and plunging into the sea. There was lots of whooping and hollering, until people realised that there was a very real chance of Manu being sucked into the ferry turbine or hit by another boat. And once the danger had subsided, everyone got bored and started drifting off. It reminded me of that scene in the film version of *The Inbetweeners*, when Simon jumps off a boat to swim to his love on the beach, only for it to take him about half an hour to get there. When Manu reached dry land, he was hooked out of the sea by his boxer shorts and promptly arrested.

The plane home was like a morgue on wings. Johnno, whose team had been dubbed a rabble, on and off the pitch, knew he was finished. There were also players in that squad who knew they had played their last game for England, and I thought I was one of them. On landing at Heathrow, we were funnelled into a private terminal – presumably to avoid the rabid fans throwing rotten vegetables – before getting a coach back to Pennyhill Park and dispersing. But I couldn't escape the darkness immediately. Not only did I think my international career was over, I'd also lost all sense of perspective. I'd convinced myself that everyone in England had read about the maid's allegations, believed them and now thought I was some kind of sex fiend. In fact, most people weren't interested. But in my mind, England's early exit, and the 'sex scandal' that had engulfed me off the field, was the be-all and end-all in every English person's life. And that kind of reputation isn't easy to shake off.

A few days later, the then team manager texted me asking how I was and if I was around. I was due to fly to Japan to start my next journey and stupidly replied, thinking he had good intentions. Instead he never replied, and I got a call from a secretary about a meeting with Rob Andrew – whose role at the RFU I never understood but his nickname 'Teflon' Rob kind of says it all. I met Rob at Twickenham, which meant I had to hire another lawyer. After some awkward small talk, Rob played the video of our interaction with the maid. And after we'd watched it, he said, 'How did we get from that to this?', before holding up a copy of the *Mirror*, with their sensational version of the story plastered all over the front page. So I replied, 'Mismanagement, incompetence, miscommunication, weakness in the face of an opportunist, complete disregard for player welfare …' I told him that either my situation was dealt with appropriately, or I'd tell the media exactly what had happened.

I gave him a long list of who had fucked up and the ramifications, including the fact that they had set a dangerous precedent. Now, every chancer knew that if they made an allegation against an England player, the RFU would believe them and possibly pay out. After the meeting, and having seen the video evidence, Rob put out a statement saying the maid's allegations of serious sexual harassment were 'entirely false'. However, they found us guilty of misconduct for allowing a woman to enter the hotel room, and me and Chris were given suspended fines of five grand each. They even tried to fine me for tweeting about the jackets I'd got from my sponsor for the entire team and management. My lawyer managed to talk them out of that one, but that wasn't the end of it. It rumbled on for years.

We never did pay the maid any money, but my legal fees had soared to more than 80 grand. The RFU, despite belatedly concluding that her account was wrong, said I wasn't entitled to legal aid, because I wasn't an RFU employee. A few weeks after arriving home from New Zealand, I flew out to Japan to start my stint with Ricoh Black Rams, which was a blessed relief. But I felt terrible for my parents because they cared so much about what the media said and what the public thought. They'd had to deal with the video sex scandal when I was at school and all the sex pest-related headlines when I made my England debut. And now my dad had got really fired up and wanted to sue the maid for defamation, get the RFU to pay back our fees for gross negligence, and stop the papers reprinting the now blatant lies. Typically, he was like a dog with a bone.

My dad reached out to various RFU people, including its chief disciplinary officer Jeff Blackett, and Bill Beaumont, who was England's representative on the IRB. Jeff tried his best to help and was amazing with his time, but those above him had no interest in helping or stepping in. My old man became bitter with the lawyers, and the media printed whatever they wanted. In the end, the legal fees having risen to well over 150 grand as the lawyers were just firing off letters hiring barristers, paralegals, etc., I had to tell him to stop as I was picking up the bill. I told him I didn't care about any of it, but he thought I was being naive. He never really got over how the RFU treated me and it put a strain on our relationship. For years, my dad wanted to get back at them (he even wanted to write a tell-all book, because he'd been in most of the key meetings and seen first-hand our pleas put down and how they had ignored sound legal advice) and I had to keep telling him not to do anything rash, because I wanted to keep playing for England.

When I received a call from the RFU, asking me to take part in their World Cup review, I told them I wasn't interested. I had my own problems, had nothing positive to say and didn't think I was going to play for England again. In the end there were three reviews – from the RFU, the Rugby Players' Association and Premiership Rugby – all of which were leaked to the media and none of which was pretty. Players were accused of being more concerned about money than their performances on the pitch, drinking too much, not training hard enough and mocking other players for being 'too keen'. There were gripes about the security, or lack of it, in New Zealand, the facilities at Pennyhill Park and media management. But it was the coaches who came in for the harshest criticism. The pre-World Cup camp was said to be too long and draining, with not enough emphasis on conditioning or skills. The coaches were accused of being divided and self-serving, lacking in people skills, unimaginative, inflexible and not having a game-plan. Attack coach Brian Smith got slaughtered, as did John Wells to a lesser degree (although I thought he was one of the best technical coaches I'd ever worked under), while only Graham Rowntree escaped with universal praise – and rightly so.

Johnno got it in the neck for picking the wrong players, presiding over a 'dour, depressing' regime, being too loyal and failing to instil discipline. While the contributions were anonymous, I was able to work out some of the voices. And most of what they said was true. One by one, the coaches either resigned or were sacked – only Graham Rowntree was spared – and some of them never worked in rugby again. The last I heard of Johnno's communications guru Gerard Murphy, who was also thrown under the bus, he was threatening to write a tell-all book. If he ever does, he should call it, 'England's 2011 World Cup: A Giant Skidmark on My Career'. That's exactly what it was to me.

People always thought me and Johnno didn't get on, but that wasn't true. Okay, we weren't exactly kindred spirits. He once asked me what I was doing with my day off and I told him I was going to see my James Haskell action figures get moulded. He looked at me like I was the spawn of Satan, and I had to tell him I was joking. But I liked Johnno a lot. He was a good man, a legend of a player, an incredible captain and the only person I was ever star-struck to meet as a young player. All he tried to do was his best for England. However, when he took the job he should have cleared everyone out and started again. He showed too much loyalty to old team-mates who I felt didn't understand how to create a winning environment, or certainly one using the players at their disposal. If he had been able to get in the likes of Wayne Smith and other leading lights to actually coach, and stuck to doing what he did best, which was lead the squad and instil the standards that he advocated within the 2003 side, then it would have worked. He should have started afresh with everything, but perhaps because he had no experience he wanted people he knew around him. I also feel he had inexperienced media people around him who panicked when things went wrong, instead of standing up to the journalists who were all over the team like vultures on a rotting carcass. Which until Eddie Jones arrived was the way the RFU did things – don't upset the media, let them have access to this and that. Whatever happens, if you don't win over the media you're going to get knifed in the back.

Some of the management selections were questionable, such as starting with Jonny Wilkinson and Toby Flood at 10 and 12 against France in the quarter-finals, when we'd never used that combination before. If we'd made it through to the semi-finals, a lot of the off-field stuff might have been forgiven and Johnno might have clung on to his job. But we didn't. And the management didn't. Because the players fucked up, we just didn't perform on the field. Management can only do so much. At the end of the day, we the players needed to take responsibility for our poor showing.

There was one last kick in the balls, which must have been located somewhere in my stomach by the end of the tournament. After the dust had settled, I got a call from O2. The bloke said, 'Sorry it didn't turn out great, but we loved the video content – and at least you made a few quid out of it.' Erm, no. In fact, O2 had been paying the RFU, who never passed the money on.

2015: POISONED CHALICE

Having thought my international career was over, I got a call from new England head coach Stuart Lancaster in New Zealand in 2012. He told me he was thinking about selecting me for the summer tour of South Africa. I obviously told him I was interested, he picked me, and after playing a couple of midweek games in the arse-ends of nowhere, Chris Robshaw broke his thumb and I started the third Test in Port Elizabeth. We were already 2–0 down in the series but we drew 14–14 and I played one of my best games in an England shirt, putting in 35 tackles. But after returning to New Zealand, I discovered I'd been dropped from the elite squad and included in the second-string England Saxons squad instead.

I rang Stuart and said, 'I know it's a new regime and all that, but why did you not tell me I was going to be dropped? I don't think that's very respectful, especially as I've just played one of my best games for England.' Stuart said he thought I'd been told by someone else, and a few days later I got a call from a furious Graham Rowntree, who claimed he'd told me I was going to be dropped at the airport on the way home from South Africa. I do not remember that happening, so we agreed to disagree.

I felt there was something not quite right about Stuart's communication skills when he was in charge of England. His approach was apparently very different to how he was with the England Saxons and afterwards with Leinster. On the rare occasions he ate with the players, he wouldn't take a seat with the lads but at an empty table, and would wolf his food down in five minutes and leave, without saying anything. When you walked past him in the corridor, you wouldn't get any more than a curt nod. At least that's all I used to get, even though I always tried to cross the divide. It wasn't because he wasn't a good guy, it was because he was so focused on the bigger picture. As far as Stuart was concerned, he didn't have time for idle chit-chat. Being head coach of England is like no other job in rugby; it's probably 15 per cent to do with coaching and 85 per cent on all the other off-field stuff.

On that tour of South Africa, we were treated like kids. It may or may not have had something to do with the fact that Stuart was an ex-teacher. I knew that after 2011 he had to completely remould how the England team was perceived, by the public and the media, and make sure the players understood the importance of what playing for England meant. But we were still adults, and some of the stuff was overkill in my mind. After one midweek game in Kimberley, we were told that not only were we not allowed to go out, we weren't even allowed to have a beer. A couple of days later, the whole squad went out for dinner. The Test team went to bed early, because they were playing on the Saturday, but us midweek boys had the following day off and knew we weren't going to be involved at the weekend. So I said, 'Listen, does anyone fancy a glass of red wine?' There was a bit of hesitancy but plenty of interest, so I ordered a bottle. That disappeared in about 10 minutes, so I ordered another one. And another. Each time we finished a bottle, I stashed it under the table, and after a couple of hours there were about 10 empties next to my feet. Before you raise an eyebrow, it was a table of 12 and some of the coaching staff even joined us, commenting on the fact that our wine was better than what they were getting, and it turned into a fun evening. Not exactly a riotous one, but boozy enough.

What I didn't know was that the team manager (the same team manager who had stitched me up before my post-2011 meeting with Rob Andrew) had been keeping tabs on us from a distance. Suddenly, he came over to me.

'James, how many bottles of wine have you ordered?'

'I dunno. One?'

'No, James. I've spoken to the waiter and you've ordered 10.'

'Have we?'

Paul Doran-Jones saw the panic on the team manager's face. 'For fuck's sake, don't worry about it. Never mind the fact the RFU has got millions and half the coaches have been in on it, we'll pay for it.'

There was a bit of back and forth, before the team manager realised he was looking a bit pedantic, and that the coaching staff had been getting stuck in as well. So he told us not to worry about it and that he'd cover the bill.

The following morning, I woke up at the crack of dawn feeling extremely dusty and slightly worried that I'd had a drink when I knew Stuart would not have wanted that. So I went downstairs to grab some water, show that I wasn't affected by the wine and get a bit of breakfast, and who should I bump into but Doz, who was thinking the same thing as me. We had a bit of a discussion about the night before, agreed that it probably hadn't been a good idea to drink so much, and while we were chatting, Stuart walked in.

'You two are up early.'

'Yes, Stuart. You know how it is, new England and all that.'

'You know what new England isn't? Ordering 10 bottles of wine at a hundred quid each.'

'Sorry?'

'You lot spend £1,000 on wine last night.'

'God. We had no idea. The waiter has done us over …'

When Doz explained that we'd offered to pay for it, Stuart informed us that the team manager had grassed us up. He hadn't mentioned we had offered to pay, but implied we'd just drunk the lot and fucked off. That afternoon, I had to get the lads together, explain the situation, and persuade them to cough up for the wine, which obviously didn't go down too well. I didn't really have a problem with paying the money, but I did have a problem with the slightly weird, sneaky way in which the situation was handled.

That wasn't the only time something like that happened. We'd have 'parties', or what could be described as parties in the loosest possible terms, at Pennyhill Park because we weren't allowed out of the hotel after games. These post-match parties appeared to just be an excuse for the management to sing karaoke badly for their families who turned up in large numbers, while the lads with their girlfriends sat in the corner and had a beer. One night, Rob Webber went off-piste and ordered something other than a round of beers, and the following morning the team manager took him aside and said, 'By the way, Rob, you owe £75.' Even after we beat New Zealand in 2012, we all had to go back to the hotel and watch staff, their family, their friends, friends of friends and seemingly anyone they knew who fancied a few beers get stuck into the bar for free, while we couldn't really drink. In the end I cracked, ordered two whiskies and got billed for them the next day.

Being treated like kids on a school trip bred resentment. It's not like we wanted to go on the smash all the time, but you should be allowed to let your hair down occasionally, especially after beating the All Blacks. Players were genuinely fearful of upsetting the coaches and getting told off. At one post-match dinner, my wife got steaming drunk on about half a glass of wine and started shouting and clicking her fingers at Stuart from across the room.

'Oi, Oi, Stuart! Come and sit down!'

I was shrinking in my seat and telling her to be quiet ('Chloe! Shut. The. Fuck. Up!') but Stuart came over and joined us. Chloe immediately got up to get some more drinks ('Just a water for me, babe'), and now it was just me and Stuart. After a bit of small talk and me telling him how much I was enjoying my time with England, Stuart asked me what the West End of London was like. I am not sure why he thought I would know that – he clearly pegged me as a party man. Then he asked me this gem.

'Are you a big drinker?

'Actually, I don't drink a lot. I used to not drink at all but now I might have a couple of beers after a game, if we've done well, and that's about it.'

I could see Stuart wasn't convinced and, right on cue, Chloe came tottering towards us, slammed two quadruple whiskies down in front of me, kissed me on the forehead and said, 'There you go, babe. The bar was a bit busy, so I bought you two, we know how thirsty you get.' Stuart gave me one of his mysterious smiles, got up and walked off, leaving me with my head in my hands, trying to explain to Chloe why it's never a good idea to suggest to a player's coach that they might have a drink problem. Not just a drink problem, a whisky drink problem.

I got on well with Stuart and respected him hugely for the tireless effort he put into the job, but I've always said I was his dirty little secret because I didn't really fit the whiter-than-white template. I was sort of kept out of the way when it suited, and then asked to entertain the lads and be my usual self – but only when they wanted. I attended one leadership meeting with Stuart and wasn't invited back for years. It was on a Monday, two days after I'd played, so I felt really sore. My neck hurt, my back hurt and my feet wouldn't work. I normally sat at the back, with the other naughty boys, but we didn't really have any naughty boys at the time, so they made me sit at the front, in this stiff wicker chair. My back and neck were in agony, I couldn't sit up properly and had to keep leaning forward to ease the pain.

It soon became clear that the 'management' meeting was about what Stuart was going to say at the next meeting to the full team. He was blathering on about this leadership pyramid he had on the screen (we had seen the same pyramid a million times), about the team coming first in every area, and when he finished he said, 'Guys, is everyone happy with that?' And everyone replied, 'Yes, Stuart, yes, Stuart, three bags full, Stuart,' or at least they might as well have done. As far as I was concerned, the players didn't need to be there. Asking us what he should have said would have made sense, but telling us what he was going to say at the next meeting had nothing to do with leadership.

When the meeting was over and I was about to leave, Stuart came over to me.

'James, do you want some feedback?'

I thought he was asking me for feedback about the meeting. So I replied, 'Yeah. You've just done a meeting about a meeting, right?'

'James, when I invite you to these leadership meetings, I need you to have better body language. You looked completely uninterested.'

Instead of saying, 'Stuart, my body is fucked and I was crammed into a small wicker chair and could hardly hold my head up because of the pain', I said, 'Yep. Sorry, Stuart, I'll work on it.' But Stuart didn't invite me to a leadership meeting for years after that, despite me being one of the most capped players in the squad. That's one of the reasons I say he wasn't focused enough on people. Had Stuart spoken to players and coaches, they would have told him that as well as training and playing hard, I was a great squad man, good at making team-mates smile and raising spirits. They would have told him that me taking the piss out of everything and calling out bullshit wasn't a toxic thing, it was a positive – if you took the time to understand me.

It could have been worse, he could have done the credibility graph for everyone. This was the most David Brent moment I have ever experienced in my life. Stuart called me in for a meeting with him (I need to flag that I already had 50-odd caps by this time), and he asked me how, in my opinion, I was doing within the squad. I said really well. He asked if he had shown me the credibility graph. I said no, but sensing this was some horrific management jargon, I told him he didn't have to. He insisted. He drew a graph with the x-axis denoting time and the y-axis credibility. There was a line across the top, which was where you were credible. His example of someone who was really credible was Brad Barritt. There was also a line below showing where you weren't credible, and in this case his example was Chris Ashton after some discipline problems and bans. He said he would show me where I was. I thought, please don't. He drew this super-excruciatingly slow line that made progress towards the credible line but stopped an inch off. He then started breaking down my moments with the squad and like a small staircase the line went up, across, up, across, stopping three centimetres below credible. He said that I was *nearly* credible. I looked around for a hidden camera, expecting him to point to himself with double-finger guns and say, 'If you want to be in the hot seat like me, all you have to be is credible.'

So 50 or so caps was not credible in his mind. That's when he truly lost me. He told me that if I worked hard I would become credible and unseat either Chris Robshaw or Tom Wood in the starting line-up. Why did he think I of all people would gain something from this, that telling me I was not credible was some management masterstroke? He must have known I would walk straight out of there and tell everyone who would listen the horrors of the condescending 'credibility graph'. He did not understand me at all, neither how to motivate me nor get the best out of mc. Eddie Jones would never have dared do this. Eddie knew I needed an arm around me and my tyres pumping up. Do that and I will run through walls for you.

I got up after our conversation and said to Stuart it would have been easier if he'd just said he liked and trusted Chris and Tom more than me, rather than drawing it out. He looked surprised and that was really the beginning of the end.

After the 2011 disaster, Stuart picked up a poisoned chalice. England were the most loathed rugby team in the world, a laughing stock, so Stuart realised that one of his main jobs was to make us liked and respected again, by the public and the media. There was all the stuff about changing the culture, being humble, not being arrogant. He asked the parents of players to write a letter to their sons, explaining how much playing for their country meant to them. That was all well and good, but Stuart didn't in my mind focus enough on what mattered most – people.

The problem with committing yourself to picking players who are whiter than white, who represent their country 'in the best possible way', is that you ignore the claims of players with edge and eccentricities. Any healthy sports team, as in any healthy company or business, contains people with big personalities and opinions. People who turn around and say, 'You know what, I don't agree. I think we should do it like this instead.' Stuart's regime had too many alpha male coaches, guys who were great as individuals but intimidating as a group. They weren't approachable or the kind of blokes who would put their arm around a player or judge the mood of the squad. And there weren't enough players with big personalities. An example of that was a review session, when one of the coaches went ballistic because someone hadn't cleared a ruck out. He was calling this player every name under the sun, including a fucking cunt, and it took every fibre of my being not to say, 'Oi! Who the fuck do you think you are? Don't speak to my team-mate like that.' I regretted not saying anything, but felt like I was on borrowed time, as I often did with England. But someone should have. That no-one felt able to stand up to that coach spoke volumes. To be fair to the coach, he apologised later and bought the player a bottle of champagne, but that just shows you how bad it was.

One of the key aspects of being a good head coach is understanding that everyone is different and has their own unique personality – and not being spooked or intimidated by anyone who has a strong personality. If you have any doubts about what a good coach is like, then watch *The Last Dance*, the Netflix documentary series featuring Phil Jackson, the renowned coach of the Chicago Bulls. He was amazing at being task-focused and people-focused. He was managing huge personalities like Michael Jordan, Scottie Pippen and Dennis Rodman, but he knew how to handle them and wasn't scared of them. He was loved and respected by his players, but was also clearly in charge. Of course, players have to train hard and play hard and behave themselves. But taking a blanket approach doesn't work. Stuart and his coaches would say they wanted players to be themselves, but if that meant a player being something that didn't fit the template, they'd get twitchy. That was very different to other coaches I'd played under, including Warren Gatland and Eddie Jones, who were all about giving players just enough rope to hang themselves with, getting everyone to open up, be honest and have difficult conversations about difficult subjects.

After losing to Ireland in the 2015 Six Nations, which put paid to our Grand Slam hopes, none of the coaches addressed the players in the changing room or, in fact, even came into the changing room after the match. Instead, they loitered outside, looking really angry, before giving us stink-eye all the way to the airport. No player stood up or said anything, because leadership was a meeting about a meeting. No player really had input in that environment. In stark contrast, after we lost to Ireland in 2018, which meant they won the Grand Slam, Eddie came into the changing room after Dylan Hartley had said his piece, and told us exactly what he thought. Some of it wasn't pretty, but they're the kinds of difficult conversations a coach needs to have with his players in the immediate aftermath of a defeat, in order to make some kind of sense of the situation. And it's also basic manners. Players don't want to lose. They always give 100 per cent. But things go wrong. What despondent players don't need – those who are broken-hearted, at rock bottom, wondering if changes will be made, if they've run out of chances or if they'll be dropped – is to be ignored.

As well as his big red diary, in which you'd see him scribbling all day, Stuart carried a book around with him called *The Score Takes Care of Itself: My Philosophy of Leadership* by former San Francisco 49ers coach Bill Walsh. Because I was struggling to understand Stuart's leadership philosophy, I decided to read this book. And suddenly it all made sense. Stuart followed it almost to the letter, from worrying about what was being sold in the Twickenham shops to making sure the boys had their shirts tucked in. It was like a military war plan, the sporting equivalent of Sun Tzu's *The Art of War*.

I didn't have a problem with *The Score Takes Care of Itself*, but I didn't understand what it had to do with us. Bill Walsh was coach of a different set of players, in a different sport, in a different era. The emotional context wasn't the same. The methods he used might not have worked with us. Earlier, I gave an example of looking to Phil Jackson on how to lead. My point was, look, don't follow it to the letter. If you win three Super Bowls, of course everything you do will be explained as a stroke of genius. But what about Bill Walsh's support staff? How did they fit into it all? If you want to follow someone, get everyone else's opinion on it from those around him. In *The Last Dance*, everyone clearly thinks Michael Jordan was the best ever, the king of the NBA. No-one really said they liked him. Bill Walsh, before he died, called up all his ex-players and apologised to them for how he treated them during his time. He was hated by all of them and only forgiven at the bitter end. It's on record that the 49ers won the next Super Bowl after Walsh left just to spite him. Stuart appears to have not read that part or chosen to ignore it. You can't superimpose someone else's masterplan onto a different scenario. And if you try to follow someone else's rules without looking around you and seeing what you've got to play with, you're going to lack authenticity.

I had an inkling things weren't going to go well at the World Cup after a team-building exercise at the Metropolitan Police's public order training centre in Kent. When it was announced, we all thought it would be a great day out. What could be better than a load of mates having a big riot in the sun, lobbing bricks through windows and kicking coppers in the shins? But of course it didn't quite turn out as planned.

Having taken about three hours to get there, we were given a set of overalls, army boots and riot shields, and told to go for a timed one-mile run. Prop Kieran Brookes was screaming for breath after about 30 seconds and someone had to carry his shield for him. Some of the other lads got blisters because the boots were brand new. Run done, they split us into two teams – one with Chris Robshaw as captain, the other with Tom Wood, because they were the main contenders to be skipper at the World Cup – and we expected the fun to start. Instead, they lined us up and gave us a long, detailed talk about what we should do if we ever encountered a riot, before running us through this one particular drill. When we approached a junction, someone had to shout 'junction', and we'd all stop on the line. One person would then shout 'left clear', someone else would shout 'right clear', and then we could walk on. I don't know how stupid normal police recruits are, but after about 10 minutes we were bored out of our minds, kicking our heels and spoiling for a fight. We were doing that drill for an hour, with not a firebomb or riot in sight.

When we finally got down to it, it wasn't Robshaw versus Wood as we'd hoped, it was all of us and a load of recruits against some older coppers, the coaches and Stuart Lancaster's kids chucking wooden bricks and petrol bombs at us. I'd never seen Andy Farrell so animated. He was swearing his head off and his eyes were filled with hatred. The problem was, they didn't really tell us what we could do, and the recruits we were lumbered with were shit. So eventually I lost my patience, started ploughing forward and chucking rioters out of the way. Once we cleared the road we would move up to a junction and go through the protocol, shout 'junction', etc. However Kieran Brookes, still exhausted from his mile run, just carried on running through the junction, looking like an idiot and leaving his team shouting, 'Stop, you fucking idiot, it's a junction!' As he ran through, this gnarly old cop swung at him with a huge haymaker, but luckily missed. Brookesy, then realising he was all on his lonesome, turned around like a naughty schoolboy, dragging his shield behind him, apologising and wheezing. Part of me wished that policeman hadn't missed with the punch, because at least it would have been an excuse for a tear-up. By the time we were herded back onto the coach, everyone was in pieces. Aside from the blisters, the lads had aching backs and necks from carrying the shields for hours, and we didn't get back to camp until well past 1 am. The following morning, we assumed the coaches would adjust training. I was complaining about the riot debacle to anyone who would listen, and most of us agreed that we needed to say something. But after drifting out in dribs and drabs, moaning as we went, Andy Farrell marched over and barked, 'Right lads, huddle up, I can sense some bad vibes. And we can't be having bad vibes, we've got a fucking World Cup to win.' Then he turned to Calum Clark, and said, 'How you feeling, Calum?'

'Fine, Faz.'

Everyone looked at Calum as if to say, 'What do you mean you're feeling fine?' because he'd been moaning all morning, along with the rest of us.

Then Faz said to Tom Wood, 'How you feeling, Tom?'

'Fine, Faz.'

And then Faz said to me, 'How you feeling, Hask?'

I could sense a sudden frisson of excitement, as if the lads were thinking, 'Hask won't fuck about, he'll tell it like it really is.' I looked around the circle and it felt like hundreds of eyes were penetrating my soul. The whole day hung on what I was about to say. I paused, took a deep breath and said, 'I am super-duper, Andy ...'

Faz grinned, clapped his hands together and said, 'Right, let's go and fucking train then!'

There was an audible groan from the lads. For the rest of the day, I had team-mates calling me every name under the sun. I just kept muttering, 'Sorry, lads. I don't know where that came from. I've never said super-duper in my life before.' After that, everyone was calling me The Deckchair, because I folded so easily.

A good professional set-up needs a doctor who will stand up to the coaches. We did not really have that at times under Stuart. A certain team doctor introduced this wellness scoring system, which meant that every day we had to enter a score out of five on a form, with zero meaning the best you'd ever felt and five meaning you were almost dead. I knew it was bollocks when I woke up one morning with a dodgy stomach and put down five on the form. I expected someone to tap me on the shoulder and say, 'Probably best if you rest today.' Instead, the doctor said, 'If it was the World Cup final on Saturday, would you train?'

'Yep.'

'Well then, are you ready to train?'

'Yep.'

But I'd be thinking, 'This makes no sense, because it's not the World Cup final on Saturday, it's one of Graham Rowntree's mauling sessions.'

Before the 2015 World Cup, everything was based on the England team being fitter than New Zealand. All the coaches ever talked about were training percentages. They kept telling us that if we trained at 120 per cent or max, by the time we got to the World Cup we'd be miles ahead of everyone else, including the All Blacks. They'd do PowerPoint presentations with graphs, charts, flashing lights and loads of sports science jargon. The players would all be looking at each other with blank faces. One of the key phrases was, 'You'll all be pinging by the time you get to the World Cup.' I can safely say we never pinged. Five years later, we're still waiting for the benefits.

At a high-altitude training camp in Denver, we'd be flogged into the ground before trying to execute line-out moves. That didn't go well because everyone was in pieces. I'm still trying to work out those moves now. The intensity of the training was unbelievable and we arguably achieved the coaches' goal of being the fittest team in the world – I'd certainly never been fitter – but we didn't focus enough on rugby. And the ball-in-play time ended up being so low at that World Cup that it didn't really matter how fit we were.

Everyone who was part of that squad thought we could win the World Cup. Okay, we would say that, but I honestly thought that if we played the right kind of rugby, we had a chance. But after we'd been dumped out in the pool stages, I couldn't understand why everyone was so angry. During every World Cup, you get fair-weather rugby fans coming out of the woodwork and throwing around cheap, uninformed opinions. And because it was at home, lots of people lost the plot and thought we were nailed on to win it. But heading into the tournament, we'd won one game in six against southern hemisphere sides. We lost to Wales by three points, but Wales were a very good side. If we'd kicked that penalty instead of kicking for touch, things might have been different, but that is a whole saga in itself. Perhaps when everyone has retired I will tell what really happened out on the pitch that day as I was in the team huddle. I can say hand on heart it was not the captain Chris Robshaw's fault in any way. He was fucked over and carried the can. It shows the mark of the man that he has never come out and said what happened.

Sam Burgess took a lot of flak for what happened at the World Cup. But Sam never said he could be Stuart Lancaster's very own Joe Montana. He didn't put himself forward as England's saviour or ask to be plucked from rugby league, where he'd obviously been quite happy. He was a great guy, a big personality, and always put his body on the line and acquitted himself in the best way he could. But rugby union is a difficult game to master, and Sam was tasked with becoming an international centre in a few months. In his autobiography, Sam said that England's early World Cup exit was down to certain selfish characters in the camp, which led people automatically to point the finger at me. Sam and I are good mates, and after our explosive chat on *House of Rugby* it was clear who Sam was talking about. I was an outgoing personality, but I was never divisive. And Stuart has to take some responsibility for those that were. I told him a couple of times to speak to players who weren't in the starting line-up and had begun to feel alienated. He never did.

Something quite telling happened after we got hammered in our next game by Australia, which secured our exit from the tournament. Having not been invited to a leadership meeting since being upbraided for my poor body language and apparent lack of interest a few years earlier, I was suddenly called upon. And I was the only one who spoke up, because everyone else was on suicide watch. I said to them, 'Guys, don't listen to the fans and the media, don't let them convince you you've let yourselves and your country down. No team has worked harder than us. No team wanted it more than us. Everyone is questioning the work we put in, from players to the coaches, but it's bullshit. It just didn't work out. We could not have done more, other than perform better on the field. We've got one more game against Uruguay – let's go out with our heads held high.' And when I was finished, Stuart said, 'That was great, James, could you address the rest of the squad?' I thought, 'Right, so now we're out of the tournament and you finally call on me?' Then, straight after that meeting, Andy Farrell, whom I have always admired, came up to me and asked, 'Can you do an awards ceremony, as a way of thanking the staff?'

'Are you sure you want me to?

'Yeah, just hand out a few bottles of wine, take the piss and don't worry about offending anyone.'

'How harsh am I allowed to be?'

'I want you to go in hard.'

It was difficult for me to get my head around. For three years, the coaches hadn't really been interested in what I had to say. Now England had been knocked out of the World Cup in disastrous fashion, they were wheeling me out to give rousing speeches and morale-boosting comedy routines.

So I put together a PowerPoint presentation and absolutely buried all the coaching and backroom staff for half an hour. I told the doctor what I'd previously been too scared to say – 'But it's not the World Cup on Saturday, it's one of Graham Rowntree's shit mauling sessions!' – before giving him a bottle of wine. As for the analyst Matt Parker, who was a Dave Brailsford protege and actually a great guy, I showed a graph with a load of spikes peaking at 120 per cent and all these lights and flames going off in the background, before saying, 'Guys, as you can see, the World Cup has gone really well. Each player has improved by an average of 7,000 quatrons and we're all pinging like mad. But where do all these numbers lead to?' And then I moved on to the next slide, which was a mocked-up picture of Matt eating a protein bar in the window of a job centre. Don't worry, he got a bottle of wine as well.

People were wincing, but most of the staff saw the funny side. The lads loved it. I didn't think I'd ever play for England again and we'd just been knocked out of our own World Cup in the pool stages, so we needed some gallows humour.

Alas, the farce didn't end there, and the turd on top of this cake was the tale of the kitman, the shares and the lost investments. Before the tournament, Dave 'Reg' Tennison sent emails to some players urging them to invest in an oil drilling company called LGO Energy. Reg explained that his mate was involved in the company, he'd ploughed a lot of his savings into it and there was only one way this company's shares were heading, which was up. The funny part was, he included the line, 'I haven't included Haskell in this email, because he's got enough money already.' Cheeky bastard! Not that I would have invested anyway, because just as I don't get my hair cut by a dentist, I don't take financial advice from a kitman.

When these shares started inching upwards, some of the players decided to invest. So that by the time we got to the World Cup camp, it was all anyone was talking about. Some players weren't happy about it, including Tom Wood, who told Reg that he didn't think it was a good idea to be persuading players to invest in shares right before a World Cup. I respected Woody greatly, loved how he spoke his mind and understood his stance, but mostly it was treated as a bit of fun. The players who invested were taking the piss out of me because, apparently, I had too much money, and I was taking the piss out of them for taking financial advice from a kitman. Some lads had gone in big, 20 grand or more, as the price had gone up a bit to start with. Reg even sent around emails suggesting that when the price hit a certain level the lads should take a box at a sporting event to celebrate. Sadly, the level it did hit meant the only box they were likely to get was the one they would now be sleeping in.

Of course, if they'd all made a few quid out of it, the media probably wouldn't have found out. But they didn't. Instead, the price dropped from £3.27 to 50p a share just before the tournament, meaning Reg and his disciples spent the World

Cup shitting themselves about their investments and it was all anyone was talking about. I, of course, took great delight in taking the piss out of Reg, whom I named CEO of Sinking Sands Investments.

A journalist from the *Sun* got wind of this sorry story and was planning to drop one of the players in it, but the player offered the journalist Reg instead. The RFU launched an inquiry and Reg got sacked, as well as losing all his savings. Reg had been in the job since 2002, was a great guy and everyone really liked him, myself included, but what do you expect if you start giving players terrible share tips before a World Cup? Reg moved to Dubai, from where he continued to send me financial advice. Don't worry, I didn't take it.

MY GUY EDDIE

Of all the coaches I played under for England, I enjoyed playing under Eddie Jones the most. If you'd told me straight after the 2015 World Cup that I'd win 20 more caps and play some of the best rugby of my life, I'd have laughed in your face. But it happened, and it was largely down to Eddie and his coaching team. Of course, international rugby shouldn't just be about winning caps, it should be about winning silverware, and Eddie also gave me and everyone else who played under him the best opportunities to do that. He knows how to win and is very good at teaching people how to win. He constantly wants to improve himself, so isn't too proud to ask coaches from other sports for advice, great people like Sir Alex Ferguson and Pep Guardiola. He's always reviewing his own staff and training model because he knows things can be tweaked and improved. And he's great with the players, pushing them to their absolute limits and setting standards that some people found too intense but which suited me down to the ground. No doubt, Eddie's the best I ever worked with.

I'd always respected what Eddie had achieved in rugby, but I'd heard he ruled with an iron fist. A few weeks into my first England camp with Eddie, I said to him, 'I heard you were like an atomic bomb, ready to go off at any moment.' And he replied, 'Nah, I was like that once, but that's the old Eddie.' He could be fiery but he was also warm, compassionate and empowering. He understood what made each player tick and how to improve them, which is why most players loved him. He strived for perfection but loved characters. We clicked because he treated me with respect and made me feel welcome.

Before Eddie, I'd played in some good and bad environments with England. People assume that because it's England, everything will be the best. That's not necessarily the case. The RFU hire whoever is available and will accept the terms offered to them, and often it's people who are malleable and won't rock the boat. A new head coach will often inherit people instead of clearing things out and building his own team. He will have backroom staff who aren't necessarily the best but who are safe and amenable and won't talk back. Eddie is the least RFU man you could get, but the environment he created was the best. That's because they let him build his own team and do things his way.

In Eddie's very first training session with England, he suddenly shouted, 'What the fuck are you lot doing?' Everyone stopped what they were doing and thought, 'Oh God, he's having one of his atomic bomb moments.' But Eddie just said, 'Why the fuck are you lot playing rugby league?' No-one had the heart to say we were playing rugby league because that's how we'd been coached for the previous four years. Then he pointed at Billy Vunipola and said, 'Billy, why the fuck are you passing? Look at the size of you, you're a fuckin' unit. Just get the ball and run over the fuckin' bloke.' Coaches too often focus on what players can't do, rather than what they can do. But Eddie was the opposite. He used to say to me, 'Hask, just carry hard and hit hard. You don't have to do anything more than that.'

Eddie didn't want us playing rugby league or like New Zealand, because you can't play that kind of rugby if you don't have the right kind of players. Instead, Eddie's thought process was, 'Right, what have I got to play with? I've got giant players with massive strength, which means I've got the makings of a monster scrum, a great line-out and aggressive defence. Get those right, and the attack will take care of itself.' Eddie had his system and he was going to stick with it, come what may. Before Eddie, we'd had coaches who fiddled and betrayed their philosophy when performances or results weren't as expected. That's what the pressure of professional sport does to most people.

Eddie was never too proud to ask for opinions from his players. Because he had total belief in his system and his coaches, including the excellent Steve Borthwick and Paul Gustard (forwards and defence coach respectively, and two of the best I've worked with), he could be open. He'd call meetings of senior players and say, 'Are you enjoying how we're doing things? Could we be doing anything different? Are you able to communicate with the coaches?' That meant we felt like we had ownership of the team. I played under coaches whose first reaction when you challenged them was to pull out the stats and tell you to start worrying about doing your own job right instead of telling them how to do theirs. Teams with those kinds of head coaches aren't successful.

Throughout my career I'd played under coaches who couldn't understand how I could be joking around one minute, and deadly serious and professional the next. Some players didn't understand it either. Warren Gatland at Wasps under-stood the need to have a bit of fun, which is why there would be lots of piss-taking during warm-ups before the serious stuff started. And Eddie was similar in that respect. He created an environment that was fun, and I laughed every day I was with him in camp. He'd bring his dog Annie along to training and chase after it during the warm-up, shouting its name. He'd take the piss out of players during meetings. Recently, someone showed me a video of Eddie making a new player stand up and thank everyone for allowing him to stay in camp for another week. If he noticed some lads laughing at something on a phone, he'd want to have a look.

Eddie understood what it meant to look after his players, on and off the pitch. When he asked why I wasn't filling in the wellness forms, which had survived Stuart Lancaster's reign, I said, 'What's the point? I could die and someone would drag me onto the training ground by my feet.' Eddie said he'd look into it, and presumably had a frank discussion with the doctor. A few days later I wrote down that I was a bit stiff, and when Eddie saw me he said, 'Right, James, you're resting today.'

'Actually, Eddie, I probably could train …'

'No!'

Eddie was the first coach I'd had who took any notice.

He especially looked after the veterans in his squads. At breakfast, he'd present me with a protein shake full of greens and say, 'Hask, mate, I made this in the blender. You're old as fuck, you need to drink this.' The lads would look at me in shock and say, 'What the fuck? Eddie's making you protein shakes now?' Once, he took me aside and said, 'Old fella, I've got a little present for you, because you trained well this week.' He'd got the head conditioning coach to book me in for a massage – not a sports massage but a massage with whale music and candles and scented oils at Pennyhill's award-winning spa. He did this for the lads he felt needed it.

Eddie valued discipline but treated us like adults, which meant we behaved like adults. After the first meeting of a camp or if there was a fallow week, Eddie would encourage us to have a few beers and get to know each other. But even when we won trophies, whether it was the Triple Crown or Calcutta Cup, we didn't celebrate. We'd have one beer in the changing room, do our recovery, head back to the hotel, maybe have a glass of wine with our partners and go to bed. No-one kicked up a fuss or felt the need to break out and get shitfaced in a nightclub, because no-one wanted to mess up the amazing environment Eddie had created or be kicked out of it. Then, at the end of a Six Nations, Eddie would make sure we had a decent night out, with proper security, so we wouldn't be bothered by mad fans or hotel maids.

I was loyal to Eddie because he was loyal to me and backed me for who I was. Because of that mutual respect, he got the best out of me as a player. Like Warren Gatland and Shaun Edwards at Wasps, Michael Cheika at Stade Français, Jamie Joseph at the Highlanders and Dai Young at Wasps again (before he got bullied into sacking me after the stag-do boat scandal), Eddie valued me exactly because I wasn't vanilla or run of the mill. You don't want too many controversial players in a squad, but you do want personalities.

8

BEYOND THE COMFORT ZONE

THE GOLDEN STALLION

I am now going to tell you the story of my first day in France. And once you've read it, I defy you to say that broadening one's horizons and stepping out of one's comfort zone does not maketh the man. A golden half-horse, half-man with a rugby ball where his cock and balls should be. But a man, nonetheless.

Shortly after signing for Stade Français in 2009, my agent called me and said, 'The owner wants you to go to Paris and do a photoshoot for a calendar.' The ink on my contract wasn't yet dry and I hadn't even officially left Wasps. And just about every rugby journalist and pundit was telling anyone who wanted to listen that I was making the biggest mistake of my life, running away to a circus, that I'd soon be living a debauched Parisian life (presumably spending my days chain-smoking unfiltered Gauloises and necking absinthe in Left Bank cafés, while wearing a beret and musing upon Sartre's reflections on existentialism), disappearing into the ether and never to be heard of again. So my immediate thought was, 'I can't be posing for a calendar. It's just going to confirm what everyone has been saying. That I'm lost, that I've disappeared up my own arse.'

Part of me wanted to do it, because I loved doing anything different, but I told my agent to tell the owner I wasn't interested. Ten minutes later, my agent phoned back. 'Listen. The owner is not best pleased and if you don't do it, it would not be a good start to your career at Stade.'

I did a bit of research and discovered that the Dieux du Stade – Gods of the Stadium, apparently – was something of a French institution, a calendar featuring arty black and white photos of various Stade Français players and stars of other teams and sports, stripped and squinting into the middle distance. It had become, I was reliably informed, a traditional Christmas stocking filler for the discerning gay Frenchman and the best-selling calendar in Europe. It was the brainchild of Stade owner Max Guazzini, who had transformed the club from third division non-entities into Top 14 titans, and who could therefore get away with kitting players out in pink jerseys and persuading them to pose for photos some might consider to be borderline porn but others – including me! – consider to be art. So it was that a week after taking that call from my agent, and with plenty of trepidation, I boarded the Eurostar at Waterloo and chugged into the unknown.

I was still only 24 and hopelessly unworldly. Like most English kids, I'd wasted most of my time in French lessons chatting shit and drawing cocks on the textbook of the kid sitting next to me. So, wanting to put my best foot forward, I spent a good portion of the journey to Paris listening to French tapes, as if that was going to make up for the years of neglect and I'd rock up in Paris suddenly sounding like Serge Gainsbourg. When I arrived at the Gard du Nord and was greeted by a stereotypically chic French lady holding a sign that read 'Monsieur Haskell', the first thing I blurted out was the suspiciously Italian sounding 'Buongiorno!' at the top of my stupid English voice and with a big, goofy smile on my face. The lady, who was sporting hair by Audrey Hepburn, a cream raincoat tied at the waist, seamed stockings and bright red lipstick, sighed, muttered 'idiot', turned on her Louboutin heels and flicked her cigarette into the gutter. Which is presumably where she thought I'd just crawled from.

Things got worse from there. Just around the corner from the shithole that is the Gard du Nord, I saw a man nonchalantly flip his tie over his shoulder, pull down his trousers, crouch down and take a dump in a bus stop. I thought to myself, 'They shit in bus stops in France? What the fuck have I got myself into?' It didn't help that my French chaperone was still refusing to talk to me, on account of thinking I was the biggest dickhead she'd ever met, and reacted to the shitting man as if it were the most natural thing in the world.

Eventually, we arrived at this nondescript multi-storey car park and I was immediately taken to an improvised dressing room, where another woman appeared and started gesticulating wildly, which I quickly worked out was French sign language for 'take off all your clothes'. So I took my clothes off, while this woman pretended not to look, before another woman popped up and handed me a pair of pink fluffy slippers and a pink dressing gown with a Stade Français logo on it, to temporarily protect my modesty. I took this opportunity to explain that I had seen some of their previous calendars and that while I was happy to get naked, under absolutely no circumstances were they to take any photos of my knob. Not even an artistic knob. Not even a black and white knob. This was to be a no-knob job.

With that, another woman marched in with a big leather holdall, which she dropped to the floor with a thud. Now I was standing there thinking, 'Normally you'd have to pay a lot of money to be in this position, naked under a dressing gown, alone but for three women and a bag of tools.' Alas, the woman then opened the holdall and pulled out one of those high-pressure spray guns that certain British women use to make themselves orange, before filling it with gold paint and gesticulating for me to shed my dressing gown. Half an hour later, I was covered from head to toe in gold, every inch of me.

Having air dried, I was led to a lift. And as soon as I stepped out onto the roof of the car park, two blokes with cameras came out of nowhere and started filming at crotch height. It was a cold day. That's all I'm going to say. But there was more to it than that. This just wasn't on. So I said to the woman, 'I thought I made it clear that there would be no full-frontal stuff.'

'No, no, no, this is for the behind the scenes video.'

'What? No-one said anything about this. What behind the scenes video? Where is this going to be shown?'

At that exact moment, I looked over the woman's shoulder and noticed a man lurking in the background, head down, hood up, his eyes hidden behind a pair of tinted glasses. It was Max, the Stade Français owner, who cleared up this mystery of the behind scenes video, which apparently was offered as a nice bonus DVD for anyone who bought the calendar.

Next to make an appearance in this French farce was my flamboyant American photographer, who entered like John Inman onto the set of *Are You Being Served?* before gushing his introductions.

'Oh, my God! It's so good to meet you, darling! I'm going to make you so gorgeous! I'm going to make you shine!'

I kicked my slippers off and handed my dressing gown to the photographer, so I was now knob-out on this car park roof. Mercifully, someone stepped forward and handed me a gold rugby ball to shield my bits, although a boiled egg probably would have sufficed as, remember, it was a cold day. But now I noticed two women looking at me through their office window, which overlooked the car park. They started shouting, 'Petit! Petit!', which I think means big in French, and I thanked them with an awkward smile and shouted, 'Oui, petit!' back, before they dissolved into uncontrollable laughter. And then I had this photographer up in my face again.

'James! I need you to look doe-eyed. Can you do that for me?'

'I can do rabbit in the headlights. In fact, I'm doing that already.'

I did my best to do what I was told and give him what he needed – chin up, chin down, look left, look right – and now there were about a dozen girls gathered by the office window, with a few of them hanging out, waving their arms about and making French noises. I bet that bloke from the Diet Coke advert didn't have to put up with this bullshit.

Next the photographer said, 'Listen, James, I need you to prance.'

'What do you mean, prance?'

'Prance! Like a pony! Like a horse!'

The cameramen were still circling like a couple of sharks and I could feel Max's eyes drilling into mine from behind his glasses, willing me to prance.

'Prance?' I said. 'Mate, you're talking to the wrong man.'

With that, the photographer started demonstrating how to prance. What he didn't seem to have noticed was that I was bollock naked but for a gold rugby ball, and there were a load of French women taking the piss out of me about 20 yards away, some of them now ironically aiming binoculars at my crotch. And it was a cold day. If you've ever done anything naked apart from have sex or potter around the house, you'll know how self-conscious it makes you feel. So my best shot at prancing looked more like a resigned donkey staggering through the doors of a glue factory, which made the photographer very unhappy.

'I can see you're a bit nervous, James! But we've all got what you've got. If it would make you feel better, I'll show you mine. After all, I've seen yours!'

Before I could say, 'No, don't do it, you mad American bastard!', he'd unzipped his fly and flopped his old chap out.

'There you are James!' he roared. 'Now you've seen mine!'

Apparently, he thought that was going to swing things (pardon the pun), that we were suddenly going to bond and I was going to start prancing around the roof like a Camargue foal in springtime. Instead, I called a time-out. Within an hour of turning up in Paris, I'd been humiliated by Coco Chanel at the station, whisked straight to a car park, been stripped, painted gold, laughed at by an office-full of French women and flashed at by an American photographer. This was a very niche situation I found myself in.

I threw on my dressing gown and stepped in to my oversized pink fluffy slippers in a real huff. Never mind looking like Liberace sashaying onto stage earlier, now I minced all the way back to my dressing room, leaving the photographer clutching his head in exaggerated horror, still with his knob out. While various gofers banged on the door, imploring me to continue, I took a long, hard look at myself in the mirror. 'This is not great,' I thought to myself. 'My confidence is at an all-time low. I'm a shell of my former self. But I can salvage my dignity. Why don't I just pull the pin and leg it? I could be back in London by the end of the day.' And then I remembered how much that man lurking on the roof, head down, hood up and hiding behind the tinted shades, was paying me. And I flung open the dressing-room door, marched back onto that car park roof and pranced like a wild stallion. I ended up on the front page of the Dieux du Stade and posed for it four years in a row. And you know what? I loved every minute of it.

MOST HATED MAN IN RUGBY

How I ended up on that car park roof remains something of a sore point. But it is a great example of how it's possible to spin bad situations into good ones, at least in the long term. I really wanted to stay at Wasps. I'd been a fan of the club since I was a kid. I'd run on the pitch after games, sometimes before the games had even finished, and gather players' autographs. People like Lawrence Dallaglio, Joe Worsley and Simon Shaw, heroes of mine with whom I'd end up sharing a dressing room and winning the Premiership and Heineken Cup. But the club's infrastructure was crumbling and I hadn't been overly impressed with the coaching since Warren Gatland left in 2005. I didn't see many decent players coming through and they didn't have the money to replace ageing and retiring players with top-class talent.

Wasps had always worked on the premise that players wouldn't mind being underpaid if they were winning things. But once Wasps stopped winning things, they simply became a club that didn't pay well and had some of the worst training facilities in the Premiership, because Acton made Broadstreet look like a high-performance centre for Real Madrid. All in all, the future wasn't looking that great in terms of success on the pitch. And, just as important, they weren't interested in paying me a wage I thought I deserved.

Over the course of two years of contract negotiations, I dealt with various CEOs and club officials, who kept telling me that I wouldn't make it anywhere else and that if I stayed at the club, I'd win things. But they wouldn't budge on the money. That's when I first learned that loyalty barely exists in professional sport. It did for someone like Lawrence Dallaglio, because he was always offered lucrative long-term contract extensions. That's why it was easy for him to be a one-club man. But most players are expendable. If they get an injury or the club thinks someone else can do their job better, they're ushered out the door. Fans don't understand this side of the game, which is why when they read in the newspapers that one of 'their' players is driving a hard bargain in contract negotiations and threatening to leave for another club, they start flapping and calling the player disloyal, a money-grabber or worse.

When it got to the point where I was able to talk to other clubs, not only did I discover that I could get a lot more money elsewhere, I also started to think that maybe I could become a more rounded player and person if I spread my wings. The first club I visited were Ospreys in Swansea, who seemed like an attractive proposition. They had a squad packed with Welsh internationals and All Black Jerry Collins, one of the best back-rows in the world. They put a big offer in, about quadruple what Wasps were promising me, but I decided that I wasn't ready to be the only English person playing in the Celtic League. I thought it would be too much pressure for me, it rains an awful lot in Wales, Scotland and Ireland, and the Celtic League just didn't really excite me anyway, just as it didn't excite a lot of Celtic players who already played in it.

That was when Max Guazzini made contact and said he was keen to sign me. Stade Français had a star-studded squad, which included a load of French internationals, Italy number eight Sergio Parisse and Argentina fly-half Juan Martín Hernández. The idea of playing with that lot was very enticing. I'd also get to test myself in the Top 14, playing against clubs like Toulouse, Toulon, Clermont, Castres and Perpignan. As a Wasps player, I got excited about playing against those kind of teams in the Heineken Cup. If I signed for Stade Français, I'd get to play against them week in, week out. The idea of living in Paris greatly appealed to me too. And when I saw what Max was prepared to pay me, I almost snapped his arm off. Legend has it he apparently only signed players he thought were good looking, and that was also a bit of an ego tickle. Max didn't put up with any gargoyles on his beloved calendar. For example, Dimitri Szarzewski was a better-looking version of that Italian model Fabio – and he was a hooker.

Back at Wasps, the new owner called all the club's out-of-contract players into a room, laid a big map on the table and said, 'We're going to build a new stadium and I want you to be a part of our new vision.' He got Raphaël Ibañez, Wasps' French hooker, to give a talk about how much he loved being at Wasps, how they'd made him feel part of a family and how shit life at other clubs was. Then the owner handed us all sealed envelopes and said, 'Inside is a non-negotiable offer – and, by the way, I'm not paying agent fees. You've got 24 hours to decide if you want to stay or go.' We were all stunned. That's not really how you do business or treat people who have put their bodies on the line for your business. And when I left the room, opened the envelope and discovered they were offering me half of what it had taken me two years of negotiating to get to, I was livid.

I got the rest of the guys into another room and went full shop steward. 'If we stick together, show solidarity and refuse to budge, they're not going to offload all of us. Just like the cast of *Friends* knew they were stronger as a collective. If we stick together and negotiate hard, we can turn this around.' Within a couple of minutes, Tom Rees had folded because they'd offered him the captaincy. I didn't blame him for that. Like me, he'd been at Wasps since he was a teenager, and he'd probably been offered a lot more money than me. One by one, the others followed suit, except for Riki Flutey, who signed for Brive, and Tom Palmer, who had been made an offer by Stade Français. (The lads used to jokingly call Tom the Night Stalker because he had the appearance and demeanour of a serial killer. The joke was that he wasn't going to France for rugby reasons but he had in fact run out of space under his patio.) So I thought, 'Fuck this, I'm going to Stade as well.'

That was when the shit hit the fan. Journalists, pundits and fans called me a money-grabber. The RFU let it be known that any players who moved to France might lose their place in the England team. Pretty much everyone was saying my England career was over. The dominant narrative at Wasps was that no-one ever came to much after leaving the club. Lawrence Dallaglio, my hero, made it known how disappointed he was that I didn't talk to him and that I was making the wrong decision. I didn't talk to him for a reason, because I knew what he'd say, that I was making a terrible mistake and would never win anything again. Ian McGeechan, Wasps' director of rugby, got the right hump and told a journalist he wasn't going to take me on the 2009 Lions tour, even though I was in the best form of my life. Shaun Edwards was also very disappointed in me. I also had agents circling, telling me that moving to France would be catastrophic for my career.

That was a very difficult period of my life, challenging, stressful and lonely. I told one journalist that I felt like 'the most hated man in rugby', which was a bit melodramatic and I later clarified was tongue in cheek. But my name was mud, and I did feel hurt and persecuted. All I'd ever known was Wasps and I loved the club, so it was a very sad situation. My dad has always been quite gung-ho and a tough business nego-tiator, but there were times when I wanted to back out of the deal with Stade Français. In the end, however, I thought, 'Bollocks to it, I'm going. I'll show them all they were wrong.' And you know what? I did.

FREE MAN IN PARIS

All the stuff that was said about me drove me to make a success of my time in France. I didn't go on the 2009 Lions tour, and I thought that might be my last chance, but I hadn't played that well in the Six Nations anyway. However, I played every England game during the two years I was at Stade Français. I became a better player and a more resilient, self-aware person. I got to play with and against many superstars of the game. I became good friends with many of them. And I had the time of my life living in Paris with my fellow Englishmen Tom Palmer, who despite the Night Stalker jibes was a top guy and a fantastic player, and Ollie Phillips, maybe the loveliest bloke in the world.

My house was in the 17th arrondissement, right in the heart of Paris and just around the corner from the Arc de Triomphe. It was an incredible place, with exterior double doors that opened onto a courtyard. Wrapped around the courtyard were five houses, with little front gardens, almost like houses within a house. After Ollie arrived from Newcastle, he moved in with me and we spent the next two years having all sorts of fun and adventures together.

On the pitch, Ollie instantly started scoring tries for fun. Ollie looked about 60 and one of our Stade Français coaches Michael Cheika said he reminded him of an accountant running around the field. But he was seriously rapid, ended up being top scorer in the Top 14 and was voted best overseas player in 2011. Typical Ollie, he also learned how to speak French fluently in about a week. Being friends with him was like being a pal of Napoleon's in a game of Risk. Wherever he went, he took the place over. He was the ultimate networker and quite possibly the best-connected man in rugby. I've lost count of the number of times people have said to me, 'I know this rugby guy called Ollie. You know him?' I've heard that line all over the world.

We shared some tremendous memories, me and Ollie. Including the time we drugged a dog. Before I tell this story, I want to make it very clear that I love animals, particularly dogs. I've always had them and I've never mistreated them. But one weekend, the neighbours went away for a few days, left this little handbag dog behind and it didn't stop barking. After a day and night of this racket, which meant we couldn't get any sleep, we took a look through a window to make sure it was okay. It had food and water, so it was fine on that front. But after a second night of barking and no sleep, we decided we were going to have to shut it up, by hook or by crook. We bought some over the counter herbal sleeping pills, wrapped a quarter of one up in a slice of ham and chucked it through their kitchen window. Unfortunately, the dog just sniffed it before wandering off. So now there was a bit of sleeping pill wrapped in a slice of ham sitting in the middle of the kitchen floor. You wouldn't have had to be Poirot to work out who'd put it there, so we were going to have to break in and retrieve the evidence.

Ollie was nominated to climb through the window, on account of being about half my size, and he managed to grab the ham and slither back out again without the dog going mental and any other neighbours seeing. But we still hadn't solved the problem of the dog's barking. So we crushed the bit of pill up, sprinkled it over the ham and chucked it back in. This time, the dog strolled straight over and wolfed it down, before me and Ollie watched with bated breath to see what would happen next. About five minutes later, the dog staggered across the kitchen and fell sideways into its basket. Mission accomplished, me and Ollie high-fived, went to bed and slept like logs. Which was a small mercy as we had a game the next day.

When our neighbours returned the following morning, we were hiding behind the curtains, snickering. They kept calling the dog's name, but he was so out of it that when he finally woke up and got to his feet, he promptly fell sideways and went back to sleep. For about 48 hours. I'm not going to lie to you, I thought we might have killed him. But we didn't, and that's the main thing. After that episode, we'd sometimes catch him staring at us through the window with an expression that said, 'I know what you two fuckers did ...'

LA MACHINE

I'd come from an unbelievably professional environment at Wasps, so French rugby was a real culture shock. I obviously wanted to carry on playing for England and had no intention of letting my standards slip, which meant doing lots of extra work. But Stade Français was like a factory: as soon as the whistle went to signal the end of training, everyone pissed off and left just me and Ollie on the pitch, plus maybe a couple of younger French players who we'd managed to persuade to do a few extra bits and pieces. The rest of them thought I was a weirdo for bringing in my own meals in Tupperware containers, spending time in the gym and working hard at my game. Some of lads started calling me 'La Machine'. I realise it sounds like I gave myself that nickname, but I can assure you it was given to me by my team-mates. They'd say to me, 'Hey, Machine, always more, always more.' I'd be thinking, 'Of course I want to do more, it's called being a professional sportsman.'

They'd give us these lunch vouchers and we'd all eat together in the Stade Français sports club or this little café that did beautiful home-cooked meals. And when they'd drunk their espressos, they'd all pile out the back and spark up cigarettes.

Lots of the players smoked – between team meetings, after lunch, even before training. You'd see them finish their tab, flick it on the grass and trot onto the field to do the warm-up. Me and Ollie would normally be out on the field 10 minutes before training started, doing our own warm-ups. One day, it got to about five minutes before training was supposed to start and there was no sign of anyone else. We could see a few team-mates loitering by the tunnel smoking, and suddenly a couple of lads appeared carrying a pasting table, followed by another couple of lads carrying bulging shopping bags. They put this table up, plonked two bottles of red wine down, as well as baguettes, cheese, sausages, foie gras and various jars of condiments and pickles. A few more lads appeared with chairs, a chopping board and a knife, and they all sat down and started tucking in. Eventually, one of them shouted, 'Oi! Rosbifs!' and waved us over, before thrusting glasses of red wine into our hands. One of the lads had brought in a load of delicacies from his home town, although why we had to eat them a few minutes before training I never worked out. But that became a normal occurrence. It was like rugby from the 1950s.

French players seemed more naturally talented than English players and the games were more physical. But I could understand why foreign players went to France and became frustrated. I could also understand why British and Irish teams with half the resources would do just as well, because they just did things better and took things more seriously. French rugby was fuelled by emotion and they were still obsessed by this notion that they could get through with flair alone, which is bullshit. By all means keep the flair, but you've got to marry it to structure, otherwise when the wheels fall off, there's no way of salvaging the situation.

Max splashed out on some of the best players money can buy, but like all French clubs he didn't focus enough on infrastructure. That's why non-French coaches never last in France, because when they come in, try to overhaul things and instil some discipline, the veteran players start grumbling, having meetings and trying to get him sacked. I always had the feeling that the club was run by those old stalwarts, who had been in the squad for years and behaved like trade unionists whenever changes were proposed. To be fair, they came in handy sometimes, like the time Max asked if we could all take a pay cut.

In my first season, we had three different head coaches. The first, Australian Ewen McKenzie, accused Max of signing players based on their looks and claimed that other players had asked to leave because they didn't want to pose for the naked calendar anymore. The second, Jacques Delmas, started taking the piss out of me in his first training session. For some reason, he kept calling me 'le poisson rouge', or the goldfish, and digging me out all the time in training. One time, I didn't win a turnover in a match, and he lost his rag and started shouting. I asked my team-mate Ben Kayser what he was saying, and Ben replied, 'I'm not really comfortable telling you, but he said, "What does Martin Johnson see in this man? How does he ever get picked for England?"' Then Delmas got right in my face and started screaming. I asked Ben what he'd said now, and Ben replied, 'He said, "If you carry on playing this shit, I'm going to tear your contract up in your face."' After a few sessions of this abuse, I actually started thinking, 'If he says anything again, just bang him out, get fired, maybe get a payout and go back to England.' Luckily, he kept picking me (apart from the Heineken Cup quarter-final against Toulouse, when he blamed me for the defeat for mucking about in training, despite the fact I wasn't even in the match-day squad), but that was the closest I ever came to punching a coach.

Some weeks we'd train terribly, with moves going wrong, people scrapping and balls being dropped all over the place. I'd be standing there thinking, 'Are these people actual rugby players?' But the team would turn up on match day and absolutely kill it. Other weeks, we'd be on fire in training, not turn up at the weekend and get blown away. It was almost accepted that teams won their home games and lost their away games. There was no rhyme or reason to anything. Before one game against Biarritz, Sylvain Marconnet, one of our props, was screaming and shouting and headbutting his mate in the changing room, and then proceeded to miss about five tackles in the first half. When he also tried to headbutt me at half-time, I said to him, 'Mate, there's no point screaming and shouting and headbutting people before a game unless you're going to front up when the whistle goes. Stop being a fake tough guy and go and hit one of the opposition players.' That went down badly. 'Oh, the Rosbif is piping up,' or whatever that is in French.

The psychology was non-existent and the physiotherapy wasn't the best (although if they deciphered any serious problems, they'd get you scanned and on the right medicine straightaway). I'd travel back to London once a week to get treatment from Kevin Lidlow, who had been putting me back together again since I was 17 and I know extended my career by years. The Stade gym was full of rusting, creaking machines and mismatched weights. The nutritionist told me my diet needed improving and that I should eat more fromage blanc, which is this white, yoghurt-like cheese. I later found out that she had a deal with a company that produced it.

We'd take eight-hour coach journeys to away games instead of flying. If we lost, Max would storm into the dressing room and start ranting and raving, telling us we had it too easy and calling us all sons of bitches. After one defeat, there was a big inquest and the conclusion was that the players were eating too many sweets on the coach. I thought, 'We were on the coach for eight hours, the hotel was *merde* and half the team smoke – and you're blaming the fact we lost on too many bonbons.' And those French boys could drink. I wouldn't go out that much, but I would occasionally have a decent night out and subsequently discover that some of the French boys had rocked up to the bar at 3 am, long past my bedtime, and gone two days without stopping.

On away trips, every hotel room would have one big bed and one tiny bed – the sort of thing you'd end up on if you stayed at your nan's. Among English players, the tradition was to play rock, paper, scissors to decide who got the big bed. Or if it were a back and a forward sharing, the forward would get it. But that wasn't how things were done by French players. Before Stade Français' Heineken Cup quarter-final against Toulouse in 2010, I was rooming with this French bloke who didn't say much and looked like that massive bloke from the film *Hot Fuzz*, who only says 'yarp'. When we arrived at the hotel, I went off to find some food and this bloke disappeared up the stairs in a puff of smoke. And when I walked into the room, he was lying on this great big emperor bed sharpening a piece of wood with a penknife. Lo and behold, the other bed looked like a fish finger. I said, 'Oi, surely it's rock, paper, scissors to decide who gets the big bed?' And he just stared at me while carrying on sharpening and chewing on a toothpick. It was like a scene from a Spaghetti Western, with Lee Van Cleef as my roomie.

Luckily, my roomie eventually decided to have a shower and while he was in the bathroom, I lifted his bed up, removed four or five slats and lobbed them out of the window (we were 30 floors up, but I didn't want him to be able to get them back), before jumping back onto my bed, sticking my headphones on and pretending to be asleep. When he finally emerged, he practically ran across the room, due to the amazing night's sleep he was going to have on his oversized bed. He actually did a Superman dive onto what he thought was comfort heaven and went straight through the middle of the bed. He scrambled back to his feet, looking furious, and while he was pacing up and down at the end of my bed, I was trying not to laugh while fake snoring very loudly. My roomie was forced to sleep down a hole, woke up with a major spinal injury and had to pull out of the game. I actually slept quite well, having found a comfortable spring to lie on. Let that be a lesson to any selfish bastards who might be reading this: if you're not going to be a good team-mate, observe proper etiquette and play rock, paper, scissors for the big bed, you will risk missing that big match with a crumpled back.

AMOUR

Despite everything – and I can't stress this enough – I absolutely loved my time at Stade Français. It was such a cool thing to be part of. We had this beautiful training facility out in the middle of a forest. I was playing big games, with and against big stars, in beautiful parts of France every week. Friends and family could hop over on the Eurostar and stay for the weekend, and my parents didn't miss a home game. That's proper fandom. And despite the structural problems at the club and Max's quirks, I much preferred him to some of the non-entity owners I'd had previously. Max was a brilliant man who made Stade Français into one of the most successful and popular rugby clubs in the world. He cared so much and looked after his players well. I'd sign for him any day.

As for big match days at the Stade de France, they were like spectacles from the Colosseum. One of my first games for

Stade was against Toulon, and Max made sure the place was packed out with 80,000 fans dressed in pink and waving pink flags. They were treated to the most outlandish pre-match entertainment I'd ever seen. There were flamethrowers going off all over the pitch, motorbike stunt riders jumping through hoops of fire, Mexican wrestlers in a ring on the centre circle, lions and elephants being led around the outside. When I ran onto the pitch for the warm-up, I was more worried about being run over, mauled or trampled to death than finding a spot to do a bit of stretching.

When I walked out into the tunnel just before kick-off, I found myself standing next to Jonny Wilkinson, who was already a full-blown Toulon hero. I obviously knew Jonny from playing together for England and had told all my team-mates that we were really good mates. So it was slightly embarrassing when I said hello and he custard-pied me, presumably because he was so in the zone (or maybe he just thought I was a dickhead). Above the tunnel exit were two big TV screens, showing what was still going off on the pitch, and I couldn't believe what I was seeing. Four giant body-builders, stripped to the waist, were pushing a giant golden egg. When they got to the centre circle, the egg cracked open and a topless woman with her fully exposed breasts painted gold clambered out and placed a gold rugby ball on the centre spot. There was much tittering and rib-digging among lads from both teams. But not from Jonny, who didn't look up once. Who knows what was going on in his head at that moment, but I can safely say it wasn't tits.

I'd just about managed to refocus when a load of Moulin Rouge girls, wearing frilly knickers, stockings, suspenders and feather boas, came running down the tunnel. My head almost fell off. And while I was working out where I was going to take Michelle the can-can lady – probably up the Eiffel Tower, if she was lucky – Jonny was still drilling a hole in the floor with his X-ray eyes. As it happened, I didn't play too badly. But as I was lying in bed that night, I couldn't help thinking, 'If I weren't so easily distracted, maybe I'd have won a World Cup and become a rugby legend and multi-millionaire, just like Jonny.'

ALMOST KAMIKAZE

I really wanted to stay at Stade Français, but they ran into financial problems and decided to let two or three players go in 2011. Wasps told me that all was forgiven, that they really wanted me back and offered me a great deal. But I wasn't ready to return to England because there were still more adventures to be had abroad. I set my heart on playing in Super Rugby and agreed to join Melbourne Rebels after the World Cup, but because the Super Rugby season started in January, I needed a stopgap. Ricoh Black Rams, who played in Japan's Top League, expressed an interest, so I flew to Tokyo the summer before the World Cup and they rolled out the red carpet for me. They put me up in this amazing hotel, gave me a tour of the stadium, I met the team and the coaches, and they took me out for an unforgettable meal, during which one of my hosts grabbed two live prawns that were thrashing around in a bowl and threw them on the grill in front of me. I didn't want to offend anyone, so I got stuck in. To be fair, they tasted unbelievable. And the deal was done.

Given what had gone on at the World Cup, it was a relief to escape to Japan. The thought of playing back in England, and all the flak I would have got from journalists, pundits and randoms on Twitter, didn't bear thinking about. But I was also a little apprehensive. Paris was a few hours away from London, so I could go back home when I needed to, and family and friends could pop over. I was also living with another

Englishman, in Ollie Phillips. But because my partner didn't want to come with me to Tokyo, I was flying solo.

Luckily, the club did everything they could to make me feel welcome. They found me a little pink two-storey house in Futako-Tamagawa, which Eddie Jones assured me was home to some of the most expensive real estate in Tokyo. It was by the river, 15 minutes from the training ground and next door to Tamati Ellison, a wonderful bloke who played a few games for the All Blacks. They also gave me a pushbike, so that I could cycle everywhere. (I did upgrade to a scooter, which didn't go down well – I didn't have insurance, it was probably illegal and it caused panic, but I just used to smile and ride off, chased by my translators, shouting and screaming at me.)

There were the usual teething problems. The language was like nothing I'd ever experienced, to the extent that I feared that if I ever got lost, I'd never find my way home. It nearly happened on the subway one day, until an elderly Japanese man helped me find the exit. I'd been going round and round for what felt like hours.

After about a week, I did an interview with a local TV station and when the reporter asked me about the standard of Japanese rugby, I started eulogising and said that the knee-high tackling was unbelievable – 'almost kamikaze'. Luckily, we weren't going out live. I couldn't make head nor tail of the local supermarket, which was the only one for miles. It was stacked with rice, noodles, vegetables and sauces, but didn't seem to have any protein. I was walking up and down the aisles thinking, 'Surely they eat meat or fish around here?' Being a meathead forward, protein is very important to me. After a few weeks, during which I must have lost a stone in weight, I bumped into an English bloke in the supermarket and said in a wheezy voice, 'Excuse me, where is the protein? The fish, the chicken. Do they sell anything meaty?'

'Downstairs, mate.'

'Downstairs? There's a downstairs? Please show me …'

Just as my legs were about to give way through exhaustion, he pointed me towards a door in the corner, hidden behind some shelves. I felt like Lucy in the *The Lion, the Witch and the Wardrobe*, entering some kind of protein Narnia. In fact, and I don't mean to sound churlish, there was probably too much of it.

Then there were the business cards, which were making my wallet bulge within days of arriving. I was told that every time someone handed me one, it was polite to go full-on *American Psycho* – 'Look at that subtle off-white colouring. The tasteful thickness of it. Oh my God, it even has a watermark …' Well, not quite, but I did examine each one with a look of awe, as if it were a Fabergé egg.

All the teams in the Top League are owned by major companies, so as well as Ricoh Black Rams there were the Sanyo Wild Knights, Honda Heat, Mitsubishi DynaBoars and Toshiba Brave Lupus. All the players are employees of the company, so when I received the contract, I genuinely combed through it to make sure I wouldn't have to assemble photocopiers in a factory if I didn't get picked. They even threw in a photocopier as part of the deal. My dad wanted it for his business and is still waiting for it to arrive. I didn't have the heart to tell him that I exchanged it for hard yen, because the chances of anyone being arsed to ship an industrial photocopier the size of a minibus from Tokyo to Berkshire were minimal.

I didn't know anything about Japanese rugby before I turned up. I soon discovered it was a massive university sport, with crowds of 50,000 for some games. And while the crowds weren't as big for Top League games, they were still decent. Each team was mostly made up of foreign professionals and a handful of Japanese amateurs, who in our case worked in the

Ricoh offices and would turn up for training in their suits. When I signed, I thought I'd be like Godzilla on the pitch, running down the field and tossing little Japanese people over my shoulder as if they were rag dolls. Alas, bigger people gravitate towards sports that require bigger people, so there were hardly any little fellas. On top of that, the Japanese players were very well drilled and demon tacklers, while most teams were chock-full of Pacific Island imports with Asian passports.

ENGLISH STYLE

In the Top League, no club really had proper home fixtures, so we'd play all over the place, with the odd game at the national stadium. Kick-off was 12 noon, so I'd wake up at 7 am, go round to Tamati's house for porridge and coffee, meet up with the rest of the foreign lads at the clubhouse, get taxis to the station, jump on a train, head into the heart of Tokyo and be at wherever we were playing by 10 am. We'd be done by 2 pm and have the rest of the weekend to ourselves, like playing rugby at school.

Before my first game, I was sitting in the changing room next to this Japanese prop. I was sticking to my very strict routine, headphones in and listening to music, when my throat started burning and my eyes started stinging. When I opened my eyes, I saw this prop kneeling and praying in front of a little incense temple he had set up in his locker. I always thought religion should be kept out of the changing room. When I was captain at Wasps, Nathan Hughes would sing Bible verses while I was trying to do a team talk. A few times I had to tell him, 'Listen, I know it's important for you to pray to God before a game, but please do me a favour and keep it zipped while I'm trying to speak.' I decided I wasn't going to give this prop a bollocking in his own country before I'd even played a game – that wouldn't have been a good look.

But then this prop started slathering himself in different oils, all over his head and shoulders, all over his body and legs. He smelled great, especially for a prop. But about 30 minutes into the game, we had our first scrum. I leant down, put my head next to this prop's thigh and it was like I'd been gassed. Because it was a hot day and he was sweating profusely, the oils had bled into my eyes, à la Cassius Clay in his first fight against Sonny Liston. I had to be led off the field at half-time and given a chemical eye bath in the changing room.

Through a translator, I persuaded the prop to stop smothering himself in Colman's English mustard, or whatever hot condiment he was using. But some translated conversations were a bit trickier to negotiate. The Japanese absolutely love a shower. They are the shower people. My team-mates would take a bucket in with them, full of shampoo, shower gel, sponges and exfoliators. They'd flip the bucket over, sit on it and be in there for half an hour, cleaning themselves to within an inch of their lives. This young bloke who changed next to me before training had a shammy leather, the sort of thing you'd use to clean your car, and he'd plonk one foot on the bench and furiously polish his spuds, like a snooker referee with a dirty cue ball. If that weren't bad enough, he'd do it about an inch from my face. He didn't speak much English, and I didn't know the Japanese for 'stop polishing your spuds right next to my face', so I had to call the translator over and relay my request.

The bushes on those Japanese boys were something to behold. They made Martin Corry look positively metrosexual. Their lush pubic foliage was made even stranger by the fact they had hardly any hair elsewhere, apart from the top of their head. They were not into their manscaping one bit, so that a few of their old boys looked like a Cadbury Creme Egg in a nest of seaweed. The first time I came bowling out of the shower, they all started making these weird noises and pointing at my crotch, because I like to keep a bit of order down there. 'English style,' I said, as proudly as I could. 'You lot should try it.' The phantom testicle polisher was as hirsute downstairs as the rest, so I said to him one day, 'Look, if you're going on tour with the Japan sevens team and single and ready to mingle, you need to sort this out. European ladies simply won't have it.' Eventually, I wore him down and he started trimming it up. Soon, most of the team were following suit. That was my legacy to Japanese rugby: manscaping. You are welcome.

LOST IN TRANSLATION

We had translators everywhere, even on the field during a game. Whenever there was a break in play, they'd run water on and deliver messages, and also pop up at half-time. On the training ground, the foreign backs and forwards had separate translators. Any time a coach said something, the translator would call us over and we'd huddle around her. When a coach got angry, the translator got angry. I'd be looking at her thinking, 'Calm down, love, what's it got to do with you?' Japanese coaches are partial to a few tears after a game, and when a coach started crying, so would the translators. They were very committed to their roles, like method actors. Except when a player wanted to give a coach a piece of his mind. You'd see the player raising his voice and gesticulating wildly and you'd know the translator wasn't translating verbatim, because the coach would still be smiling, even though you'd heard the player say he wanted to run him over.

Some of the Japanese lads liked a drink and could get very loose on a night out. One of the amateurs, who sold photocopiers by day, trained by night and was like a tackling machine. He would get utterly steaming on this stuff called *shochu*, which is a potato vodka. That meant he wasn't very popular with his compatriots. He wouldn't normally say much, but suddenly he'd be talking non-stop in broken English and you couldn't shut him up. But I soon learned that you weren't allowed to discuss any off-field shenanigans. If you went on a team social in England and players misbehaved, you'd walk into the changing room whenever the next training session was and tell everyone – very loudly – what you'd seen, in graphic detail, with embellishments. The point was to make it as uncomfortable and embarrassing as possible for the players involved. But after I saw a couple of Japanese lads on the piss in Tokyo and brought it up in the dressing room, they denied all knowledge.

'Alright, lads, good fun the other night?'

Blank faces.

'I saw you in that bar. Taking your shirt off.'

'No, no, not possible.'

'Come on, I saw you standing on the table, being sick on that girl's head.'

'No! That wasn't me!'

'It was you! I've got pictures!'

One of the foreign lads had to take me aside and explain that in Japan, you can do what you want on a night out, short of murdering someone, and it must never be mentioned again.

GAIJIN

Us foreign pros (or *gaijin*) became very tight, including the Pacific Islanders who weren't officially part of the club's overseas quota because they had Asian passports. We had this

Tongan guy called Emosi Kauhenga, who was a 20-stone lock. I'd never heard of him, but in his first game, they kicked off, he caught the ball in one hand, ran half the length of the field, rumbling straight over tacklers like a tank, before doing a back of the hand spin pass to the winger, who scored. I was standing there thinking, 'Where the hell did you find him? And why has an English club never signed him?'

Because the Japanese don't celebrate Christmas, we played on Christmas Day. We woke up in a hotel, had rice, miso soup and a couple of cold boiled eggs for breakfast, then piled onto a bullet train to Ota City, home of table-topping Panasonic. Seconds after the game started, I hit this Aussie guy, landed on top of him and said, 'Merry Christmas!' He smiled and replied, 'Fuckin' 'ell, mate, what a way to spend it.' Us foreigners celebrated Christmas the following day. One of the Islanders had spent all night rotating a pig on a spit, and we all went round to his house and spent Boxing Day having a pig feast. It was an amazing day spent with great people.

One of my Ricoh team-mates was Ma'a Nonu, All Black legend and my absolute hero. He'd just won the World Cup and was at the peak of his powers. He was the best centre in the world by a long way – immensely powerful, athletic and skilful, with a great kicking game. But he was also a lovely, generous bloke. He was the first guy to give me a real insight into Samoan culture. If you wanted something, he'd give it to you. Even if you didn't want something, he'd give it to you. After one defeat, Ma'a stood up in the changing room and announced that the foreign boys were going to sing a song to cheer everyone up. This was news to me. Suddenly, he launched into Bob Marley's 'Three Little Birds' – '*Don't worry, 'bout a thing, cos every little thing gonna be all right ...*' I got up and joined in, although I didn't know any words beyond the first verse, while all the other foreigners put their heads down and left us to it. Meanwhile, the Japanese players were all looking at each other in astonishment. When we were done, we got a polite, awkward round of applause. But even the translators looked embarrassed.

As for the Japanese fans, they were certainly different to the fans I'd experienced elsewhere. The cheering at games wasn't spontaneous, it was organised. At Ricoh, the cheerleader was a guy in a dinosaur suit – I never found out why he wasn't in a black ram suit – and as soon as he started shouting and hollering, the fans would come to life. But I can't say a bad word about Japanese rugby fans. They were polite and respectful, and really took us foreign players to their hearts. One family befriended me and took me sumo wrestling, which was an incredible spectacle. Young fans would draw cartoons of the players or take lots of photos, put them in a book and present it to us. I was sad to leave Tokyo, but I was committed to testing myself against the best players in the world in Super Rugby, which is about as broad as horizons get.

SUPER RUGBY

However, the next stop on my world tour wouldn't be Melbourne, as planned. The Rebels pulled out of the deal because of the World Cup scandal – they clearly thought I was a wrong'un – and I couldn't make it work with the Crusaders in Christchurch, whom I'd always been a fan of. So I hastily arranged a deal with the Highlanders, from Dunedin, which was where England were based during the World Cup. Fortunately, they didn't seem worried about the chambermaid controversy and I quickly learned that unless you were an All Black, the public left you alone. The Highlanders would only pay me NZ$60,000 (about £40,000) for the season, but I wasn't bothered about money. All I was interested in was testing myself and finding out exactly how good I was.

I'd seen plenty of Super Rugby highlight reels, with players like Doug Howlett, Joe Rokocoko and Ma'a Nonu scoring all those incredible length-of-the-field tries – and if you listened to Stuart Barnes and most of the other British rugby pundits and journalists, you'd think New Zealanders played a brand of rugby that no-one in the northern hemisphere was able to comprehend, let alone emulate. But I took that as a challenge. I was the first English player to play for a Kiwi side in Super Rugby, the Highlanders had a rich history, full of unbelievable players, and I was regarded by some as a has-been, drifting aimlessly. People thought I was going to flounder, so I had plenty to prove.

I'd learned so much about myself while playing in Japan. It would have been very easy to become lazy and coast on the other side of the world, away from home and the English media. No-one was really judging me, so I could have done pretty much what I wanted. But I discovered that my biggest critic was myself. I always maintained high standards, was as professional as possible, because I wanted to be the best player I could be, for me and the team. I discovered I was resilient, because I had to do a lot of my own training and go out of my way to eat well. I also discovered I was very independent, self-reliant and comfortable in my own company, even a loner at times.

If I have an audience, I come alive and act up to it. But I don't need to be in a crowd. My room-mates would often be disappointed to discover that I could be quite serious one-on-one. My Wasps team-mate Simon Shaw once sat on the end of my bed and said, 'Come on then, entertain me.' I can't remember what I was doing – writing, editing a book, uploading fitness content, putting together a playlist, who knows – but I replied, 'I'm busy. Seriously. I'm working here.' Apparently Shawsey had requested me as a room-mate, but never again. I like going out for coffee on my own, eating on my own, reading, listening to music, preparing a DJ set or just fiddling around with some new piece of technology. My wife sometimes says, 'I get a shit version of you,' meaning the quiet, introspective one. But it's not like that. That's just who I am. And I'm happy I'm like that. Plenty of British players have signed for foreign clubs and only lasted a season because they can't handle being in an alien environment, with no friends or family. But it never really bothered me.

I was on my own again in New Zealand, although Tamati Ellison, my old Ricoh team-mate and next-door neighbour, had also joined the Highlanders. He and his lovely wife basically adopted me as another member of their wonderful family. I owe them a lot, as they looked after me so well in Japan and in New Zealand. I rented a house from Samoa's former Highlander Seilala Mapusua, which was right on beautiful Saint Clair beach. I'm not a bright lights, big city man anyway, so it was perfect for me. That surprised some people because they assumed I'd go half-mad with boredom. I joined a boxing gym – New Zealand Fight and Fitness – for extra conditioning, did a bit of jujitsu, drank a lot of coffee and ate a lot of meals for one. It was just a nice, laid-back existence.

A SERIOUS BUSINESS

I'd contacted Highlanders' strength and conditioning coach Andrew Beardmore (a top man, who would become a friend) before I arrived, to find out how fit I'd need to be – because I knew Super Rugby would be faster and more physical than Japanese rugby – and ended up doing Highlanders fitness sessions after training with Ricoh. All that extra work paid off because I hit the ground running. I landed on the Thursday morning, did the team run on Friday and played my first game for the Highlanders on the Saturday, coming off the bench against the Chiefs, for whom World Cup winners Sonny Bill Williams and Aaron Cruden were making their debuts. I put in some hits, effected the match-winning turnover and was quite happy with how I played. More importantly, we got the win away from home against a bloody good side.

That's not to say I wasn't apprehensive, because the Highlanders had some seriously good players – and my chip and chase and out-of-the-back-door passing weren't the best (despite what anyone says, they were in the locker somewhere, gathering dust – search YouTube for rare footage). They had scrum-half Aaron Smith and full-back Ben Smith, who would both win the World Cup with New Zealand in 2015, as well as winger Hosea Gear and hooker Andrew Hore, who was a World Cup winner back in 2011. On top of that, the head coach was Jamie Joseph, a former All Black who had a reputation as one of the best teachers in the game.

I soon learned exactly how seriously rugby is taken in New Zealand. In England, as in most countries, being a rugby player is right down the list of things people want to be. Things are changing, but when I was in New Zealand every kid growing up wanted to be an All Black. That was the greatest thing anyone could achieve. Everyone had a rugby ball in their hands from an early age and seemed to have played at some level, whether for their local club's fifth team or a bit of touch on the beach. Kids are coached from an early age to play with the ball in hand and hone their footwork, speed and athleticism, and the school competitions are fiercely competitive, with big crowds and games on TV.

In New Zealand, the relationship between Super Rugby and club rugby is fluid, so that if you're not getting a game for the

Highlanders, need to find some form or get up to speed after an injury, you might play for the Maniototo Maggots, which was officially my club side. That local rugby was just as important to people as the All Blacks, and allowed youngsters not long out of school to play with and against – and learn from – some of the best players in the world. If you listen to a number of the British pundits, you'd think New Zealand rugby was something mystical, but I soon worked out it was quite simple. It's about perfecting the basics and doing things quickly, directly and accurately. And it all comes from a deep-rooted love of the game. Plus, everyone wants to do it, so you are getting the very best of the athletic talent.

There is no promotion or relegation in Super Rugby, which means teams can start a season with a game-plan and stick to it. In England, a coach can have the best intentions in pre-season about playing expansive, fan-pleasing rugby, but if his team is dicing with relegation in January or February – and playing on muddy pitches in sideways rain most weeks – any thoughts of style are likely to go out of the window, at least until the end of the season. A Super Rugby season also isn't as long as a European season, which means players have more time to rest their bodies and work on their skills in training.

There was so much talent on display in Super Rugby, particularly in the New Zealand teams. For every two or three lads you see on the TV, there are two or three more who are just as good playing for the second team. There was also much more variety than in Europe. The New Zealand sides were fast and powerful, but not insanely physical; the Australian sides were more formulaic in their attacking play and less powerful, but very well organised; the South African sides were just brutal – after playing the Sharks or the Bulls, I'd feel like I'd been in a car crash.

One thing that amused me was that Kiwi players had no concept of English rugby. Shortly after arriving, I filmed some of my team-mates for my YouTube channel and asked them what they thought English rugby was like. All of the answers were along the lines of, 'Don't you just maul it? Pick and go?' None of them watch northern hemisphere rugby, they're just not interested. I'm not even sure it's on TV in New Zealand.

Before my first game for England against the All Blacks at Twickenham, a couple of their players were asked about their England counterparts and fudged their answers. It was quite clear that they didn't really know who they were about to come up against. At first I thought, 'You disrespectful bastards.' Then I thought, 'Actually, I love that. It shows that all they're interested in is what *they* need to do to win.' We spent too much time talking the All Blacks up, waxing lyrical about their virtues, polishing their aura. We knew about every single player in their team in forensic detail. But they didn't give a shit about us. They were going to play their way, and that was that. It wasn't arrogance. Who we were and what we did just didn't impact on their game-plan. I thought we needed to be more like that, stop blowing smoke up their arses, and concentrate on what we were good at and how we could hurt them. We got there in the end, when Eddie Jones took over, but it took a long time.

ONCE WERE WARRIORS

One of the biggest cultural shocks was the Kiwi sense of humour. In the UK, the humour in rugby teams is very sharp and utterly ruthless, bordering on aggressive. But when I first arrived in New Zealand, I'd get involved in a bit of to and fro and someone would chime in, 'Jesus, bro, that was a bit harsh.' I'd have to apologise and explain that I was still working out the levels of humour. I never really got to grips with it, although saying it looks like the council cut your hair is apparently a step too far in New Zealand. But despite the odd humour-based misunderstanding, they were great people.

One team-mate I became good friends with was Andrew Hore, who invited me to come shooting on his farm. I didn't know it at the time, but Andrew and a couple of mates had been convicted of shooting a protected seal in 2005, which was caught on camera by a tourist. A few years after I left the Highlanders, he was done for supplying a shotgun to an un-licensed person, who then almost shot his arm off while shoot-ing ducks. Had I known this, I might have thought twice about accepting the mad bastard's invitation. I say 'might', because I love shooting and he was actually a lovely bloke.

Because I did a bit of shooting back in England, I'd packed all my gear. So I rocked up to this place in the middle of nowhere – which was just a dot in a mass of green on my satnav – wearing tweed sports jacket and trousers, a gingham shirt and tie. Everything but the deerstalker. I even brought a hipflask and a bundle of New Zealand dollars for the beaters. When I got out of my car, they thought I was the funniest thing they'd ever seen, because they were all wearing manky T-shirts and denim shorts. They immediately nicknamed me Lord Farquaad from *Shrek*, before telling me they didn't even have pheasants in New Zealand. They had Kiwis, but they were endangered, and not even Andrew Hore shot them. Instead, the shoot involved us hanging off the back of a pickup travelling at 50 mph, with a beer in one hand and semi-automatic shotgun in the other, blasting anything that moved, mostly rabbits. Well, that's the story I am sticking to anyway. We didn't receive any messages and Captain Blackadder definitely did not shoot the delicious plump-breasted pigeon, Sir.

Unsurprisingly, my Highlanders team-mates, just like my team-mates wherever I went, liked a party. And one of the worst ideas I ever had was having an end-of-season party at my house – or more accurately Seilala Mapusua's house – after an all-day session following our last game in Australia. We played the game, got smashed, flew back to Dunedin and the lads came directly from the airport, carrying slabs of beer on their shoulders. I got on the decks with Adam Thomson early and started spinning some tunes before the whole thing descended into carnage.

On hearing a commotion coming from the garden, I wandered outside to discover they'd stacked some of Mapusua's garden furniture under the eaves of the house and set it on fire, along with some of my clothes. As I've already said, my fashion game's not great, but it's not that bad. And compared to Kiwis, I was like David Beckham. I obviously lost the plot, and as I was in mid-flow, Lima Sopoaga jumped up and smashed an egg on my head. The yolk hadn't even had time to start dripping down my face when I charged through what was now a raging fire, like some deranged stuntman, and knocked Lima cold with an overhand right. I thought I'd killed him. Seconds later, I was pinned against a wall by a second-row, and Kade Poki, who was only a little bloke but very good mates with Lima and ferocious as anything, landed with a lovely right hand that split my nose. Then from nowhere, and for reasons he probably didn't even know, our lunatic scrum-half Jimmy Cowan tried to punch Elliot Dixon, who was a 6 ft 4 in back-row. Dixon, whose right arm was in a sling after shoulder surgery, slipped the attempted blow and knocked Cowan out with his left hand.

Now we had two blokes out cold in the garden and it was like a scene from that New Zealand film *Once Were Warriors*, except instead of someone shouting, 'Cook the man some fucking eggs!' someone was smashing raw eggs on my fore-head. When my team-mates who were still conscious refused to leave, I ended up calling the police. 'I've got an out of control party at my house, which might burn down at any minute – get round here now!' As the lads were piling into their cars and about to drive off, a couple of police cars pulled up. But instead of giving them a bollocking, they offered them lifts home, because, like everyone in New Zealand, they were rugby fans.

Now it was just me and Jimmy Cowan in the house, me with my busted nose and him with a big cut above his eye. It looked like we'd just gone 12 rounds. Having put the flames out – which wasn't easy – and finally persuaded Cowan to get lost, I got a taxi to A&E. Luckily, the doctor was an English rugby fan and did a beautiful stitching job.

The following morning, I was relieved to find the place hadn't burnt down. But the carnage was even worse than I remembered. The house was littered with bottles and someone had spewed on the floor in the kitchen. I also discovered that they'd tried to light another fire at the other end of the garden, right next to the propane tank. Had that fire taken off, it would have blown us all up. When I met up with the lads for another team social that evening (having got some deep cleaners in), it was as if nothing had happened.

'What the hell were you boys thinking?'

'Oh, it was only a bit of fun.'

I saw Mapusua at the 2019 World Cup in Japan. I said to my wife Chloe, 'Shit, hide, he's going to want to know where all his garden furniture went.' But he clocked me from across the room, grinned from ear to ear, gave me a big hug and didn't mention it. I'm not sure he would have been so forgiving had we incinerated his house.

MY GREATEST ACHIEVEMENT

The Highlanders didn't make the play-offs that season. I managed to get myself banned for four weeks after a game against the Cheetahs, in which some bloke grabbed me by the bollocks and wouldn't let go, so I let fly with a combination I'd been learning in the gym, missing with a right but landing with a left hook. Despite that moment of madness, it was probably my best game in a Highlanders shirt and, remarkably, we won 36–33, having been 30–9 down. It might surprise you that I consider playing in Super Rugby, and elsewhere in the world, as my greatest achievement in rugby, and not only because I proved so many people wrong. Working with people from different cultures makes you think and do things differently. I learned so much from foreign players, both in England and abroad. When you view superstars from a distance, it's easy to convince yourself that they're otherworldly beings, almost mystical talents that you could never hope to emulate. But when you play with and against these people, you soon realise that they're not supermen, they're just ordinary human beings. It's like being shown under the bonnet of a Ferrari – 'Aaah, I can see how it works now. It's a beautiful engine, that's for sure, but there's no magic to it.' The best players become the best players because they work bloody hard and never stop honing their skills. Playing in New Zealand even made me view the Haka in a different light, albeit still with all the respect it deserves as an incredible cultural tradition. When I was younger, I had the Haka on my iPod and I'd listen to it before games, whether we were playing against the All Blacks or in an ordinary Premiership game, to hype myself up. But when I met and became friends with All Blacks, I suddenly no longer found the Haka intimidating or threatening. I saw it for what it was: a magical challenge rooted in culture, delivered by people I then knew personally. Yes, at times it was hard to maintain eye contact with the aggressive stares of guys you'd been out for beers with. But that just about sums up any cultural experience – it can be magical, while also erasing some of the magic.

Playing with the likes of Aaron and Ben Smith in New Zealand and Ma'a Nonu in Japan, I learned that being ultimate professionals didn't necessarily mean doing things the same way. They had developed their own ways of doing things that worked for them and the greater good. At Stade Français, I discovered why Sergio Parisse was the best number eight in the world. He knew he was held in high regard by his coaches and team-mates, which meant he played with confidence and without fear of making mistakes. When a great player is allowed to play without fear of making mistakes, he'll take risks. Sometimes those risks won't come off, but more often they will and the team will benefit. Sergio taught me to be less hard on myself, to trust in my preparation and skillset, and play with more freedom. It was the same for foreign imports I played with in England. Australia flanker George Smith was coming towards the end of his career when he signed for Wasps, but working with him was special. He was so thorough, which is why he was so good. In fact, he was probably the best player I ever shared a changing room with. And when you know why someone is good, you can at least try to emulate them.

Every player should test himself in foreign environments if he's offered the chance, which is why I thought Maro Itoje being blocked from playing in France for a year was petty bullshit, because he would have learned so much. Maro's club Saracens had been relegated because of salary cap breaches, and he wanted to make the best of a bad situation by playing for Racing 92 for a season and making plenty of money doing it. But the Premiership club owners decided they'd rather see Maro playing against Hartpury in the Championship.

I absolutely loved my time in New Zealand and didn't want to leave. Jamie Joseph, who was a great guy and one of the best coaches I ever worked with, didn't want me to leave either. And had Tom Varndell not made a late, try-saving tackle on Sam Vesty against Bath in the penultimate game of the 2012–13 season – maybe the only tackle he ever made – and Wasps had been relegated, I would have stayed. But Wasps had made me a decent offer and I'd agreed to re-join them, as long as they were still playing in the Premiership.

I didn't exactly return to Wasps a conquering hero, but I did feel vindicated. Despite all the warnings, leaving England and trying something new hadn't been a terrible mistake. My stints in Japan and New Zealand proved I hadn't gone abroad for the money. I hadn't lost my place in the England set-up. I had worked bloody hard and become a better player. People could say what they wanted about my rugby ability, but I'd been a key component in every team I played for. That was so important to me. And players who had criticised me for leaving England were now taking me aside and saying, 'I wish I'd done what you did.' Not many have followed my lead.

9

TAKING FLAK

THE MEDIA

My attitude towards journalists was that I knew they had a job to do – but I didn't trust them because they'd stitch me up in a heartbeat. Wherever I played, there was widespread contempt for journalists. Some players would walk in the changing room and say, 'I can't believe what so-and-so has written about you. What planet is he on?' Others would nudge you in the ribs and say, 'Have you seen what so-and-so has written about you?' They'd do it for a laugh, but it would still irritate you. Even now I'm retired, if some journalists ask me for an opinion, I won't talk to them. Why would I, when they wrote so much nonsense about me when I was playing? I even block them on Twitter.

I'd always give journalists the benefit of the doubt, and some of them were fine. But there were plenty of weasels, and if someone did stitch me up, I let them know about it. I thought some of them wrote about sport because they weren't good enough to play it, which is why they were so cynical and vindictive. But the biggest problem with journalists is that they have to add spice, which means sensationalising everything and having strong opinions and angles. Their job demands it, that's how they sell newspapers and get punters to click on their stories. And if there is no angle, they'll chisel one out, which might involve knifing someone. Many players will ask friends and family to stop telling them bad things they've read about them, because it can be soul-destroying. I had to tell my dad to pack it in. He'd call me and say, 'James, so-and-so has given you 5 out of 10 ...'

'Thanks, Dad. Love you ...'

I was never openly contemptuous towards journalists because I knew it was a game and they had a job to do. I actually enjoyed dealing with the media and had a lot of fun deadpanning when they were trying to create a bit of hype.

'James, will there be a bit of extra spice on Saturday, because of what happened last time?'

'No. We're professional sportspeople, we don't hate anyone.'

'James, you must have been appalled by so-and-so's behaviour?'

'No. We're professional sportspeople, these things happen.'

If I liked a journalist, and they weren't asking daft questions, I'd have a nice chat with them. I understood that they could help me as much as I could help them – almost like a business transaction – which is why I tried to reveal as much of my real personality as possible. But I did have a couple of tactics when dealing with journalists whom I didn't like. I'd answer questions they didn't ask, or say, 'That's a terrible question. What are you trying to insinuate? I know your game.' Or if they'd written something unreasonable, I'd look them in the eye and say, 'I read what you wrote. It's not based on any truth.' They'd bluster and stammer, while trying to justify themselves, because they didn't like it up 'em. They might have thought I was being contemptuous, but I saw it as being honest. I'd also take the piss out of them because they're often such sensitive little sausages. At press conferences, I'd pick them up on their suspect hygiene and 'special' shoes or ask them if they got dressed in the dark.

No player likes to be slated, but I realise it's part of a journalist's job to criticise performances. Informed, constructive criticism is fine. What irritated me were some of the outlandish and ill-informed opinions, or what they called 'insight'. A journalist would write a story about some off-field, behind-the-scenes incident, the atmosphere in the changing room or a certain player's state of mind, and I'd read it and think, 'This is not what's going on. In fact, this bears absolutely no resemblance to what's happening.' Despite what they want their readers to believe, most journalists are just people looking into a house through a frosted window. Unless you're inside the house, you can't possibly know what's going on. So journalists spend a lot of time guessing. Even I don't claim to know what's going on, and I haven't been retired long.

There was also the constant flip-flopping. One week, Eddie Jones was the best thing since sliced bread. The next, he was out of his depth. One week, I was brilliant and should be in the England team. The next, I was terrible and everything that was wrong with England. And there was no accountability. They'd never put their hands up and say, 'Actually, I got that wrong about so-and-so.' Own it! Don't pretend you never said it! It's fine that you made a mistake, we all do. As a player or coach, all you want is for the media to be fair and consistent. But nuance isn't prized in rugby journalism. Does that person saying I'm suddenly terrible know why I played badly? Do they know that I'm carrying an injury? Has he or she even asked? I know it's difficult being a sports journalist nowadays because access to players is limited. But some of them don't even bother to try.

PLAYING GAMES

After Stuart Lancaster tried to befriend the media, they knifed him when things went wrong at the 2015 World Cup. Some pundits even suggested we weren't fit enough, which was complete nonsense. So, when replacing him, Eddie Jones soon worked out that they were going to write what they wanted, whatever happened and whatever he said. His attitude was, 'I don't really care what they write. Most of them don't know what they're talking about and there's no point pretending to be friends with them.'

When you call out journalists on their bullshit, they'll re-double their efforts to bring you down. Like when England lost to France in the 2020 Six Nations and some in the media made it out to be a catastrophe, despite the fact they'd beaten the All Blacks to reach a World Cup final only a few months earlier. But Eddie is a very clever man who knows exactly what he's doing. He never says anything he hasn't given a great deal of thought to – unless he's really annoyed about something – and has been playing games with the media ever since he took the job. Like the time he suggested he might move Jack Nowell from the wing into the back-row. That was the old magician's trick of showing the media something with one hand while doing something else with the other. He was just throwing some nonsense out there, knowing that the media would be all over it like dogs with a bone and losing their minds – 'Oh my God! What on earth is Eddie doing?' – leaving him to concentrate on the important stuff. Behind the scenes, Eddie would have been saying, 'Don't worry about those muppets, lads, we know what we're doing.' I used to love sitting back and watching the media get their knickers in a twist over that kind of stuff.

Eddie used to use me as a human shield, to blunt and frus-trate the media. For example, if we were playing Scotland, he'd

say to me, 'Right, Hask, I want you to go into the press conference and not mention Scotland once.' And I'd sit there and
stonewall for half an hour.

'James, what do you think about the new Scottish back-row
combination?'

'Well, obviously, I think we've got our preparations spot on.'

'James, are you surprised that Scotland have dropped
so-and-so?'

'Well, we'll be giving it 100 per cent, as we always do against
Scotland.'

The journalists would be looking at each other as if to say,
'This bloke is a pain in the arse.' But afterwards, Eddie would
give me a big grin and say, 'Brilliant, mate, I'm gonna buy you
a massage for that performance.'

Eddie has even managed to plug the leaks in the England
camp, which were a constant source of tension between
management and media. Before one autumn international
against South Africa, Martin Johnson pulled me aside and
said, 'We're going to put you in the team this week, but don't
tell anyone.' I hadn't played in the first two games of the
autumn internationals, so it wasn't expected. But the
following day, the *Telegraph* had a big headline: 'Haskell
recalled to beef up England.' Johnno went mad in the team
meeting. 'I can't believe this has happened. No-one speaks to
the fucking press!' As he was saying this, he was banging his
finger on a flip-chart with the team line-up written on it, right
next to my name. Afterwards, he said to me, 'Did you tell
anyone?'

'No. Honestly.'

'Are you sure you didn't tell your dad?'

'No!'

I could tell he didn't believe me, and all my team-mates
started calling me 'the mole'. England teams always got leaked

in those days, and I think I know who the real mole was, because it hasn't happened since he left.

PUNDITS

Some former players were as harsh as the career reporters. Paul Ackford, former England lock turned *Telegraph* journalist, seemed to hate me. After one game against South Africa, he gave me a 4 out of 10 and said my defence started to wane after half-time. That was one of my best games for England and I put in something like 35 tackles. He always had something negative to say about me, to the extent that it felt like a personal vendetta.

Those player ratings are often miles off because the journalists don't even watch the game. During the Lions tour, which I watched from the stands next to the media box, I would see journos with their heads down for 90 per cent of the first half, beavering away on their laptops. After England's Six Nations game against Wales in 2015, in which I famously ran into the post, the *Daily Mail*'s Sam Peters gave me a 4 out of 10 (sound familiar?), accompanied by some scathing words, despite the fact I was only just pipped to the man-of-the-match award by George Ford. His excuse was that he had to get the words submitted by half-time to make the next day's paper (it was a Friday night game), and I had missed a tackle that led to a try. He admitted that he'd got it wrong, but giving opinions on just the first half of a game is not fair at all. He was not the first person to do it, and he won't be the last.

Former England hooker Brian Moore once called me a 'half-wit' while commentating on a game between England and Italy, because I made a mistake and got sin-binned. Brian Moore, lest we forget, has a reputation as one of England's lairiest ever players. He also wrote that despite never having met me, he thought I was a wrong'un with my own website who was clearly obsessed with money, so I went on Twitter and said to him, 'How dare you judge me when you don't even know me?' A few years later, I did a radio show with him. It was just after the release of his autobiography, in which he wrote about being abused as a kid. He spoke about it so articulately and movingly that I said to him after the show, 'It was a real honour to listen to that, it's amazing that you've spoken out about it.' And he replied, 'I know we've had our spats on social media, but you really don't want to go up against someone like me, because I can make or break your career.' With that, he walked off and got in the lift. I honestly couldn't believe my ears.

I look at some pundits and think, 'You don't know what you're watching. This is not the same game you played.' What would astound most fans reading this is that half these outspoken journos have never once been into England camp, watched a session, spoken to the coaches or grasped what we are trying to achieve. For example, Paul Ackford, with all his bluster and hard words, never came in to interview any of us. Clive Woodward the same, Stuart Barnes the same. You can't be of an opinion on the national team with no knowledge of the national team. I know Lancaster got a couple of the usual no-shows in to explain what we were trying to do, but sadly they knifed him and wrote what they were going to all along. That's why Eddie's 'Fuck 'em, I'll say what I want' attitude is so loved by the players.

Ernest Hemingway said it better than I ever could. 'Critics are men who watch a battle from a high place then come down and shoot the survivors.' Remember that when you read your papers or go to tweet or post on social media. You have to be in it to win it. If you don't have direct inside knowledge, then you know next to nothing.

I sometimes feel like I'm not qualified to comment on rugby after not playing for 12 months, so I get very frustrated when I hear people commenting on rugby when they haven't played for decades. Clive Woodward is deservedly feted for leading England to World Cup glory in 2003 and I love him. But as a pundit, he does my head in. One week he'll say so-and-so is terrible and England should cast him into the wilderness, then a few weeks later he'll say England desperately need so-and-so back. As I've said, I don't mind people changing their minds, but you have to acknowledge you've changed your mind! And Clive must realise that when class players have a bad game, they haven't suddenly become bad players. Then Clive will start talking about what he would have done if he was still coach. That's madness. England have a completely different set of players from 2003 and Clive hasn't worked in rugby since 2005. It's now 2020 and things have moved on. He doesn't really understand the situation, yet he'll say all this stuff deadly seriously, as if it's gospel. What concerns me is that people look up to the likes of Clive for their knowledge of the game, and rightly so, but when most of it is sensationalist stuff just to get headlines, it can really muddy the water (and don't worry, I'd gladly say all this to his face).

I have current players on *The Good, The Bad and The Rugby* – just as I did with *House of Rugby* – because they're young, relevant and know what they're talking about. But I watch some of the television coverage and it's dry and dull. When the BBC had Dylan Hartley on as a pundit during the Six Nations, he made the others look out of touch. Dylan had only recently retired so had true insight. Wheeling out legends of the game is all well and good, and both Jonathan Davies and Jerry Guscott are true legends of the game and achieved feats I could only dream of, but both retired over 20 years ago! Often the same old message is put out there about the lack of flair in modern rugby and players not running into space, but there is no space in modern rugby. I am not entirely convinced a lot of these old boys would have lasted that long in the modern game. I know it's a moot point, as the players would have adapted to the game they were playing, and if the skill and talent is there, perhaps the mentality adjusts with it. Jerry Guscott, for example, was not a huge fan of tackling. In fact he didn't appear to like contact full-stop! Which is going to be tricky when most of the space you find on a rugby field these days is between a forward's ears.

When a lot of rugby fans reference the 'golden age of rugby', they're talking about a time when a lot of these legends-turned-pundits were playing. But when you watch those old games back, you realise that defending was almost optional, tacklers dived vaguely in the direction of attackers' legs and everyone fell over if someone did a double-dummy switch move. Just go onto YouTube and have a watch of some of these 'mega' games; it's like watching the Under-8s play now. Everyone is in a herd running from one side of the field to the other as soon as the ball gets into some space, and there are holes every-where, as the defence instead of being in a line seems to be resembling a sort of dot-to-dot. I believe most of those players and teams would get battered in the modern game.

Maybe it's because *The Good, The Bad and The Rugby* doesn't pretend to be straight punditry – me, Mike Tindall and Alex Payne don't talk about the week's action in forensic detail, because there are loads of other podcasts that do that, some of them very well – but I don't feel the need to criticise. If a player elbows someone in the face or kicks someone in the head, I'll obviously say what a terrible decision it was. But if they make a mistake or don't do something well, I'll be honest about it without being unpleasant. I can understand how play-ers tick because I was doing their job not long ago. My rule of thumb is, 'Be honest, but say nothing you wouldn't feel comfortable saying to someone's face.' But even though I try not to be unfair, I sometimes feel uneasy after recording a podcast. I worry if I've been too critical about a player or if a journalist will put a spin on it. I hate to think I might have pissed someone off or upset them. I even get my missus to listen, just to be certain.

Rugby punditry is easy from the commentary box, dissecting the game under no pressure, telling viewers how things should be done. But in the heat of battle, you don't see things that pundits see. You might only see them when you watch the game back. And when a game has taken a certain course, it's very hard for a team to come together and change things, especially when you're playing in front of 80,000 people in the Millennium Stadium, blowing out of your arse, it's so loud you can't hear your team-mates, and there's another team on the pitch stopping you from doing what you'd like to do.

There are journalists and pundits who are not much more knowledgeable than fans, in that they don't understand the game in any kind of detail. They'll see someone make an eye-catching break or put in a big hit and think that means they had a great game. But they don't notice a player's more subtle defensive work, organisational skills or physicality. It's possible for a player to have a great game and not really be noticed by the uninitiated.

HASKELL, YOU'RE SHIT

There are fans who are nice and polite and genuinely think they know what's going wrong with the team. One day, I was at Pennyhill Park with England and this silver-haired, middle-aged bloke came up to me and Dylan Hartley and said, 'I've got a letter for Eddie Jones, the contents of which will help England.'

Dylan and I looked at each other, trying not to laugh.

'What like?'

'Just a bit of advice about England's attack that will fix all your problems.'

We were both tempted to steam it open, because we do get some mad fan mail sent to the hotel, from bizarre pictures of fans in a state of undress, propositions for some no-strings fun and pure hate mail. I was also tempted to open it as there was part of me that thought this bloke maybe had the key to all our ills. I imagined the envelope to contain blueprints, charts, the meaning of life and GPS coordinates for the Holy Grail. But I handed it over to the boss, and when he showed it to us it was a bit of a let-down. The bloke had written, 'Modern rugby is all about deception ...', and asked if he could come in, watch a few sessions and he would then reveal some more secrets. I desperately wanted Eddie to invite him, but he wasn't having it.

Some rugby fans are very odd. I'll have people come up to me and say, 'Hello, mate. Big fan of yours, but I'm a Saracens supporter.' It's as if they think I'm going to shake my fist at them and reply, 'Grrr, be gone, you Sarries swine!' Instead, I'll reply, 'No worries. I like Saracens, too. I've got great friends at the club.' People think they have to apologise for who they support, but it's not tribal for players, like it is for fans. We don't give a shit about that kind of stuff. There might be individual players on other teams who you think are arseholes, but when you're playing 35 games a season, tribalism goes out of the window.

Sports fans are among the most irrational people on earth. So many of them have no concept of patience, what it takes to be a professional sportsperson, the structure of a team or the business. No player I've ever met has deliberately not given 100 per cent in a game, yet you'll hear fans say, 'He's not trying. He doesn't care about the shirt. He's not loyal to the club.' They think their team should win all the time, and think something is wrong if they don't, which is obviously ridiculous. If teams didn't lose sometimes, there would be no sport or betting industry.

Some rugby fans are so irrational, they think it's quite acceptable to tell you you're rubbish to your face. One afternoon, me and my old mate Doz were having a quiet drink in a pub in London and this bloke came over and said, 'Haskell, Haskell, how are you?'

'Good, mate, just having a beer.'

'Nice. I just wanted to say, I've watched you play for England quite a lot and you've often been shit, to be honest.'

'Thanks, mate.'

'Oh, I've seen you play a few good games as well.'

'Brilliant. What do you do, out of interest?'

'I'm an accountant.'

'Right. Well, imagine if someone you'd never met before walked into your office, strolled up to your desk and said, "Mate, you are a shit accountant most of the time. You don't get the best deal for your clients, you lose your company money. You're an embarrassment to your trade."'

'But that's not the case. I'm a good accountant. And I pay £80 to watch England play at Twickenham, so I'm allowed to give my opinion.'

'Yes, mate, you can have an opinion, but you don't have to share it directly with me.'

'No, you're wrong. If I want to tell you, I can.'

It was then that I gave Doz the special nause signal we came up with years ago, which was an SOS to get us the hell out of these types of conversation. Paul, spotting the signal, walked over, put a heavy arm around the bloke's shoulders, hugging him in tight, slightly picking him up so his toes were making minimal contact with the floor and said, 'Come on, mate, enough of that, let's go and find your friends.'

Judging by the accountant's level of chat, I think it may have been easier for Doz to find some dragon's eggs.

KEYBOARD WARRIORS

There have always been nutters about, offering opinions on anything they fancy, usually subjects they know nothing about. But back in the day, fans would watch a game and discuss it down the pub. The end. Now, they've got hundreds of different platforms, whether it's Facebook, Instagram, Twitter or whatever. The internet means sports fans feel more involved and closer to the action. But the vast majority of these people have never even played the game, let alone got anywhere near being a professional. Yet they go on social media and slag off players and coaches and tactics – 'Drop him! Sack him! He should never play again, the wanker!' – and presumably when they see how many likes their comment gets, they get a buzz from being part of the narrative. I don't get it, because I freely admit I'm not qualified to give an opinion on anything, except playing rugby and coffee, which I actually know a lot about.

There was a time when you lost a game and just got criticised by your coaches and the media, but now you can plumb straight into bollockings from thousands of angry people across the globe. People who think it's funny to abuse players on social media should be a fly on the window of an England coach after a loss. It will be deathly quiet, because players will be depressed about how they performed and wondering if they'll ever play for England again. And they'll be on their phones, looking at Twitter and Instagram, reading all this hatred. 'You're fucking shit!' Kill yourself!' 'Hang up your boots, you cunt!' It's basically a form of self-harming and a horrible thing to be a part of.

I hear people say, 'You put yourself out there, so you've got to expect to be shot at.' I don't accept that. No-one should expect to be abused. Most of these keyboard warriors wouldn't walk up to a player on the street and abuse them, because that would be harassment. If they did it too many times, their victim would call the police. But these people can harass people online to their heart's content, without fear of punishment. And if you do fire back at them, it can get you into trouble. One bloke messaged me on Twitter, telling me how shit I was at rugby, that I was a cunt, and that I should retire. I went back at him hard, having looked at his profile and gleaned all the ammo I needed, which was lots. Bizarrely the people with the least to shout about seem to shout the loudest, so I said some-thing along the lines of, 'Mate, your teeth are so yellow when you smile, cars slow down and your missus looks like she was set on fire and was put out with a hammer.' Strong, I will admit, but if you are going to go back, then I operate a full scorched-earth policy. Plus his teeth did look like he brushed with a hammer and his missus was unfortunate collateral damage. This bloke came straight back with a long, angry message, telling me how upset he was and that he'd be complaining to the RFU, and surely we as professional sports-men had codes of conduct and couldn't talk to a fan like that. He even implied that his wife had been through similar to what I described. He said, 'As for bringing my wife into it, after the recent unfortunateness that is unacceptable.'

I went back and said I was so sorry, I had no idea that his wife had actually been set on fire and put out with a hammer, which shows you that these people are so desperate to justify their behaviour, they will make up the weirdest lies. It turns out the trolls don't like being trolled.

Another time, someone blocked me in at the Ricoh car park on team run day (it turned out to be team-mate). Which was no mean feat as there are about 5,000 spaces, and it was pretty empty. So I filmed a little video, which consisted of me removing a metal fence from in front of my car and wrapping it around the car that had blocked me. This video got loads of views across various social media platforms, and it actually went viral, bizarrely. However, not everyone found it amusing. This one character sent me a particularly angry message, calling me every name under the sun, including a thick English cunt, and told me that if I had done that to him he would have knocked me out and burnt my car out. So I screenshotted his picture and posted it on Instagram and Facebook, with the message, 'If you have one rule in life, don't be like this bloke.' The problem was, everyone started hounding him, which meant he kept sending me these long, rambling messages, saying that even though I was a cunt, could I please take it down as he and his Mrs were getting abused. He contacted me on every channel, Twitter, Facebook, LinkedIn, with increasing urgency. However, he never once apologised in any of the messages, he just didn't like getting abused. It was bizarre and I kept ignoring him. Eventually he said, 'If you don't take your Instagram message down, I'm going to track you down and break your legs.'

I was sitting in my JCB, doing a bit of digging at a neighbour's house, when this message came through. And I was so angry that this bloke had threatened me – absolutely apoplectic – that I got straight on the phone to Doz. The moron's address was on his Facebook profile and he was only an hour's drive away. I don't consider myself to be a tough guy at all, but I said to Doz, 'This weasel has threatened me and I'm sick of it. I have his address and I am going go fuck him up, but it would be good to have some back up if you are around.'

Doz, appearing reserved on the phone and probably thinking he might be an accessory to GBH, obviously tried to calm me down, but because I was so wound up, I was intent on going through with it.

The best and worst thing about Doz, and why our friendship is so good, is if I say, 'Right, let's do something,' he says, 'Okay, I'm in,' which has led to some ill-conceived plans, some of which I have covered in this book and some you will never know about.

Luckily, on this occasion Doz's wife Zoe was in the car with him (hence the reservation in his voice) and they/she managed to talk me out of it. Had Doz not answered his phone, or if his wife hadn't been with him at the time, there's a chance I might have gone round to this bloke's house and given him a battering.

As an aside, it has to be said that Doz is a changed man these days. He even goes by 'Paul, the artist formally known as Doz'. And whenever I invite Paul out, I imagine he and Zoe have very similar conversations to Frank the Tank and his wife in the film *Old School*.

Paul: 'Can I go out with Hask?'

Zoe: 'Just as long as you promise to take it easy.'

Paul: 'What do you mean?'

Zoe: 'You know exactly what I mean. You've come a long way since Dozza and we don't want him coming back, do we?'

Paul: 'Honey, Dozza is not coming back, okay? That part of me is over. Water under the bridge. I promise.'

After one game, I posted something on Instagram and this kid replied, 'You're a wanker, mate!' Another wrote, 'You are gay,' another, 'What a prick,' etc etc. Because these people are often idiots, I was able to find out everything about the first kid just by clicking on his profile, as well as the fact that some of his mates had been abusing me too and they were all part of this little gang. And because I was bored, I phoned up his school, which happened to be in Twickenham, and spoke to the headmaster. He was very apologetic and promised to punish the miscreants accordingly, but I suggested I come into the school and speak to them instead, so that maybe they could learn a practical lesson from it.

A couple of weeks later, I visited this school with Chloe (I thought me turning up on my own – a 6 ft 3 in, 19-stone unit – might look a bit aggressive). We were shown into the head-master's office, before they wheeled in these ten tiny 12-year-old kids. I kicked off with, 'Guys, I think you had some things to say to me,' and one of them started crying. Undeterred, I said to the kid who had called me a wanker, 'I thought you wanted to call me something?' Obviously, none of them wanted to say anything to my face, so I said, 'Lads, I didn't come here because I was angry about what you said to me, I came here to teach you something I wish I'd learned earlier. I've made some mistakes on social media, said things I shouldn't have. But I eventually learned that you are accountable for the things you say online. And you don't really know who you are abusing online. They might be a nutcase and want to take revenge in person. And that horrible thing you wrote when you were a kid might come back to bite you when you go for a job interview, because this stuff doesn't just disappear.' I pointed out that it took me one click to find them, and that being online is a dangerous place. I was very calm and stayed seated the whole time. They all sent me written letters of apology, which I replied to individually – and when my team-mates found out what I'd done, they all started calling me a snitch. You can't win!

Sometimes, I'd have a pop back at someone and people would spring to their defence, like the time I told someone they looked like Ronnie Corbett in a dress. People went mental.

'You can't say that to someone!'

'That's bang out of order!'

'You're abusing your privileged position!'

'What if they've got something wrong with them?'

In the end, I stopped reacting. My wife said I should be more like The Rock. Would The Rock reply to people insulting him on Twitter or would he rise above it? Of course, The Rock rises above it. And if it's good enough for The Rock, it's good enough for me. Nowadays, if anyone is being horrible, I block them. It makes life much easier. A lot of players have done the same, or come off social media completely. I can understand it, because the abuse piles up so fast you need a pair of wings to stay above it.

Problem is, you can't block people who comment on newspaper articles. And they're so bloody tempting, the online equivalent of crack. Newspaper comments' sections are where people's souls go to die. I imagine those commenters sitting at home in their pants, wallowing in misery, feeling unloved by anything apart from their cats, typing away in the dark, the glow of the laptop on their angry, sweaty faces. I once made the mistake of reading the comments under an article about me, and it wasn't the smartest move. One person had written, 'You can sum up everything that's wrong with English sport – not just rugby – in two words: James Haskell.' Another person had written, 'James Haskell is the rugby equivalent of an unflushable turd.'

10

CELEBRITY

THE FIRST BRUSH

My first brush with fame came when I was a teenager at Wasps. Me and a few other academy players were invited to a now extinct event held for a Cheltenham Ladies charity. John 'Bentos' Bentley, ex-England and British and Irish Lions, was the compere, and when we turned up, he said, 'It's gonna be an interesting night, lads. Make no mistake. When I announce your name, you'll walk in, they'll go wild and you'll take a seat at the table that makes the most noise. We've got 300 ladies in the house and there will be some opportunities that you will need to consider very carefully.' Bear in mind that I was only 17.

We were in this bar adjacent to the main room and all we could hear was the laughing and screaming of 300 women. It was similar to that scene in *Gladiator* when the lads are waiting to enter the Coliseum. I didn't think I'd actually get eaten, but I couldn't be sure. When Bentos walked out, the noise almost blew our heads off. It was like Queen taking to the stage at Live Aid. And once he'd restored some semblance of order, which took about five minutes, he started introducing us in his unmistakable Yorkshire brogue.

'Ladies, the first young man we have for you is a young Harlequins player called Ugo Monye. He's fast as they come, good-looking, I think you'll like him …'

Ugo got ushered through the doors and the place went berserk. It was like these women had been locked in this room for a year, with only champagne for sustenance. There were knickers flying everywhere, stocking tops being shown, and Ugo was put in a headlock and dragged to the nearest table. It reminded me of the toothy-mouthed monster in *Return of the Jedi* or the giant Venus flytrap in *Little Shop of Horrors*, Ugo basically being fed to women.

Now I was absolutely shitting myself. Dry mouth, sweat trickling down my back, gulping down air. The noise from the room was vibrating the doors that I was standing behind. The baying for blood was reaching a crescendo. These ladies were hungry, and Kitty needs to eat.

And then I heard the fateful words.

'Next up, a young lad from Wasps. He's tall, he's handsome – some people are calling him the new Lawrence Dallaglio – put your hands together for James Haskell!'

I slowly pushed the doors open and had only put one foot in the room when a woman grabbed me by the tie and started pulling me towards her table, like a farmer with a prize heifer. Her mates were grabbing my wrists and ruffling my hair and probably doing lots more that I was far too numb to notice. And when I finally sat down, having been touched more times than Michael Palin's passports, I slowly started to get a grip on things and began thinking that tonight was going to be a good night after all. Once I had straightened my tie, closed my torn shirt, and clocked a few promising faces, I decided to take a seat at the closest table. Just as I was ready to release the handbrake, the woman next to me said, 'I've just been diagnosed with cancer.'

Which as you can imagine slightly tempered the mood. I have to say, however tragic it was, it's a bit of a strong opening gambit, not even to say your name before you hit me with that bombshell. I came straight back down to earth faster than Felix Baumgartner.

'Wow, I am so sorry, I hope you are okay.'

Thinking that perhaps this was not going to be quite the table I had hoped for and looking for a smoke-bomb exit, I looked across the room. Ugo had about five different women kissing his face and another woman's hand on his inner thigh. My confidence was restored. Luckily, we rotated courses, and without writing a kiss and tell, the night was not unsuccessful.

BANTER

If I do qualify as a celebrity, I am Z-list. Bottom rung. Barely on the ladder. As far as I'm concerned, unless you're someone as famous as Tom Cruise, Ricky Gervais or Beyoncé, you're just scrabbling around on the floor for crumbs. When I attended the National Television Awards, I had to queue up for the red carpet and found myself being bumped out of the way by reality TV stars. I'm not going to lie to you, that gave me the hump. I thought, 'I had an actual job before I did reality TV. In fact, I've got more jobs than you'll find in a job centre. And I'm being jostled aside before I even reach the red carpet by some bloke who is kind of famous for lying on a sun lounger for a few weeks, drinking sangria and chatting up women, all so he can have his photo taken and maybe appear in a *Daily Mail* article about the awards' best-dressed people.' The actual big-timers get whisked through, while the rest have to fight it out like cattle, all trying to get papped, each person thinking they are better than the next. People were jumping the queue all over the place. This other bloke was screeching hysterically and waving his arms in my face. He bumped into me about four times, then skipped the queue. It crossed my mind to punch him in the back of the head, perhaps not a good look with all the media and super-keen fans in attendance. In the end I said to Chloe, 'Fuck me. This is great and all that, but I'm not doing it again.' Luckily, I don't think I will ever get invited back. I've had my moment in the sun.

I remember sitting on the back of the coach once with my old Wasps team-mate Simon Shaw and he said to me, 'Hask, you are desperate to be famous.' And it didn't matter how many times I told him I wasn't, he wouldn't have it. But being famous for the sake of being famous holds no interest for me. What Shawsey failed to understand is that I just want to make a bit of money so I can have a comfortable life and a few nice things. And to make a bit of money, I have to put myself in certain situations that raise my profile. If I could make millions of pounds without being famous, I'd do it. On the other hand, I remember going to a family party when I was a kid and my dad introducing me to a former England player. I shook his hand but had no idea who he was. Afterwards, my dad said to me, 'Why were you not more excited? He played 60 times for England!' That's why I never turn down a request for a chat, selfie or autograph, because I'll be that player in a few years' time, faded into obscurity.

When I did get recognised as a player, it was usually lovely. It was an honour and a privilege that people knew who I was, because it suggested I was good at my job. But sometimes when someone asked me for a selfie or an autograph, I'd think, 'Why are you asking for my autograph? You should be asking for that nurse's autograph over there. I didn't help anyone, all I do is chase a ball around a field and hit people.' Other times, people would be shaking so much that they couldn't hold the camera still, and I'd think, 'Come on, mate, relax, I'm really not that important.' My wife hates it when she's trying to have a serious conversation, or worse still an argument with me, which I have probably caused, and some bloke marches over, completely ignores her and roars, 'Hask! Can I just shake your hand? You are a bloody legend!' Most people can see if a couple are having 'words', but these people don't care, they just barge in anyway. Chloe will stand there fuming, desperately wanting to say, 'He's not a legend, he's a fucking prick.' People pumping up your tyres can make you lose your grip on reality, but that's not likely to happen to me with Chloe around, thank God.

Most people are nice and polite, but not everyone. People film and take photos of me while pretending not to. Or walk past, point and shout, 'Fucking hell, it's James Haskell!' Or 'Hask! Hask! Hask!' at the top of their voices, as if I'm going to break into a big smile and give them a hug. Recently, I was doing a live *House of Rugby* podcast, we invited some people on stage and some bloke said, 'Haskell, you're a fucking cunt.'

'Sorry? What?'

'You love it, you cunt.'

So it went on. When I had a photo with him and his mates, he got all arsey because I wouldn't then shake his hand.

'Come on, Hask, shake my hand.'

'Let me explain something to you. I've never met you before and you just called me a cunt five times. That's very rude and inappropriate.'

'Fucking hell, Hask, but I thought you love the banter!'

Then there are the people who come up to me and say, 'I thought you were a wanker, but you seem all right.' Why would you say that to someone? And what are you meant to say in response? Thanks? Or the people who don't know what to say, panic, look at my hair and say, 'Mate, you're going bald. Time to shave your head.' People meet me and seem to feel the need to banter – and I learned to hate that word. I've used it many times in the past, but it seems to have become synonymous with being a prick to someone.

One time, this young guy came up to me looking very sheepish at a live show and said, 'Hi, I think I was very rude when I met you last time. I'm sorry and I hope you accept my apology.' I actually remembered him – he had said something like, 'My Mrs says we look the same, except I am not going bald,' then laughed to himself nervously.

I was shocked and said thank you so much. It was the first time ever that someone realised they had gone too far and apologised. I shook his hand and said no worries, that's really kind of you to take the time to say sorry.

NAUSES

The fact that rugby players aren't footballers, cash and fame-wise, is good in some ways, but not in others. For example, at no point in my career did I have women (normal women, not Cheltenham women) throwing themselves at me. Instead, I got invited to a lot of children's parties, or Harry Potter-themed parties or to DJ at people's weddings for the princely sum of a 'couple of pints with the lads', which I never went to or did, for obvious reasons. You soon learn to be wary of people hanging around and invading your personal space, which some fans find hard to understand and take badly. If you're not playing a lot, because you're injured or are bin juice, you end up being dragged to a lot of corporate dos and seeing the same old faces, who can get very in your face and nausey, because they make the mistake of thinking they're your friends.

One fan asked Trevor Leota to be godfather to his baby. Trevor obviously didn't turn up to the christening, but

Lawrence Dallaglio's mum did, and ended up being stitched up as godmother. Imagine trying to get out of that one.

There was another Wasps fan who was really into darts. He very much reminded me of Jed from *I'm Alan Partridge* ('I'm just a fan, James, your biggest fan ...'). He'd come up to me and say, in this thick Lancashire accent, 'Do you like darts?'

'No.'

'Are you sure you don't like darts?

'Yes.'

'Oh, I made you a darts board.'

He'd got a circle of wood and drawn the numbers on by hand, not even using a ruler for the measurements. He had made the classic mistake of going too big with the 20 and then had to squish the other numbers in. He may or may not have had a tattoo of my face on his chest and drunk tea from an Arielator. Unlike Partridge, I never made the mistake of ending up in his living room.

At Northampton, a fan made some brownies for Dozza, and being the streetwise man he is, he didn't touch them but offered them around. Tom May was the first cab off the rank and bit into one excitedly. The smile of delight on his face quickly turned into pure dread. This particular treat contained more than chocolate and nuts. It was full of hair, from fuck knows where. He was retching into a bin in the corner, while the rest of the lads were on the floor laughing. A rule to live by is if a fan makes you anything, lob it in the bin without hesitation. Nothing good can come of it.

On my mate's first day in Gloucester, a woman came up to him in the street and said, 'You're the new signing, aren't you? Great to have you at the club. I don't know if you're single or not, I've got no tits and a fanny that doesn't work, but I'd love to have a go on you.' I mean, what a thing to say to someone.

Surprisingly enough, even knowing the bloke as well as I do, he turned her down and went off reeling down the street in a daze, thinking, 'What the fuck?'

Then there was the bloke who kept messaging the lads, asking for their used pants; the bloke who kept asking for photographs of players' feet (usually in rugby socks); and the bloke who kept saying he'd pay to watch us pleasure ourselves. The lads would walk into the changing room and very casually say, 'Has that bloke contacted you recently?'

'Yes. He wants to see you wank off, but says he isn't gay, that the one?'

In the end, I called his bluff and told him I was up for doing a show for him if the money was right. He never replied. I out-sickoed the sicko.

As for celebrity fans, they're thin on the ground. The vast majority have no idea who I am, which became abundantly clear at the National Television Awards. The journalist Martin Bashir, who made his name making Michael Jackson look suspiciously like a paedo, is a big fan. And I once made eye contact with Ricky Gervais and he gave me a nod (which as a super-fan was the greatest day ever for me). He didn't say anything, and immediately went off to talk to someone more famous than me – which could have been almost anyone else in the room – but I'm almost certain he knew who I was, and I'm happy with that.

I did go to Harry and Meghan's wedding, where there were some proper big names. That afternoon, I was chatting to Tom Hardy, as you do, and someone tapped me on the shoulder. I spun around to see Elton John with his husband David Furnish. Elton said, 'James, how are you?', and I spent the next few minutes telling him how much I loved him, especially in the movie *Kingsman: The Golden Circle*, where he cameoed as himself. His character is a diva who shouts at everyone and tells them to fuck off. He beckoned me closer and said, 'To be honest, James, I didn't really have to act.'

Tom Hardy was yesterday's news. He could have dropped down dead beside me and I wouldn't have noticed. Elton Fucking John: what a legend.

THE JUNGLE

How I went from chatting to Elton John at Harry and Meghan's wedding to sitting in a jungle chatting to Minty out of *EastEnders* is a tortuous tale. I'd been asked to do *I'm a Celebrity* ... a few years earlier but was still playing and didn't think taking the time off would go down very well. Then after I retired, I was asked to do *Strictly Come Dancing* but didn't think that was a good idea either, because everyone seems to end up shagging each other. It must be hard to pretend to be sexy with someone for 12 hours a day without actually getting sexy. So many relationships have bitten the dust because of it, and I wasn't sure I'd last long anyway because of my various injuries and the fact that I move like a cow on roller skates.

Then *I'm a Celebrity* ... got back in touch and said they wanted me and Chloe to be the first couple to do it. Then they changed their minds because they were worried that me and Chloe would spend the whole time hanging out together, as if we were a couple of lovesick teenagers. So they asked if I wanted to do it on my own. I'd never wanted to do reality TV because I thought it was dangerous. First, me on camera 24 hours a day didn't sound like a good idea, because I'd struggle to get through a couple of hours without saying something 'problematic'. I'm also not very good at dealing with miserable, opinionated people. And the chances of encountering a few of them in the jungle seemed quite high. So I ummed and ahhed before finally saying yes.

I joined eleven other contestants going into the jungle: former Girls Aloud singer Nadine Coyle, *Good Morning Britain's* Kate Garraway, reality TV star Caitlyn Jenner, actress Jacqueline Jossa (spoiler alert: the eventual winner), radio DJs Roman Kemp and Adele Roberts, comedian Andrew Maxwell, Cliff Parisi out of *EastEnders*, Myles Stephenson from boyband Rak-Su, football pundit Ian Wright and *Corrie's* Andrew Whyment.

Beforehand, I was obviously a bit worried about the nutrition side of things. I was 122 kg when I went in, which is just over 19 stone, and putting away about 4,500 calories a day. I knew food was going to be an issue for me, but when they assured me I'd get a minimum of 1,200 calories a day, I thought that was probably manageable. But on day one, I discovered that each meal equated to about four spoonfuls of rice and four spoonfuls of beans. That didn't amount to 1,200 calories a day; it was nearer to 150 calories for 90 per cent of the day. When you're as big as me, that's quite dangerous. So after a few days, I started freaking out. I just could not stop thinking about food. There were times when I felt like crying. Just the act of getting up made me exhausted and I got dizzy walking up stairs. My way of dealing with the boredom was to do things, like collect the water. Which by the end meant as soon as I had done one trip, I was gasping for air as if I were playing the All Blacks, my vision was blurry, and I had to lie down and sleep.

Because no-one knew about rugby or me, I didn't have to be the usual James Haskell, full of bravado. I could just be nice. I kept telling myself: don't take the piss out of anyone, just be kind and supportive. I tried to imagine it was a pre-season camp with a load of weird new team-mates, terrible accommodation and training sessions consisting of collecting buckets of water, cooking rice and drinking kangaroo testicle milkshakes.

I loved sitting around chatting and telling stories, and particularly enjoyed getting to know Caitlyn Jenner. She was one of the most inspirational people I've ever met, an absolute hero. The only problem with Caitlyn was that she was deaf as a post. She had hearing aids, but had set the volume through her iPhone before they confiscated it and set it far too low. She was like those two old spinsters from *Fawlty Towers*, constantly mishearing things. It made for some comedy moments that I will never forget. I used to have to stop her wandering off mid-scene, and she would then shout at me for telling her off. We were like a very funny married couple. She is such a legend, and what she achieved and went through is insane.

It wasn't all plain sailing. I had a weird row with Kate Garraway about chivalry, of all things, snapped at Andy Whyment after he wouldn't stop going on about a roast dinner a few of us were treated to and he missed out on, and after one argument, I had to lock myself in the dunny and let off some steam. They were trivial disagreements that in a normal setting would have been forgotten in seconds. But this wasn't a normal setting. We were in a jungle, with a load of strangers, with hardly any food, with a load of cameras pointed at us. It didn't help that the people who made the programme were terrified of anyone saying anything that some viewer in Tunbridge Wells might have been offended by.

One night, Andrew Maxwell said to me, 'If things get desperate, the first person we're eating is you. As soon as you fall asleep, we'll be all over you with our knives.' A few of the others joined in, the joke being, of course, that because I was miles bigger than everyone else, I'd make the best meal. The following day, we were all lying around the makeshift camp fire, basking in the sun. Andrew was getting into me again, calling me 'Lunk', which was his nickname for me, saying that as soon as I drifted off it was meal time.

I said, still lying on the ground, 'I tell you what, Maxwell, I'm going to take that big kitchen knife and open you up like a holdall, so we've got something to carry the food around in.'

It was obviously a joke. He laughed, Ian Wright laughed, Kate laughed, hell I even laughed at my own joke. But later that day, I got called to the Bush Telegraph room and was told to stop making jokes about murdering people. Apparently, I was scaring the senior producers. The fact that I had been on the menu was lost on them. That really upset me, and to be honest I felt like walking out. Just because I looked big and apparently scary, I was being threatening. It was a wake-up call that I was being pigeon-holed from the off.

Then there was the story with Cliff Parisi, Minty from *EastEnders*. The whole time he was in there, I kept telling him to eat. He wasn't even eating the rations he was getting because he didn't like the food, which meant he was asleep all the time. One day, he started having palpitations and passed out, so I volunteered to do the next challenge for the both of us. But before I went off to do it, Cliff took me aside and told me to lose on purpose, so that he could go home. The challenge turned out to be a drinking race (blended pig's brains, among other things, naturally), so I won my race and threw Cliff's race as he'd asked me to do. I wasn't prepared to get Myles Stephenson nominated to leave for a bloke who had asked me to lose for him. Little did I know that back in camp, Cliff was being interviewed and telling them that he thought I'd do my best to save him, which then of course made me look like a bit of a bastard. Especially as Caitlyn didn't hear me say off air (no hearing aid, of course) that I was going to make it look convincing but lose, as Cliff had asked me to. She said on camera rather too loudly, 'Don't beat Myles.' I replied, 'Don't worry Caitlyn, it's not my first rodeo.' This was beamed out live to the nation.

So not only do I make women go first, and stop northerners asking about roasts, I now fuck off TV heritage.

But while I was in the jungle, I thought it was going okay. I was bonding with people, exchanging stories, getting stuck in to the challenges and generally being a good campmate. I spent 99 per cent of my time making sure that those who were struggling were okay. I would go up to each campmate and help them. I wasn't really arsed about anything except the lack of food. Years of being a sportsman had prepared me to deal with pressure and compartmentalise. So when I got voted out and left the jungle, I got quite a shock. Back at the hotel, Chloe told me the horrible truth, which was that after the first two weeks, when I had come across as favourite to win, I had then been edited to look like an ogre and a bully. I couldn't believe it. I was for a short time public enemy No. 1. And it had been far worse for Chloe. She'd been dealing with all this shit on my behalf, trying to defend my honour. She'd even gone on TV's *Lorraine* to fight my corner.

I kept asking her, 'Did they show the conversation we had about men's mental health?'

'Nope.'

'What about the conversation about gender equality?'

'Nope.'

'What about when I was comforting Roman?'

'Nope.'

'Me bonding with Caitlyn?'

'Nope.'

I'd been naïve. I knew they had to edit things to create certain storylines and drum up a bit of drama, but I honestly didn't think they edited people to look horrible when they weren't. Thinking that everyone in Britain now thought I was a bully was difficult to take. Especially when I thought I'd made lots of new friends and made a decent fist of it. The day after leaving the jungle, I had to sit in a room with all the contestants' family and friends. Bear in mind, I've now discovered that they all think I was bullying Kate and Andy and stitching up Cliff, because they only see what's been edited. Kate's husband and kids were giving me side-eye, Cliff's wife wasn't talking to me because she thought I'd got her husband thrown out. I was really anxious because I honestly thought my life had been ruined. It sounds melodramatic, but I was incredibly tired, over-emotional, and felt so isolated and vulnerable.

Only when I did an interview for the *Extra Camp* programme did I think that everything might be all right. They did the segment where I watch my campmate's reactions to me leaving, and they were all lovely about me. Jacqueline cried and said I'd been like a big brother to her; Roman cried as well and said what a great support I'd been; Ian said he didn't know how he was going to get through the rest of it without me; and Caitlyn said to Ant and Dec that me being voted out had 'ripped the heart out of the camp'. It was one of the most emotional moments in my life. And one of the best. I sobbed uncontrollably at the table, because of the relief and because I'd never heard a group of people be so nice about me. Ant and Dec said on TV that they had never in 19 shows seen a reaction to someone leaving like that. Everyone's reactions was all I needed, having my camp team-mates' approval is all that has ever mattered. It doesn't matter what the media say, what the fans say, if your peers respect and like you, then that is all you need. I'm not sure what that says about rugby players, but it's the truth.

That saved me. Suddenly, the *Sun* were doing stories about *I'm a Celebrity* ... fans being furious that they'd been 'duped' into thinking I was a bully. Unsurprisingly, they wondered why my campmates seemed so upset about me leaving when I'd been portrayed as this horrendous, overbearing ogre. And they concluded that the editors had stitched me up. It was my life in miniature. Now, people who only know me from the jungle come up to me and say, 'I thought you were great on *I'm a Celebrity* ...' And, unlike rugby fans, they don't feel the need to add, 'I thought you were a dickhead before that.'

11

RETIREMENT

A FRUSTRATED SPECTATOR

I'd always been adamant that if I was no longer good enough and the door to playing for England was closed, I'd hang up my boots and do something else. Sportspeople are always the first to know if they've no longer got it, but sometimes they are the last to admit it. I'd see players continue to plod on when they were well past their sell-by date, only being picked on reputation and keeping a younger, better player out of the team. I didn't want that to be me.

I suffered a toe injury in 2016 that was very difficult to recover from but managed to fight my way back into the England team. However, I also started to take notice of what other people were saying. And when they're talking about your age and suggesting you're not quite the player you were, that worms its way into your head. Instead of thinking, 'Don't listen to them, you can get through this,' you start thinking, 'Maybe I should just pack it in.'

I did a lot of work with my psychologist, who kept saying to me, 'Stop talking about yourself like that. You might not be able to do some of the things you used to, but you're still as good as these young kids, and with more experience.' And for a while, she was right. I played some of my best games for England under Eddie Jones and was man of the series in our whitewash of Australia in 2016. But an ankle injury I picked up over years of playing flared up again at Northampton at the end of 2018 and effectively finished me off. My wife said it was like watching me voluntarily torture myself. Every day, I'd spend hours at the club I loved, with team-mates I loved, but I was a frustrated spectator, because I couldn't actually play the game I loved. One day, a drunk wandered into Franklin's Gardens while we were having a training session. I went over to show him towards the exit and he started shouting in my face, 'You're shit! Why are you bothering? You're never gonna play for England again, you are finished!' I kept my cool and helped him out. It was odd because his words really hurt. It was such a shock that I knew he was talking directly about me through his drunken haze. I so didn't want him to be right, but sadly I only played twice more for Saints after that.

I saw countless experts, got second, third and fourth opinions, and eventually someone said that the only option was fusion surgery. I was never coming back from that. And who was going to sign me anyway? I was hardly a young buck. I felt like I hadn't achieved everything I should have achieved in rugby and desperately wanted to play for England in the 2019 World Cup, especially after the 2011 and 2015 debacles. I'd even fantasised about lifting the trophy ... and the book deals ... and the Haskell action dolls ... but I just couldn't do it anymore. Just like the drunk said, it was time to admit defeat.

WHAT AM I?

When I told my Northampton team-mates I was retiring, I cried like a baby. I didn't expect that (I didn't even cry on my wedding day, as Chloe was quick to point out), but I probably should have. The end had come a lot sooner than I'd imagined, because I still felt like I was 21 and as competitive as ever. I felt like I'd let the club and my team-mates down because they'd welcomed me, my wife and my family with open arms after my bad ending with Wasps. And I'd also failed to prove the fans wrong, especially those that thought I was a bad signing and let me know about it. Including the drunk.

For 25 years, I'd spent almost every waking hour trying to be the best rugby player I could be. And now what was I? I felt like the prison librarian Brooks from *The Shawshank Redemption*, suddenly having to contemplate life in the real world. I didn't think I was going to hang myself in a cheap hotel, but I did feel institutionalised. I worried how I'd cope without daily structure or goals at the end of the week. I worried that I'd lose my identity and be unsure of my place in the world. I wondered what would happen to all that adrenaline that I was used to channelling into rugby. Many ex-players had told me how hard they'd found retirement. Some had struggled with depression and other mental illnesses. Others had struggled to find a new purpose in life. Some people, usually those who had never played professional sport, would say to me, 'You'll be fine. Just think of all the things you achieved.' I tried that but it didn't make any difference. I still thought I could have done more. And I was still terrified.

But forget about the discipline and the training and the games, the thing that scared me most was that I'd no longer have team-mates. What would life be like without the sheer excitement – and excitement is exactly the right word – of a team-mate walking into the changing room wearing a terrible pair of new shoes? Or with a bad haircut? Or having done something awful on a night out? That's what I loved most about rugby, that wonderful camaraderie. A load of lads, all different personalities thrown together as a team, sitting around in a changing room taking the piss, chatting nonsense and having a good old sappuccino. I wasn't afraid of no longer hearing the cheering, I was afraid of no longer hearing the laughter.

NO LONGER THE DICKHEAD

It was that camaraderie that nursed me through the first few days of retirement. There were dozens of calls and messages from former team-mates, opponents and coaches from all over the world, plus glowing tributes in the media. I didn't know how to take it, because when you're playing, compliments from your peers are few and far between. That's just how professional sport is. But people telling me what they really thought was a great boost, because the respect of your peers is all a sportsperson really craves. Journalists even wrote positive things about me, but what really blew me away was the reaction from the public. There must have been several thousand messages on various social media platforms, which genuinely shocked me. I read every one of them, and 99 per cent were complimentary. One person wrote, 'Why did it take for him to retire for people to be so nice to him?' They had a point.

Throughout my rugby career, I was portrayed as a dickhead by the media. It never made much sense, because if I was actually a dickhead why would some of the greatest coaches in rugby – Warren Gatland, Shaun Edwards, Michael Cheika, Jamie Joseph, Eddie Jones – have loved working with me? But that's the way it almost always was. Matt Hampson has said that before we shared a room with England Under-21s, he thought I was going to be a dickhead, simply because I was posh. Every club I went to, team-mates thought I was going to be a dickhead. I would walk into the changing room, look at people's body language and know they were thinking, 'Oh God, I've heard all about this bloke …' When I got into the England team, team-mates thought I was going to be a dickhead. When new players came into the England squad, they thought I was going to be a dickhead (when Ellis Genge came on *House of Rugby*, he said he wanted to hit me on his first day in the changing room). When I got picked for the Lions, players from other countries thought I was going to be a dickhead. Rory Best says that when he heard I'd been called up to replace the injured Billy Vunipola, his first reaction was, 'Oh, for God's sake, why him?' But I became great friends with Rory and his fellow Irishmen Sean O'Brien and Johnny Sexton. Like just about everyone else who thought I was going to be a dickhead, they soon realised that I was a great craic and a good guy. In fact, everything I'd been in the jungle but that the bastards had edited out. Now, players from all over the world come on *House of Rugby* and tell me what a great team-mate I was, which is all I ever wanted to be.

LAYING THE GHOST TO REST

When I first retired, people honestly thought I'd become so addicted to piss-taking that they started asking Chloe if I was now unloading it all on her, as if she were now a surrogate team-mate. They assumed that I was walking into the living room, putting in a big tackle on Chloe and roaring, 'Fucking hell! Look at the state of your shoes! What the fuck have you done with your hair? Have you ever thought about getting your teeth done?'

In truth, Chloe was more worried about me. Any sportsperson will tell you how important it is to have a supportive partner. Sportspeople are, by their very nature, selfish individuals. They have to be, at least the successful ones. I'd have to wake up at the right time, go to bed at the right time, eat exactly the right food at the right time, train at the right time. It caused a lot of problems during my career, because girlfriends would have to fit their lives around mine. They could only go on holiday when I could, they didn't see me at weekends, I'd disappear for months with England in the summer. When I was injured, I could be a nightmare. When the team lost, I could be withdrawn. When I got dropped, I could be difficult. If I didn't know whether I was going to be picked or not, I'd be on edge all week. I might come home one day, announce I'd signed for a team in France, Japan, New Zealand – or Northampton – and ask if they'd like to drop everything and come with me. A sportsperson's life is a never-ending rollercoaster, with your partner strapped in next to you. So while you might be upset when they dump you, you can't really blame them.

When I first met Chloe, she didn't give a shit about rugby or want anything to do with me. But a few days later, I was out on a Wasps team social in Richmond, gave her a call and asked her to come down. She didn't fancy it, so I hit her with the killer line: 'Look, I want to go home with someone tonight and I'd like it to be you.' What a charmer. Chloe claims that I told her right at the beginning after our first row about me being selfish and not being able to plan ahead – 'Let me be very clear, this is the James Haskell train, and either you're on it or you're not.' Chloe understood what I was trying to say. She accepted my obsessive routine. She compromised her own career to fit her life around mine. When we went out and random people talked to me and completely ignored her, she bit her tongue.

She learned enough about the game that I could discuss it with her but didn't bang on about it all the time. I'd heard team-mates' partners analysing games in great detail, criticising the refereeing and tactics, and the wife of one England coach would completely lose her shit and bully him if the team lost. At one event, she poured a pint of beer over his head, which was embarrassing to witness.

After the Six Nations game against France in 2015, when I got yellow-carded and people accused me of costing England the title on points difference, I could see Chloe looking at me, all mortified and depressed, and thinking, 'What have I got myself into?' But she likes the task of making people feel better. It's not as if she strokes my head and whispers, 'Are you all right, Pudding?' But she does liken it to trying to coax a toddler out of a sulk.

'James, would you like pizza?'

'No.'

'It's got lots of pepperoni on it.'

'Oh, go on then …'

'What about a nice glass of whisky?'

'Yes!'

For two or three years, Chloe watched me fight tooth and nail to recover from injuries and get myself back on the pitch. She'd seen me getting out of bed in the morning like an old man, in terrible pain. A couple of times when I was in hospital with an injury having surgery, she would ask to sleep beside me, even though the hospital said she couldn't or that they had no beds. She would not take no for an answer and would even pay her own money to get one. She always insisted on staying just to take care of me. When I had the toe injury and ankle surgery and could barely move, she did everything for me, and I mean everything. Many sportsmen's partners aren't like that. They're not interested in the hard times. They're good-time girls who are just in it for the perks, often until they run out.

Chloe would sometimes say, 'You know it's going to end?' That's when we started having lots of conversations about the inevitable. She was incredibly supportive, as well as realistic, and brought a lot of sense and clarity to the situation. We spent a lot of time identifying problems that might arise in retirement, such as mental health issues, and how I could keep them at bay. And together we planned for the future.

I thought I made the transition quite seamlessly, at least after the initial concerns. I did a lot of travelling – including our honeymoon, finally – and let my hair down in a way I hadn't been able to do before. My mum and dad seemed more heartbroken than I was. For 25 years, so much of their time had been taken up with my rugby, whether I was playing for the local minis or for England. And suddenly it was finished. I just hoped my retiring would at least reduce the stress in their lives. Every bad write-up they read about me, whether it was about an on-field performance or some off-field scandal, they took to heart. And if the media weren't talking about me, my dad would want to know why. My dad's a fun guy, my mates love spending time with him, he's a bit of a legend. But if I played a bad game, he'd get down, just wouldn't know how to compute it. After that yellow card against France in 2015, he couldn't even look at me, out of sheer disappointment for me. He knew that I might not get another chance, and what the media would say. But now I've hung up the boots, I want my mum and dad to stop worrying and relax, safe in the knowledge that I'm grateful for everything they've done. Because of them, I've had a great life.

But while I thought I was coping well with being an ex-rugby player, Chloe will tell you I was a bit all over the place for the first few months. And she'd be right, because in my head I was still a rugby player – an England rugby player – and not ready to give that up. But Eddie Jones inviting me into England's World Cup camp for a week in the build-up to the tournament and then during the final week, made a huge difference. I got to hang out with the lads one last time, share some laughs, have a coffee and moan like the old days, and even do a bit of training. And when Eddie thanked me for everything I'd done for England in front of the team, I got quite emotional.

I left that camp a different person. I'd laid the ghost to rest. Suddenly, I wasn't a rugby player. And, more importantly, I was okay with that. It helped that I was more prepared for retirement than most sportspeople because I'd always had other interests. When Matt Hampson broke his neck and severed his spinal cord, that was a game-changer for me. Seeing a team-mate go down on the training ground and stay down made me realise how precarious a career in rugby was. After that, I tried to immerse myself in as many things as possible. When I was in the gym, on the training ground or playing a match, I was 100 per cent focused. But I learned to switch off and pursue other interests, to create equilibrium, whether it was writing, DJ-ing, public speaking, online coaching or flogging supplements. I was basically the Del Boy of rugby. I would have a crack at anything if I thought I'd enjoy it and be able to make money out of it.

In some ways, players from the amateur era had it better. They combined playing top-level rugby with day jobs, so were more rounded people. When they hung up their boots, the transition to full-time normality was smoother. Many players from earlier in my career, while fully professional, were of the same mind. Tom Wood was always playing with knives and knots and captivated by the great outdoors, and before he retired he realised he needed to upskill himself and start planning for life after rugby. Now he's a tree surgeon. Andrew

Sheridan was clearly going to do something in wine because he was doing Sommelier exams during the 2011 World Cup. Most evenings, you'd see him staring at a bottle of red, making notes. No-one ever asked him if he was drinking it, because he was quite an intimidating character (as well as a complex one who sang, played guitar and released a couple of folk albums). I also had a team-mate who became a male escort, which was more lucrative than his rugby career. What a life! Although I'm not sure he's still in the business – he'd be well into his forties by now – and he had to live with the nickname 'Man Whore'.

Not everyone from my era planned for a life beyond rugby. I saw players spiral into panic in the last few months of their career and then, a few months after retiring, they were doing something completely mind-numbing, because they hadn't thought of anything else to do. Spending year after year running out at a packed Twickenham and suddenly finding yourself selling anti-virus software is a sure-fire way of getting depression.

I recently became a trustee of the Rugby Players' Association charity Restart, which supports players suffering from injury, illness or hardship. I was astounded when they told me how many former and current players call their hotline because they're struggling with retirement – the lack of direction, routine and adulation, and of course the mental health issues. These retired players had gone from being top-flight athletes to not having a reason to get out of bed in the morning. Others aren't retired yet but are depressed at the prospect. They're looking over their shoulders at young kids coming up behind them, having to decide whether to take less money for more beatings. They're terrified of being axed and walking out of the changing room for the last time. Some of these people are in life or death situations, gripped by mental illness and unaware of how the hell to get out of it.

I was also amazed to discover that neither the RFU nor the clubs contribute to Restart. Instead, all the money comes from private donations, dinners and the RPA awards. So my role is to raise awareness and educate players that this charity exists and can help them, if only they take that first step and reach out, whether it's providing therapy sessions, rehab or helping people into work post-rugby. It's also about making current players care about their peers, and cajoling England players and clubs into getting more involved.

Whereas players used to be discouraged from doing too much outside of rugby, now they're being educated to get off their arses and cultivate other interests. But I worry about younger players just coming into the game, because many of them don't seem to be interested. Players in general are more professional nowadays but also seem to be less mature and worldly-wise. There aren't the same big personalities in changing rooms, and I wonder whether that means they'll be less resilient than players in the past.

I recall an introductory meeting at an England camp in 2015, when quite a few young players got up and said, 'Hi, my name's so-and-so, and I like to go for coffee with the lads.' I felt like saying, 'Boys, there's more to life than going for coffee with the lads. And that's not a career, because if you could get paid for going for coffee, I would be front of the queue! When you retire, you can't pay the gas and electric bills with framed shirts and England caps, you've got to find a job and pay for these things. Start planning ahead now.' As well as going for coffee with the lads, a lot of young players waste their downtime playing video games. England hooker Luke Cowan-Dickie was the best in the world at search and destroy in *Call of Duty*. How much time do you have to spend on your computer to become the best in the world at *Call of Duty*?!

Then again, I told a few young players they would never earn money from gaming, and that they needed to get a life, and the response came back, 'That's where you are wrong.' And I *was* wrong. Thanks to the invention of online streaming platforms like Twitch, some lads are making great money button bashing. It might be time to dust off the Xbox.

CAGE FIGHTER

Before I retired, I drove to the Northampton Hilton to see Eddie Jones. It's not like he had any plans to pick me, but I just wanted to tell him why I was retiring and thank him for everything he'd done for me. If not for Eddie, I don't think I would have won a Grand Slam, a man of the series or as many caps for England. When I told him about my plans, he became quite serious. I think he was genuinely concerned about how I would cope.

'What are you going to do now?' he asked.

'I'm not really sure.'

'Do you want to go into coaching?'

'No, not really.'

'Good. Because unless you're at the top, there's fuck all money in it. You are better off earning it elsewhere and coming back to it.'

I'd done a bit of coaching and enjoyed it. And maybe I'd consider a consultancy role. But teaching people when I could still be learning and performing doesn't appeal to me. I also liked the idea of not having a boss for the first time ever, which trumped the fear of not having a monthly salary.

I sometimes wish I'd been a Special Forces soldier, which is something that would have tested me to the absolute limit. But I don't think they take on knackered old rugby players in their mid-thirties! So having turned down an offer to work for

Goldman Sachs in the City – I would have thrown myself out of the window after a week – I thought I'd have a go at mixed martial arts instead.

I've been a fan of MMA for years and used to do UFC shows for BT Sport on my days off, just me and a couple of camera crew. I had also done some work for BAMMA, the British Association of Mixed Martial Arts. So when my agent phoned me after about five weeks of retirement and said, 'Someone from Bellator [an MMA promotion company] has been in touch, they want to meet you,' I thought they wanted to speak to me about doing some commentary. But when I met them, they said they wanted me to fight. At first, I thought it was a bit of a joke. But then I considered it more seriously. It was a chance to be a professional sportsman again, but an individual one. That appealed to me. As did the fact that it was another chance to prove people wrong.

My entire life, people have been telling me what I should and shouldn't do. And not just journalists and pundits. People would stop me in the pub or in the street and say, 'You shouldn't have left Wasps … you shouldn't have joined Stade Français … you shouldn't have posed for that calendar … you shouldn't have gone to Japan or New Zealand … you shouldn't have tried to run a business while you were still playing rugby … you shouldn't have been a DJ …' and so on. But that kind of negativity is like a red rag to a bull and made me who I am.

That's why I've got a tattoo that reads, 'The best revenge is living well.'

So I got in touch with the guys at Shootfighters gym in London, where I'd been training for years. And when I explained the Bellator proposal, they agreed to coach me. But they were adamant it wasn't going to be a showbiz stunt. Paul Ivens, one of the owners, said, 'If you don't commit to it 100 per cent, you could get hurt. You need to live and breathe it.'

Training as an MMA fighter is the hardest thing I've ever done – a lot harder than rugby. In rugby, I had two contact sessions a week and played a game at the weekend. In MMA, I trained five or six days a week, four at peak intensity. It takes you to some horrific places, physically and emotionally. From day one, I was training with experienced fighters and I didn't get any preferential treatment. I went from being a top dog in rugby to bottom of the food chain in MMA. I wasn't very good, but they saw I was a hard worker and quickly accepted me.

I enjoyed learning new skills – and there's no better feeling than putting new skills into practice – but everything was just so incredibly technical. I played rugby for so long that I could do most things without thinking. But in MMA, I had to think about everything I did. I didn't sleep before my first sparring session because I was terrified. I'd done lots of rolling, wrestling, jujitsu sparring and pad work, but I didn't know how I was going to react when they stuck me in the cage. Elite rugby players are tough, but it's a different kind of toughness. It's hard to want to punch someone when they haven't really upset you. Unlike boxing, an MMA fight only really begins when you're on the ground. Being choked is horrific because you feel like you're drowning. One day, I got choked out four times in training and I couldn't swallow properly for the next few days. I asked the coaches and they said it's normal, get on with it. I was blood-tested after a couple of training sessions, and the results showed that the damage to my body was as high as I endured in playing a Test match ... and then another Test match straight after. And that blood test was done just after a normal training session and sparring session.

In no time at all, I was a full-blown professional sportsman again. I was taking ice baths three times a week, spending long hours in the sauna and evening after evening being manipulated and massaged by my physio. My body was permanently wrecked. It caused friction between me and Chloe, because she obviously didn't want to see me get hurt. But I liked it too much to quit, and I am not really built to start something and then stop, unless injury puts a halt to things. I actually tore my pec badly just before the Covid-19 lockdown but only told my physio Kevin and the coaches. I spent the first six weeks rehabbing it every day and would have been fit, but in the end it was coronavirus that put paid to my first scheduled fight. I am not sure what will happen next with it. There is talk of fighting in empty arenas and huge delays. It's a six-days-a-week job that I need to really consider getting back into. During lockdown, my body appears to have got worse for the rest.

There is a fear that I might get exposed in MMA. But that's kind of why I wanted to do it: I was a tough guy in a team sport, but could I be a tough guy on my own? We will have to wait and see if it ever happens.

DJ

My other fantasy job is being a superstar DJ. I can't even begin to imagine the buzz of being someone like Carl Cox or Simon Dunmore, playing to 10,000 people in an arena. I wasn't really into music when I was a kid, and it was my psychologist who taught me how important, and useful, it could be. I wanted to find a method whereby if I put music on before a game, it didn't matter what had happened that day – whether the boiler had broken or I'd had a row with my missus – I could get in the zone and stay there. But it was only when I went on holiday to Ibiza that I started getting into house. I also started spending a lot of time in Las Vegas, where we'd go clubbing every night and listen to people like Calvin Harris, Steve Aoki and Tiesto. It wasn't just the music I liked, I also found DJs bewitching – the way they controlled the mood, the way they got people moving exactly as they wanted, the fact that thousands of sets of eyes and ears were focused on them. It was like they were puppeteers, with thousands of people on strings. That appealed to me and I really wanted to give it a go.

I discovered that quite a few DJs were rugby fans, including Jaguar Skills, Simon Dunmore and Seb Fontaine, who is good mates with Lawrence Dallaglio. All of these guys were kind enough to give me advice, but I felt I needed to take a more rigorous approach to learning the trade, rather than relying on pointers. So I signed up for lessons at SubBass Academy of Electronic Music in London, which was effectively a step-by-step DJ-ing course for beginners. Graduating from the course included doing a gig at Ministry of Sound, which is a bit like playing your first game of rugby at Twickenham. I was incredibly nervous beforehand, but my dad gave me a pep talk, it went off okay and from that moment I was hooked on DJ-ing. It was the closest feeling I'd found to running on a rugby field and almost had the same intensity. Most sportspeople never find something to replace the buzz of competing, but I'd stumbled upon my thing.

I was soon doing gigs for 5,000 people, and DJ-ing has become my biggest passion in life. I'd honestly give up everything else if I could just do two or three DJ sets a week. I've got a booth in my house, I practise all the time and still have lessons from my DJ teacher and guru Alex Grover. Eddie Jones used to say, 'There are a lot of people who are comfortable being professional rugby players. But if you're comfortable, you're not doing it right.' That's why I approach DJ-ing – and everything else – the same way I approached rugby, as a trade that you never stop learning.

Bizarrely, I'm making more money DJ-ing than I did playing

for my last club Northampton, and I'm only doing two or three gigs a month. Some gigs are better paid than others, with the top clubs paying less because they know you're desperate to play there, and corporate gigs paying the best. University gigs pay okay but can be frustrating because you get drunk, and sweaty students stand by the booth all night, asking for high-fives or selfies and not really listening. I want people to book me because I'm a serious DJ, not because I'm James Haskell the rugby player, or that bloke from the jungle. I love it when someone says to me, 'Fucking hell, you can actually DJ,' to which I reply, 'Yeah, what did you think I was going to do? Turn up and press play?'

I suspect that Chloe thought that when I retired, I'd magically become a different person. That hasn't happened. I'm still a workaholic and too often prioritise work over friends and family. I'm planning more books and have an F45 gym franchise in Bath, which my dad is very involved with. I also do a bit of motivational speaking, which ties in with my love of performing. I'd love to do more TV presenting and even have a crack at acting, although I fear I might end up being typecast as 'Doorman 2' or 'Thug 3', rather than some all-action hero like The Rock. Whatever I do, I'll give it my all. That's the only way I know how.

12

PRIDE

Despite my podcast, sometimes I forget I ever played rugby. I spent so long in the game, but it feels like it happened to someone else. That's good in a way, because it means that I've severed the cord, that I'm not looking backwards, that I don't need to be living that life anymore. But I haven't forgotten about it completely. And I never will. My shirts are stored in labelled boxes and when I finally buy my forever home, I'll make sure it's got a man cave to display them.

When people bring up my achievements, it makes me proud. I enjoy talking about the old times and have learned to be grateful for the career I had. I never even thought I'd be a rugby player. I deferred my university entrance for a year, thought I'd give rugby a go and I was still doing it almost 20 years later. Far better players than me didn't achieve what I did, either because they didn't work as hard as me or were beset by injuries. But one of my biggest regrets is not savouring the highs as they happened. People sometimes bring up England's whitewash of Australia down under in 2016 and bang on about what a great feat it was. But at the time, I didn't think it was a big deal and barely celebrated. People thought I was arrogant, but it was because I was never satisfied and, for all the bravado, was riddled with self-doubt.

I say to young players now, 'Enjoy the good moments, because before you know it, it will all be over. And you can't go back.'

But, of course, I'm tremendously thankful for so much. Winning the Premiership final with Wasps, alongside my hero Lawrence Dallaglio and old pal Tom Rees in the back-row, is what dreams are made of. Heineken Cup winners' medals don't grow on trees, but I've got one of those as well. I won a Grand Slam with England, and people don't realise how hard it is to win every game in a Six Nations tournament. I also won man of the series in Australia (for which I was awarded a trophy consisting of one of my trainers with 'man of the series' written down the side, stuck on what appeared to be a cake stand. Thanks, guys). I would have liked to have won 100 England caps, but 77 ain't bad. In fact, I'm the 14th most-capped England player in history, and plenty of unbelievable players earned fewer. I'm one of only a few players from the northern hemisphere to play in Japan and New Zealand. And while I still regret not winning a cap for the Lions – and, for that reason, don't like to say I am a British and Irish Lion – that tour of New Zealand was the best I ever went on. I will treasure those memories forever.

I also did some stupid stuff in my time, most of it just so I had a story to tell the lads. And I was Marmite with the media and the public. But I eventually worked out that as long as I had the love and respect of my wife, family, close friends, coaches and team-mates, it didn't matter what anyone else thought. For as long as I live, there will be people who say, 'That dickhead Haskell messes around too much.' But I suspect I'll be doing all right.

ACKNOWLEDGEMENTS

It's pretty clear that without the help of a huge number of people this book would never have got off the ground. It would instead have stayed in my head, which for some would have been a good thing, or eventually been found inscribed on a wall somewhere in bodily fluids.

The first person I need to thank is the brainchild behind this book. Oliver Malcolm sent me a few Instagram messages suggesting I tell my story, and from those messages six months later we have *What a Flanker*. The truth is, I ignored Ollie for ages as I thought he was some weird superfan who might have been trying to lure me into the back of a van and later some shallow grave with the offer of a book deal. It turns out Ollie is a legend of a bloke, an absolute publishing guru and king of HarperCollins. Thank you, Ollie, for being persistent and for being the easiest publisher I have ever worked with.

Thank you to my long-suffering literary agent, Clare Hulton, who had a baptism of fire with my first book *Perfect Fit* and who turned Ollie's stalkerish messages into an amazing deal. Clare is always on the phone ready to listen when I vent, however this time there has been no venting, no complaints, and if anything I have made life too easy for you. You are welcome.

My ghostwriter Ben Dirs captured my voice and humour straightaway. Ben, you have been brilliant from the get-go and had me in stitches when I read back our interviews. Thank you for never being precious and letting me make edits. I really enjoyed our Three-Hour Chats; it's not often someone is paid to listen to me just talk. Most people walk away after the first hour. Without you, *What a Flanker* would not be what it is.

Zoe Berville, my incredible editor, crafted a wonderful book and shaped my own edits beautifully, turning gibberish into the finest prose. Well, the finest prose for a rugby player. Thank you so much, Zoe. I also love how you have never been flustered once by changes or terrible grammar. I think my last editor is just about out of the asylum.

Thanks to my team at HarperCollins who have helped create the book and the audio version. Simon Gerratt (Editorial Management), Fionnuala Barrett and Charlotte Brown (Audio), Lucy Brown (Publicity), Orlando Mowbray (Marketing), Sim Greenaway (Design) and Alan Cracknell (Production). All of you have been brilliant professionals and so easy to work with.

Mum and Dad, without you I would not be here today. If it weren't for your love, drive and support, I wouldn't have had the career I have had, or achieved all the things that litter the pages of my books. You are always there for me in the good times and bad. Sorry for all the stress and drama, but I did tell you it would make a good story one day. You are both amazing, and I love you.

Thank you to my wife Chloe, who pushed me to tell my story. You have been with me for six years now and have seen a lot of what's in this book play out. You have picked me up when I was down, have pulled me back to earth when I got too carried away with myself. You nursed me back to health after injury and supported me when I came up with mad ideas to be a DJ or a cage fighter. You are the best thing that has ever happened to me. You are my censor, and my guide on what's funny and what's not. I am so proud of the empire you have built for yourself. I love you lots.

All of the adventures contained in these pages would not have happened if it wasn't for my amazing and long-suffering agent Duncan Sandlant from Esportif. Duncan, you have taken me around the world – England, France, New Zealand, Japan – got me the best deals possible and gone into bat for me more times than I am sure you ever thought possible. I have not been easy to look after and I've had my fair share of scrapes. You always gave me sound advice and protected me wherever possible. If it weren't for you, 2011 would have been far worse, as some of these pages attest to. Thank you for always putting up with my dad's calls and odd demands, like for photocopiers and match-day boxes.

Finally, I want to thank my team-mates, the good, the bad and the ugly. From Papplewick School, Wellington College and Maidenhead RFC through Wasps, Northampton Saints, Stade Français, Ricoh Black Rams and the Highlanders, to England and the British and Irish Lions. Without you, I wouldn't have had this ridiculously entertaining, fun, challenging and amazing life. I have been spoilt in getting to play and work with the best coaches and players in the world. I have had my chance to travel and test myself against the best. To all those who have kept me laughing every day from 15 to 35, thank you.